D0336373
112

# The Humanist Outlook

# The Humanist Outlook

*Edited by*

A. J. AYER

PB PEMBERTON
in association with
BARRIE & ROCKLIFF

First Published 1968 by
Pemberton Publishing Co Ltd,
88 Islington High Street,
London N1,
in association with
Barrie & Rockliff (Barrie Books Ltd)
2 Clement's Inn, WC2

SBN 301 66764 0

Printed in Great Britain
on Caxton Antique Wove paper by
Richard Clay (The Chaucer Press) Ltd, Bungay, Suffolk

## Contents

# Introduction

A. J. AYER

# A. J. Ayer

MA, FBA. Wykeham Professor of Logic, University of Oxford. Fellow of New College, Oxford. Hon. Fellow of Wadham College, Oxford. Grote Professor of the Philosophy of Mind and Logic, University of London, 1946–1959. Visiting Professor at New York University, 1948–1949. City College, New York, 1961–1962. President of the British Humanist Association, 1965–.


Publications include: *Language, Truth and Logic*; *The Foundations of Empirical Knowledge*; *The Concept of a person and Other Essays*; *British Empirical Philosophers* (edited with Raymond Winch); lectures and articles in philosophical and literary journals.

# Introduction

## A. J. AYER

The contributors to this book are all members of the Advisory Council of the British Humanist Association. What this implies is illustrated by their essays. It is not so much a matter of their adhering to a given set of doctrines as of their having similar moral interests and a common intellectual approach. On the assumption that this was a sufficient source of unity, no attempt has been made to give the book a central theme. Each contributor was asked to write on any subject of his own choosing. With the exception of Sir Karl Popper's essay, which he has translated from the script of a broadcast, addressed originally to a German audience, all the essays were written in response to this request.

Humanism is defined in the *Oxford English Dictionary* as any system of thought or action which is concerned with merely human interests. The point of the word 'merely' here is that it excludes theology. The early humanists, who took Erasmus for their master, were believers in Christianity; but they did not think it right to apply religious tests to every form of intellectual activity. In particular, they attached an independent value to the study of the languages, literature, history and mythology of ancient Greece and Rome; it is for this reason, indeed, that classical studies still go by the name of the humanities. At the same time, they took the first step towards freeing scientific inquiry from religious control.

That the scientific movement of the Renaissance was seen as a threat to religious orthodoxy is shown by the persecution of Galileo. Nevertheless Newtonian physics was not in fact so very difficult for Christian apologists to accommodate; it could even be welcomed as lending support to the argument from design. The most serious outbreak of intellectual hostility between science and religion occurred in the nineteenth century, when the advance of geology and the theory of evolution undermined the biblical account of Creation. It was partly as a result of this conflict that the anti-clerical scepticism or deism of the eighteenth century Enlightenment gave way in the nineteenth century to a broader movement of Rationalism or Free Thought, which was not merely anti-clerical but hostile to any form of religious belief. Present-day humanists are in fact the intellectual heirs of those nineteenth-century free-thinkers.

Freedom of thought was a form of resistance to authority. It rested on the principle, for which Professor Flew argues in his contribution to this book, that one should not be required to accept as dogma what is not known to be true. The adherents to this movement were not rationalists, in the philosophical sense of the term. Though they had confidence in the power of human reason, they did not believe that reason alone, unaided by observation, could discover how the world worked. They put their trust in scientific method, with its implication that every theory is liable to revision. This open, critical spirit has continued to be a distinctive mark of Humanism. It was characteristic of the Cambridge Heretics to whom Professor Sargant Florence pays tribute, and it comes out particularly well in the essays which Dr Bibby and Sir Karl Popper have contributed to this book.

The hostility of the rationalists to religious dogmatism was not evinced only in their fidelity to the natural sciences. It extended also to questions of human conduct. This did not mean that their moral principles were necessarily different from those which were held by their religious antagonists. The difference lay in their denying that morality either had a religious basis or needed a religious sanction.

In maintaining that one cannot look to religion to supply a logical foundation for any code of morality, they were demonstrably right. The decisive argument in their favour is that no moral system can rest solely on authority. It can never be a sufficient justification for performing any action that someone wishes or commands it. Not only has it first to be established that the person in question has a legitimate claim on one's allegiance, but even when this has been established, it still does not necessarily follow that what he commands is right. Neither does it make any difference to the argument whether the authority is taken to be human or divine. No doubt the premiss that what God wills is right is one that religious believers take for granted. The fact remains that even if they were justified in making this assumption, it implies that they have a standard of morality which is independent of their belief in God. The proof of this is that when they say that God is good or that he wills what is right, they surely do not mean merely to express the tautology that he is what he is or that he wills what he wills. If they did mean no more than this, they would be landed with the absurd consequence that even if the actions of the deity were such as, in any other person, we should characterize as those of a malignant demon, they would still, by definition, be right. But the fact is that believers in God think of the goodness which they attribute to him as something for which we ought to be grateful. Now this would make no sense at all if the deity's volition set the standard of value: for in that case, no matter what he was understood to will, we should still be obliged to think him good.

It is no answer to this argument to say that the possibility of God's being anything other than good is excluded by his nature. There is, indeed, no logical objection to building goodness into the definition of God so long as it is compatible with the other attributes which go to make up the concept. The drawback is only that it adds to the difficulty of supposing that the concept is satisfied. But so far from this proving that God's nature can serve to define goodness, it proves just the opposite. If one did not know what one understood by goodness, independently of ascribing it to God, its inclusion in the definition would not be intelligible.

Not only is it a fallacy to think that moral principles can logically depend upon the will of God: it is also a fallacy to look to human morality for a proof of God's existence. The underlying assumption is that only purely selfish behaviour is natural to man; so that if it ever happens, as it not infrequently does, that people behave unselfishly, they must be inspired by a higher power. But, as Mrs Knight remarks in her essay on Morality, this assumption is false and the conclusion which is drawn from it is invalid. The assumption is false because the only criterion for deciding what is natural to man is what men actually do. Antecedently to experience, there can be no reason for expecting people to behave in one way rather than another. If experience shows that they act unselfishly as well as selfishly, we can only conclude that both types of behaviour are natural. No doubt the self-regarding impulses are the stronger, and in many persons remain so, but this does not alter the fact that many actions are motivated by concern for others. If the capacity for evil is part of human nature, so is the capacity for good.

It is not, however, enough that the capacity for good exists: we are still left with the problem of the extent to which it is exercised. The most important question here is that of moral education, to which Dr Hemming's essay makes a valuable contribution. One thing which is clear is that this is not an isolated problem. It is bound up not only with the question of children's health, about which Dr Henderson writes, but also with that of their material and social background. What social reforms are needed and how they can best be brought about are problems to which the solution calls for the exercise of intelligence as much as goodwill. These are questions in which we are, and ought to be, emotionally involved. But, as Professor Eysenck shows, the very fact that we are emotionally involved makes it difficult for us to treat these questions scientifically. No doubt we do not rely on science alone for our understanding of human nature. In a different way, as Miss Nott rightly argues, this function can be admirably performed by works of art. Yet when it comes to questions of social organization, the lack of a scientific approach will tend to deprive us of the information that we need to put our good intentions into effect.

This is not to say that science can supply us with our values. We have to distinguish the question how moral principles are formed, and how they can be implemented, from the question of their justification. To the question of justification, the correct answer, in my view, is that moral principles cannot be justified in terms of anything other than themselves. We have already seen that they cannot be founded on authority, and I believe that it can also be shown that they cannot logically be derived from statements about matters of fact. That is to say, I do not think that any conclusions about the way things ought to be can be logically deduced from a set of premisses which merely report the way things are. Of course, this does not mean that we cannot appeal to matters of fact in support of some moral decision: it is only that when we take the facts as justifying the decision, the acceptance of some moral standpoint will be presupposed. For instance, in very many cases, a sufficient reason for concluding that one ought not to pursue a certain course of action is that it will cause suffering to other people: but the reason is sufficient only against a moral background in which it is assumed both that, other things being equal, suffering is evil and that one has a duty to consider the interests of others beside oneself. These are assumptions from which very few people would dissent, at least in theory, but they are not susceptible of proof, or, for that matter, of disproof. If they are to be criticized, it can only be on the basis of a different moral outlook, which will equally operate as a judge in its own cause. This is not a ground for scepticism, still less for moral nihilism. It is just that when it comes to the conduct of life, each one of us has to decide what ends he thinks it right to pursue and what principles he is prepared to stand by. This is a point that Kingsley Martin's essay brings out very clearly. I should add that there is no escaping this responsibility. Even those who surrender their independence of judgement, or those who merely go by current fashion, are tacitly making a fundamental moral choice.

In explaining how such choices come to be made, there are many social factors that have to be taken into account: and one of them, undoubtedly, is religious belief. The fact that there is no logical connection between religion and morals does not entail that there is no causal connection. On the contrary, it is historically obvious not only that religious belief has had a considerable influence in shaping man's moral outlook, but that it has operated, at times very powerfully, as a moral sanction. It is the idea of its being indispensable as a moral sanction that is implicit in Voltaire's saying that if God did not exist it would be necessary to create him. From what I have already said, it should be clear that I am not in agreement with this view. I believe that comparatively few people nowadays are at all strongly motivated either by the hope of being rewarded, or by the fear of being punished, in an after-life: even among professed Christians there is a decline in the literal belief in hell. Yet it does not appear that the loss of this belief, or indeed the weakening of religious faith in general, has caused people to behave worse to one another. On the contrary, I agree with Professor Ginsberg that the balance of the evidence is on the side of moral progress. In spite of the wars, the dictatorships, the cults of violence, the political and racial persecutions which have disfigured the history of this century, I believe that the average man is more humane, more pacific and more concerned with social justice than he was a century ago. This is not to say very much: we have very little ground for complacency: but since it is becoming the fashion to decry ourselves, I think it worth remarking that the belief in social progress is still empirically defensible.

If there has been a movement towards the decrease of man's inhumanity to man, it is one in which the Christian Churches have played a part. Whether, in the whole course of its history, organized Christianity has not done more harm than good is a question which it would be difficult to settle and perhaps not very profitable to argue: it is, however, fair to say, at least of the Anglican Church, that in recent times it has shown itself to be more favourably disposed towards social reform, more ready to question its moral and even theological positions, and more tolerant of other groups than it has been in the past. I think that the same is true even of the Roman Catholic Church, though to a very much smaller extent. This is one reason why I think it would be a mistake for the humanist movement to expend its main energy on an anti-clerical crusade. But whatever view one holds of the extent of the political and social influence which the Churches have managed to retain, and of the uses which they make of it, one will have to take account of the reasons for its existence. This will involve a more general enquiry, along such lines as Professor Firth has followed, into the psychological and social causes of religious belief. It is important also to consider how far the needs for which the practice of religion caters are capable of being satisfied in other ways. Miss Brophy's study of the part that might be played by imaginative literature is a contribution to this end.

One desire which the arts are not equipped to satisfy is the desire for personal survival. Though a belief in personal survival has commonly been held as a corollary of the belief in the existence of a deity, the two are not logically connected. It would be perfectly consistent for an atheist to accept the hypothesis of life after death, perhaps on such evidence as has been assembled by the Society of Psychical Research. Dr Besterman devotes his essay to a consideration of these paranormal phenomena, and concludes that they are explicable in other ways. This is a field in which it is especially difficult to maintain an impartial outlook, but I think I can fairly say that, apart from the logical difficulties about personal identity which are involved in the hypothesis of survival, it does not seem to me that the evidence which has been adduced in its favour is strong enough to overcome the scientific objections to which it is exposed. I take it, therefore, to be a fact that one's existence ends with death. Professor Crew, in his most moving essay, shows how this fact can be emotionally acceptable.

If Professor Crew is right, as I believe him to be, it follows that our accounts of happiness and self-fulfilment are closed at death. This has the harsh consequence that very many people are left with an unfavourable balance, which will never be redressed. Partly for this reason, I think that it is morally incumbent upon humanists to do everything in their power to bring about the material and social conditions in which the great majority of people will have a fair opportunity of finding satisfaction in their lives, and I think that, so far as possible, their concern should extend beyond the national or professional groups of which they happen to be members, to mankind as a whole. There are three essays in this book which bear, in an especially concrete way, upon the possibility of a general increase in human happiness. Professor Longuet-Higgins writes about computers and their power to economize labour. Lord Ritchie-Calder writes about the growth of population, with reference to the need for birth-control, and the choice of priorities for expenditure on research. Lord Boyd-Orr writes, in the same connection, about the problem of food-supply. The case which he makes out for a world food-authority seems to me over-whelming.

Underlying all such discussions is the problem of creating the moral and political climate in which the ends which we agree to be desirable can be achieved. In common with other humanists, I believe that the only possible basis for a sound morality is mutual tolerance and respect: tolerance of one another's customs and opinions: respect for one another's rights and feelings; awareness of one another's needs. It is easy to refer in a general way to the social changes which are necessary for this to come about: the spread of education, the erosion of class distinctions, the eradication of national and social prejudice, the general increase in material prosperity. It is not easy to see, in all instances, how changes of this sort are actually to be effected. Neither are they sufficient. It would be naïve to assume that it is only poverty and ignorance that stand in the way of universal brotherhood. There are irrational forces in human nature that need to be better understood. Even when they are understood, there will be difficult problems about the ways in which we ought to try to master them. But, though these questions are hard, I do not think that they are intractable; and one thing which will make them more tractable is an extension of the spirit which informs the contributions to this book.

# Towards a Scientific Humanist Culture

CYRIL BIBBY

## Cyril Bibby

MA, MSc, PhD, FLSX. Principal of The Kingston upon Hull Teachers' College. Publications include: *Health Education, A Guide to Principles and Practice*; *Race Prejudice and Education*; *Self-Education*; *The Human Body, How Life Is Handed On*; *T. H. Huxley—Scientist, Humanist and Educator*.

# Towards a Scientific Humanist Culture

CYRIL BIBBY

The meaning of the word 'humanist' has varied through the ages, and in each age has covered a range of attitude and opinion. It is sometimes applied to early Greek philosophers such as Democritus, whose point of view was in some ways remarkably similar to that of modern science. It has been applied to certain twelfth century admirers of classical antiquity and to Roger Bacon of a century later. It is commonly used of Renaissance figures like Leonardo and Boccaccio, and especially of the great Erasmus and his fellow-opponents of arid scholasticism. And, of course, we now apply it to a whole cluster of liberal thinkers of the eighteenth and nineteenth centuries. Two things at least these men have had in common. The first was so well expressed by Terence that frequent repetition has made it very familiar; *Homo sum: humani nihil a me alienum puto* ('I am a man: nothing human do I count alien'). The second, as Benjamin Farrington[1] has reminded us, was well put by Pliny the Elder: *Deus est mortali iuvare mortalem* ('A mortal's god lies in helping his fellow-mortals').

That is to say, whatever the special characteristics of Humanism in particular historical periods, it is always interested in human potential and human welfare. It is more than a rational intellectual attitude, for that can go with narrow interests and social unconcern. Humanism has connotations of cultural width and of generosity of spirit and of at least some degree of philanthropy. It implies not only an intellectual interest in everything relating to humanity, but also a conviction that humanity is worth caring for. Even though all available evidence of the workings of the universe seems to indicate that the present has followed inevitably from the past, and it might seem that the future will follow inevitably from the present, nevertheless the humanist has faith that he can in some way influence the future. Without such a faith, he could well be a rationalist and philosophical materialist, but he would scarcely be a humanist. With such a faith (and the word is justified, for the belief it expresses has not been and probably never could be proved) the humanist has something in common with the religious man. It is not so much that the latter is a believer and the former an unbeliever, but rather that the one puts his faith in a deity and the other in humanity.

Today, one who describes himself as a humanist implies first of all that he has no faith in revealed religion, but generally there are other implications also. Most Humanists are, in philosophical terms, materialists rather than idealists, believing that there really is a world of matter of which they have some genuine if limited knowledge. On the other hand, in the popular usage of those words as indicating degrees of selfish absorption in material advancement, humanists tend to be idealists rather than materialists. Almost invariably, they accept that our species has evolved from earlier anthropoids and possesses a neurological equipment with enormous potential for intellectual development and social improvement. And, of course, it is this which permits them to contemplate the absence of a god not with dull dismay but with comparative equanimity and even with some degree of optimism about the ability of mankind to forge for itself a fine future.

The contemporary tendency to use the word 'humanist' rather than other available near-synonyms has some interesting implications. In part, it has arisen from the desire for a term not already the traditional trade-mark of one of the organizations which have been seeking some form of federal unity, but there are other more important reasons. 'Atheist' sounds too dogmatically certain, too aggressive, too exclusively concerned with theological (or, rather, atheological) belief. 'Agnostic' is open to the objection that it is too negative, that it denies something but does not obviously affirm anything. 'Secularist' seems to relate too much to anti-clericalism which, while having positive implications for some aspects of social policy, is largely irrelevant in many others. 'Free-thinker' appears too dated in a decade which is fairly permissive towards behaviour and almost completely so towards opinion. 'Rationalist' has an excessively cerebral tone, almost ignoring those many aspects of life in which factors other than reason are significant. In contrast with all of these, and yet absorbing the essence of each, 'humanist' is more positive, directing attention to the belief that humanity must rely on itself, to the hope that it will do so successfully and to the determination that every effort shall be made in that direction.

A common objection to Humanism is that it is unable to provide an ethical system and in effect, lives parasitically on the ethical capital of one or other of the great religions. It is said that only some sort of theological belief can tell us what we *ought* to do, as distinct from what we may feel inclined to do; and many humanists are deeply troubled by this claim. Yet, in fact, this apparently weighty argument rests largely on linguistic ambiguity. To elaborate an illustration once used by Antony Flew,[2] when we tell a man that he ought to catch a certain train, we may mean either of two different things. We may mean that he is under some moral obligation to do so, but more commonly we mean that it is necessary for him to do so if he wishes to reach his destination by a certain time. That is to say, *ought* often means no more than 'this is the necessary procedure to produce that result'. And, once this is recognized, much of the logical difficulty about humanist ethics disappears. A deist may say 'Thou shalt not steal', or 'Thou shalt not commit adultery', meaning that such actions would be offences against divine injunction. A humanist may legitimately say the same, meaning 'It is necessary for each individual to refrain from theft if we wish to maintain the convenience of certain private property rights', or 'It is necessary for married people to refrain from extra-marital intercourse if we wish to maintain the institution of marriage in something approximating to its present form'.

This still leaves it logically possible for an individual to reply, 'I do not wish to maintain any private property rights', or 'I do not wish to maintain anything approximating to the present form of marriage'. In that event, society as a whole may insist through its institutions and laws, 'But we do have these wishes, and we are going to arrange that aberrant individuals are made to conform'. Or any single individual may similarly say that he has these wishes, and will therefore do his utmost to persuade others to exercise the specified restraints. Then there is room for a second element of personal and social judgement: whether, granted the wish for a stated result, the advocated behaviour is the best or necessary means of attaining it. An individual might, for example, argue that theft will not necessarily weaken private property rights or that adultery will not necessarily undermine marriage. In that event, another individual or society as a whole might reply with a contrary estimate of the consequences of such actions, and thereupon determine to use argument and/or social sanctions to discourage or prevent them. That is to say, despite all the difficulties which may lie in the way of making correct decisions about this or that particular moral problem, there is a thoroughly logical framework available for a system of humanist ethics.

In determining the ultimate aims of his ethical system, the humanist can, in the nature of the case, call for no divine guidance. He is on his own: but 'he' is here a collective noun, implying the whole of mankind in so far as knowledge and experience and wisdom are placed in a common pool. This pool, for the humanist, takes the place of revealed morality in the ethical systems of most religions. Since, however, only a minute minority even of church members ever claim to have had direct divine revelation, while the overwhelming majority rely on mediation through other human individuals, the average humanist is at no great practical disadvantage in this respect compared with the average believer. For the former, the general consensus of his society operates in much the same manner as the latter's second-hand or more remote divine injunction. And, despite exceptions among both believers and non-believers, most people in practice accept the greatest happiness of the greatest number as the most general aim of social organization and moral education. Nobody has ever strictly proved that this should be so, and it is doubtful whether any such proof is logically conceivable. It is, however, equally doubtful whether it is necessary. The professional philosopher may still wish to explore the question, but the great mass of mankind will be content simply to assert that happiness is in general desirable, and concentrate on the best methods of achieving it.

It is at this point that the humanist is forced to conclude that he should be a scientific humanist. Science has no more and no less to say than any other field of knowledge or method of inquiry in helping us to decide what are our deepest desires: the wish for happiness is there, dependent upon no special learning or mental discipline. When, however, we come to the often difficult and complex task of deciding how best to achieve this ultimate aim, science could be of the greatest help. To return to the examples already discussed, it is, in principle, scientifically discoverable how far the maintenance of private property or of marital fidelity may contribute to the most general end of universal happiness, and thus warrant acceptance as intermediate ends.

And so, down the scale, until a range of moral laws of varying degrees of generality has been established. These would be laws in the scientific rather than in the theological sense, although they might have much in common with the theological concept of natural law. They would be generalizations about the nature of humanity and of social functioning, just as the law of gravity is a generalization about the properties of matter. And, like other scientific laws, they would be subject to modification in the light of advances in knowledge and might in many cases be only approximately true or applicable only within a certain range of circumstances. But, in so far as they were established, they would provide society with a *rationale* for the establishment of laws in the legislative sense and would give the individual guidance on matters of personal behaviour. They would, in fact, constitute the framework of that science of 'eubiotics' for whose establishment T. H. Huxley[3] appealed so long ago.

Ever since C. P. Snow's[4] Rede Lecture on 'The Two Cultures and the Scientific Revolution', a great deal has been heard of the cultural gap between the natural sciences and the arts, and many suggestions have been made for bridging it. Why there was this sudden snow-balling of discussion on this theme is a little difficult to understand; for, although everything that Snow said was relevant, none of it was very novel. It is, for example, interesting to look back at Matthew Arnold's[5] earlier Rede Lecture on 'Literature and Science', and perhaps even more at Huxley's[6] Mason College address on 'Science and Culture'; to say nothing of the careful consideration given to the cultural role of science by a whole group of great Victorians. At times, indeed, one is tempted to think that, if only people would cease confusing contemporaneity with novelty, and if they had the humility to spend some time carefully studying what was said and written on this subject during the latter half of the nineteenth century, a good deal of repetitive discussion would be saved and a fair number of inconclusive conferences seen to be superfluous.

None of this reduces our debt to Snow, for he seems to have chosen just the right moment to make our own generation vividly aware of many important points and to have succeeded in shaking some influential people out of their complacency. Unfortunately, however, that very quotable phrase, 'the two cultures', has rapidly become something of a cant phrase, repeated without much thought as an indicator of educational modernity and even, by its very repetition, tending sometimes to encourage resigned acceptance of the very dichotomy which its originator deplored. And, so quickly did the phrase gain acceptance, few people seem ever to have questioned its validity. Why, one wonders, should we speak of two cultures rather than of three or four or five? And, if for simplicity we are to identify one main cultural divide, is it in fact between the sciences and the arts? What, indeed, do we mean by 'the arts'? Usually that term is applied to those subjects for which universities award the degree of

Bachelor of Arts rather than Bachelor of Science, but it is a poor service to conceptual clarity to base anything whatever on the confused and largely irrational complex of university regulations and nomenclature.

If, in fact, we must identify two main cultural camps, we shall be forced to conclude that Snow has drawn the boundaries incorrectly. The great division lies not between the scientist and the non-scientist, but between scientists and creative artists on the one hand and purely verbal scholars on the other. We pay too much attention to the factual contents and the modes of presentation of different fields of study, and not enough to their tempers and methods of operation. Consider, for example, the phenomenon of colour as studied by the painter, the chemist, the biologist, the physicist, the literary critic, the philologist, the psychologist and the philosopher. Each of them seeks to identify and systematize relevant data, and then to apply any emergent general principles in the manner most appropriate to his own discipline. But the scientist and the artist experiment with pigments, assess their properties, explore the actual coloured stuff of the material world. The man of letters, on the other hand, treats of colours only in a secondary or derivative sense, dealing with words implying coloration rather than with coloured things themselves. One can study all that has been written about colours, and still remain remote from material reality; but both scientist and artist must actually handle coloured things, and this is one reason why they have so much in common.

Both working artist and working scientist explore the properties of the universe; both manipulate the materials of the world and discover what happens when they are modified by movement or by forces; both seek for significant patterns inherent in nature, and both select from nature individual elements which they then arrange into other patterns; for both, the thing is primary and the word secondary. And, of course, neither can get very far without the involvement of the whole personality—mind and muscle, sensuous response to sensual stimuli, reason and imagination, holistic apprehension and atomistic concentration, critical analysis and speculative synthesis. For each, the time comes when things must be brought to a point, decisions made despite remaining uncertainty, gambles taken and failures clearly recognized as such. Scientist and artist alike are always producers, with many of the attributes of the base mechanic and using some of the same tools. Perhaps that is why, in our still essentially aristocratic culture, they are both often looked down upon by those cultural mandarins whose special studies need no implements other than pen and paper and whose hands at the end of a day's work are still quite clean.

If Snow's dichotomy is a false one, why has it been so generally accepted? The answer may well be largely of a linguistic nature, and may perhaps be best reached by posing a subsidiary question: why do we speak of 'scientists' and 'non-scientists' rather than of 'litterateurs' and 'non-litterateurs', or of 'literati' and 'non-literati'? After all, the word 'literati' has been in the language since at least 1621, while Whewell did not coin 'scientist' until 1840. Yet it is the newcomer which is used as the verbal indicator of the dichotomy, and this says a good deal for its conceptual potency. Most people, indeed, find it difficult to believe that the word 'scientist' is of such recent coinage and, when once satisfied of the fact, wonder how the world managed for so long without it. Some guidance may be gained by looking at other dichotomizing verbalization-pairs, such as 'white' or 'non-white', 'U' and 'non-U', 'believer' and 'non-believer', or even 'sense' and 'nonsense'. Although as dichotomy-indicators they would be equally effective, people do not normally speak of 'coloured' and 'non-coloured', or of 'L' and 'non-L', or of 'sceptic' and 'non-sceptic': why not? It seems that there is a general, even if generally unconscious, tendency for those who formulate such distinctions to do so in terms of that group which is regarded as in some way the superior moiety. And this seems to imply a similar semantic significance in the use of 'scientific' and 'non-scientific'; an unadmitted and usually unrecognized deep-down feeling that the scientist is in some way superior. Or, to put the same point from the other side, the literati are not only uneasily aware of their own ignorance of science, but even more uneasily aware that very few scientists are quite so ignorant in the field of letters. No doubt that is why they so frequently utter jibes against the so-called 'narrow' scientist: it is a defence-reaction similar to that of the little boy who cocks a snook at the policeman; it is a comforting and fairly safe gesture of defiance directed at one who is uncomfortably recognized as in some measure representing higher authority. And the sad thing is that the gesture is unnecessary, for those who make it are not so excluded from that authority as they commonly imagine.

By about the middle of the nineteenth century, it was already becoming clear that the future lay with science and that no culture which ignored it could hope to continue as a powerful unifying force in society. The fact is that the attitudes and the temper of science have become the attitudes and temper of the best part of modern culture, so that most educated people are at least partially scientists. We have not yet reached that happy state foreseen by Huxley[7] when, in a lecture to the Working Men's Club and Institute Union, he said that 'Scientific knowledge is spreading by what the alchemists called a "distillatio per ascensum"; and nothing can now prevent it from continuing to distil upwards and permeate English society, until, in the remote future, there shall be no member of the legislature who does not know as much of science as an elementary schoolboy'; but, outside the legislature, the permeation has proceeded pretty far. Almost the whole of modern thought has become impregnated with science, and many self-professed 'non-scientists' would be as surprised to discover that they have for years been thinking scientifically as M. Jourdain was to learn that he had long been speaking prose. Snow was justified in chiding those who claim to be well educated and yet are ignorant of so central a scientific generalization as the second law of thermodynamics, but he failed to notice something much more significant. This is, that even the most scientifically ignorant of the learned habitually think in terms of a universe of flux, in terms of the transfer of energy, in terms of evolutionary processes, in terms of matter of such fantastic complexity that we have as yet barely begun to comprehend it. As architecture was the great imaginative triumph of one age, and music of another, and poetry of another, the greatest achievement both of human thought and of human vision during this last century has been that of natural science. And it is because science is a triumph of the imagination as well as of the intellect, a thing of beauty as well as of utility, that only the most crustacean of academic troglodytes have been able to resist its radiance entirely.

It is sometimes suggested that, today, everyone's education must be solidly scientific so that they can operate effectively in an increasingly technological society. This argument is not at all persuasive. It is perfectly possible to drive a motor-car without ever having heard of a four-stroke heat-and-pressure cycle, just as it is to watch television with discrimination while knowing next to nothing of cathode rays. Society certainly needs a number of innovators to invent new machinery, a larger number of technologists to devise methods of mass-production, and a yet larger number of technicians to effect maintenance and minor repairs; but the average citizen, if he knows how to use a telephone to call in a servicing assistant, needs less understanding of his highly sophisticated tools than earlier men did of their much simpler ones. Nor is universal school science teaching essential in order to provide society with more and more professional scientists. It is, in fact, perfectly possible to produce good scientists from intelligent young men and women who until the age of eighteen have done very little in this field. The progressive raising of faculty entry requirements during these last twenty years has had little to do with the actual needs of the students, and a good deal to do with the convenience and egotism of their teachers. Today, no Newton or Darwin or Huxley or Rutherford would get into a science faculty of an English university: the situation has become quite preposterous.

No: the real reason why science must move right into the centre of culture is so as to ensure that each citizen is part of the spirit of the age. Only so shall we produce men and women unafraid of advance because confident that its direction can be determined, accustomed to question all authority not justified by the nature of the world, unwilling to allow great issues to remain mere matters of opinion when it is possible to discover which opinion is right and which wrong. Only so can we ensure that society does not pass into the control of an all-powerful scientific hierarchy, which would be as pernicious as any other priesthood.

The fear that an unambiguously scientific culture would be arid and dehumanizing is totally unjustified. Science engages the whole person. It is demanding and it is rewarding, it encourages the exercise of scepticism and yet allows the tentative acceptance of well-based authority, it is adventurous and creative, it promotes self-confidence while repeatedly demanding humility. At its rare best it may do all these things almost simultaneously, and that is why scientists sometimes love their work with the sort of passion which may radiate from an inspired painter or sculptor or dancer. This dithyramb to the splendours of science is, unfortunately, remarkably remote from the pedestrian dullness of most teaching of the subject today; and not surprisingly so. We pay far too much attention to inculcating the facts of science and not nearly enough to fostering the growth of the scientific spirit. Pedagogues are still arguing whether they can manage to squeeze one or two more science periods per week into the school timetable, instead of asking themselves whether the whole shape and spirit of the curriculum is not at least a century out of date. Professors of science subjects are acting as if each undergraduate were a Methuselah, who could reasonably spare a decade or two to store his mind with what can be better kept in works of reference, instead of firing their students with the spirit of inquiry. Professors of literary subjects, paying an oblique but highly dubious compliment to the rapidly mounting prestige of science, are persuading their pupils to waste time on desiccated little pieces of so-called 'research', in which the type of technique appropriate to microscopy is misapplied to poetry, instead of urging them actually to emulate the poets. And, in our colleges of education, all sorts of exciting and potentially valuable approaches to pedagogy are being inhibited by a haunting fear that the university professors might not approve. Not until we effect a revolution in all these fields will it be possible for a real culture of scientific Humanism to flourish.

In such a culture, the earliest stages of child education will scarcely distinguish between the natural sciences and the creative arts. Nursery and infants school teachers, fortunately, have already to a considerable extent grasped the importance of giving children an understanding of things without fragmenting them in the manner so prevalent in formal education at its later stages. In general they have already a vague awareness that both science and art are explorations of reality, using the same senses and offering similar opportunities for sharpening the powers of sensual discrimination. When this awareness has been made explicit and definite, they will realize also that the same objects of examination will serve for the promotion of aesthetic sensitivity and for that of elementary scientific investigation. As teachers of older pupils come to adopt similar pedagogic attitudes, it will become possible for science and art to continue in harness higher and higher up the school. The art specialist will see that painting lessons offer a perfect opportunity for education in the science of colour, and lessons in light crafts for a study of the properties of matter. The science specialist will encourage pupils to exclaim at the beauty of lepidopteran wing-scales, to contemplate the lovely shapes and colours of crystals, to take pleasure in the almost infinite variety of oscillograph patterns. And, even in our universities, where pedagogic understanding is at present so abysmally low, we may hope for some degree of recognition of these things. Or, if that recognition is too long in ascending to these higher academic reaches, we must hope that a generation of students properly educated in the schools will manage to survive the treatment meted out to them for three or four years thereafter.

Just as science is in some sort a soul-mate of art, it could be a fortifying companion of letters. Too often, specialist teachers of science and specialist teachers of language and literature have ignored what they have wrongly regarded as the others' private domain. On the one hand, literature has been taught as if it consisted solely of poetry and novel and drama, to the complete exclusion of those many gems of clarity and grace which may be found in the writings of some of the greatest scientists. On the other hand, science has been taught as if the language in which its procedures were described and its results expressed were of no consequence. This latter failure, moreover, has become more conspicuous in recent years, during which scientific journals have increasingly been written in an obscure gobbledygook characterized by an apparently compulsive use of the third person passive, an almost universal phobia of illuminating imagery, an andemic tendency to verbal flatulence. Instead of allowing this sort of writing, which has already filtered down into the undergraduate essay and the secondary school laboratory notebook, to contaminate the earlier stages of education, we must see to it that the whole process is reversed, so that once more professional scientists come to use that 'close, naked, natural' language enjoined by the founders of the Royal Society.

Science teachers must remind themselves that their subject is essentially a social activity, in which exact communication is as important as exact observation and experiment. They must recognize the deeper truth, that he who goes no further than observation rarely gets as far as observation; that in order to get thus far, it is necessary to go further, as far as communication. They must utilize their science lessons to provide their pupils with repeated practice in that clarity and coherence of apprehension and expression which is the great distinction of the educated mind. Similarly, teachers of language and literature must more vividly appreciate that the skilled and sensitive use of words is best learned in situations relating to the real world and its sense-impressions, and that the rich stores of science could be daily used to this end. In neither case, of course, will this humanizing and cultural widening of their specialist subjects be possible without a willingness to spend vastly more time than at present on individual items of the syllabus; and that will not be possible until syllabuses are very heavily pruned. But, since most children at present forget most of the facts they have learned at school within a few years of leaving it, and retain for life only something of the general attitudes and spirit of the teaching, it is difficult to believe that they would be any the worse for covering syllabuses of only half their present length.

A culture centred on science would, inevitably, make much use of the language of mathematics. So much so, indeed, that already many people have fallaciously come to regard mathematics as a science, with the ludicrous result that in most universities it is not permitted to study mathematics jointly with other languages such as English. Moreover, the dependence of certain branches of science upon mathematics for the expression of their methods and results is so marked that some scientists, whose eminence in their own specialities is matched only by their naïvety in philosophy, have been misled into imaging that the world is a delusion and only the equations a reality. A scientific culture that was also humanist would make short shift of both these errors. It would also abandon the pernicious delusion that an inexact quantitative observation is in some way superior to an exact qualitative observation. And, of course, it would ensure that children were given some elementary understanding of the nature of variation, of sampling procedures, of sets and groups, and thus help to immunize them against the tendency to venerate almost any piece of sociological or psychological information which happens to be expressed in mathematical or statistical terms.

A culture of scientific Humanism will no longer occupy innumerable hours of children's time in the repetitious teaching of much that today passes for history and geography. Schools will, naturally, provide their pupils with the over-all sweep of these subjects as interesting background material, but they will be more concerned with recent and contemporary aspects of social life. And they will not continue to ignore the fact that our society is one of a particular species, *Homo sapiens*, which has inherent biological characteristics[8] predisposing it to particular forms of behaviour, some presenting peculiar difficulties and others offering especial opportunities for the sort of ethical development which most humanists would like to see. Inevitably, in its social and moral education, scientific Humanism will challenge all religion in the form of demonology or miracle-mongering or unhistorical assertion. But it will recognize that religion sometimes has the aspect of wonder in the face of the great mysteries of the universe, of spiritual aspiration, of humility; and such religious attitudes will also be its own. It will, in short, seek to live by the text, 'And ye shall know the truth and the truth shall make you free'.

The twenty-first century is only thirty-odd years away. If, by then, we have not evolved some sort of unified culture, the world will be an appalling place. And, since the only possible unified culture in the present historical epoch is one of scientific Humanism, we must do everything we can towards its achievement. If we succeed, we may look forward to a future of material wealth, sensual delight, æsthetic sensitivity and moral grandeur. Mankind has reached the parting of the ways: we go on to all or to nothing.

REFERENCES

1. Farrington, B. (1965), 'Plain Humanism', *Rationalist Annual for 1965* Pemberton, London, p. 21.
2. Flew, Antony (1964), 'How far can a Humanist Ethic be Objective?', *Rationalist Annual for 1964*, Pemberton, London, p. 9.
3. Huxley, Leonard (1900), *Life and Letters of Thomas Henry Huxley*, Macmillan, London, Vol. II, p. 385.
4. Snow, C. P. (1959) *The Two Cultures and the Scientific Revolution*, Cambridge University Press, Cambridge.
5. Arnold, Matthew (1882), *Literature and Science*, Cambridge University Press, Cambridge.
6. Huxley, T. H. (1880), 'Science and Culture', in *Collected Essays* Macmillan, London, 1893, Vol. III, pp. 134–159.
7. Huxley, T. H. (1877), 'Technical Education', in *Collected Essays* Macmillan London, 1893, Vol. III, p. 421.
8. Bibby, Cyril (1964), 'Biological Predispositions and Social Morality', *Aspects of Education*, Institute of Education, Hull, No. 1, pp. 24–31.

# Gods and God: An Anthropologist's Standpoint

RAYMOND FIRTH

## Raymond Firth

PhD, DPh, LLD, DLit, FBA. Emeritus Professor of Anthropology in the University of London. Hon. Secretary, Royal Anthropological Institute, 1936–1939, and its President, 1953–1955. Fellow, Centre for Advanced Study in Behavioural Sciences, Stanford, 1958–1959. Honorary member of scientific societies in the USA, New Zealand, Australia and Denmark.

Publications include: Anthropological studies based on research into Polynesian, New Zealand Maori and Malay communities; *Human Types*; *Elements of Social Organisation*; *Man and Culture: An Evaluation of the Work of Malinowski*; *Two Studies of Kinship in London* (editor); *An Evaluation of the Work of Malinowski* (editor); *Essays On Social Organisation and Values*; *Tikopia Ritual and Belief*.

# Gods and God: An Anthropologist's Standpoint

RAYMOND FIRTH

Anthropologists are accustomed to looking at religious systems in a relatively neutralist way, as social analysts. Some do so while committed to some variety of religious belief, which predisposes them to the assumption of an ultimate reality of a more or less mystical order behind all the social behaviour which they register and examine. Others, probably the majority, regard all religious ideas and institutions as explicable solely in human, social terms. They look upon assumptions of extra-human entities or powers at work in the universe as so much additional material, for consideration in the same terms of social inquiry. But anthropologists of either frame of mind have rarely looked directly at Western religious beliefs in the way in which they are used to examine primitive religions. This essay briefly indicates my own standpoint in such analysis from a comparative point of view.

Many years ago, it is reported, a judge in a Maori Land Court in New Zealand was hearing a case in which control by spiritual beings was adduced as evidence for long-standing ownership of a piece of land. The court showed no surprise at hearing gods cited to support a claim in the case. But when the name of one god was mentioned a witness said, 'That god is dead.' The court demurred, 'Gods do not die.' The witness replied, 'Gods die when people cease to believe in them.'

We may commend the robust commonsense of the Maori witness, a pragmatic anthropologist who had seen the passing of his ancient religion. And yet, at the back of our minds may linger a memory of early social conditioning, that a god as a spiritual being cannot be subject to the laws of mortality. If in the Western idiom we think of monotheism and write God with a capital initial, it is inconceivable to most people that God could die. If people cease to believe in Him, we are apt to think that He nevertheless continues to exist for them, even though unrecognized. Even, if putatively, all people in the world cease to believe in Him, on the conventional Christian view he would still be there, invisible, holy, omniscient, omnipotent, ever-loving—though presumably sorrowing. When in the Christian faith God did die, to take upon Himself the sins of the world, it was His human semblance that died—God the Son; God the Father continued to reign supreme.

But among primitive peoples all over the world anthropologists have seen or had report of the death of gods. Religious proselytization, Muslim in Africa, Hindu in India, Christian the world over, has destroyed pagan cults, has converted polytheists into monotheists or has restricted the range and altered the labelling of the spirit entities worshipped in the traditional systems. Such spirit personalities have been denied as false, and, their names forgotten, have passed into oblivion. In similar style historians have noted the disappearance, the 'death', of many gods once current in the world of classical antiquity—Attis, associated with death and resurrection, with fertility and the annual spring renewal of vegetation; Isis, queen of heaven, mistress of the elements, associated with rites of purification; Mithra, linked with sacrifice, with the dualism of good and evil and doctrines of rewards and punishments in the afterworld.

Yet what is meant by the death of a god? With a human individual we have a fairly clear-cut index of death, the cessation of the functioning of the physical body. Even here the criteria are not as final as used to be thought, with the advent of new modes of resuscitation. Granted that the confusion is merely semantic, and that cessation of the beating of the heart is best described as suspended animation, which becomes death only if the heart is not revived. Still, however, something of the person survives. Genetically, some portion of his substance, infinitesimal maybe, continues in his descendants. Ideationally, his personality lives on in the memory of his family and friends, and, if he has been a productive scholar or artist, in the transmitted materials of his writings, paintings or other works. So, even if there be no belief in a survival of his soul after his bodily death, as a person and not simply as a physical individual, he cannot be said to have completely died.

Something analogous occurs in the death of a god, or indeed in the history of any concept given a personalized form. For the prime fact about a god or God is that he/she/it is a quality or set of qualities conceptualized as a person. Equivalent to the physical death of a human individual, a god can have a material dissolution. This likewise can occur in two forms, cessation of behavioural function and physical decay. At intervals over a period of nearly forty years I have observed this process in a small, remote Polynesian community in the Western Pacific, on the island of Tikopia. Half pagans, half Christians when I visited them first, the lives of them all were deeply affected by the pagan cult with its elaborate cycle of ritual performances of worship with offering and prayer. Later, as proselytization became keener, the number of pagans declined, the offerings became fewer, the rites curtailed.

In 1966, when I returned for the third time, all the people had been Christian for a decade, the ancient temples were in ruins, the wooden symbols of the gods in decay, the traditional rites completely abandoned. Physically, the gods were dead. What the people called their 'bodies', their material embodiments, had rotted away; their 'doings', that is, the ritual which recognized, honoured and perpetuated their names and attributes, had perished and begun to be forgotten.

As an anthropologist, this is what I class as religious conversion, the change of people from one religious system of observances to another. The major indices of conversion are of overt commitment—alteration in style and rhythm of ritual behaviour, and alteration in name of the extra-human entities to whom the behaviour is oriented. Believers regard this as a change from darkness to light, laying prime emphasis on change in belief. But the belief situation may not follow such a simple pattern.

It may be the worship of a god which dies, while belief in his existence still remains. On this island of Tikopia, as late as a year ago, it was the belief of many people that the traditional gods were not dead but in limbo. The worship of them had been abandoned, for what seemed good reasons. These gods stood for the principles of fertility in vegetation, prolificity of fish, health and welfare of man, as well as for sex complementarity and differentiation, cultural invention and other major social interests. In the public view, as circumstances changed the gods had failed in their major tasks. They had proved to be relatively inefficient in confrontation with the modern external world. Though they had on occasion demonstrated their power by striking sacrilegious trespassers with illness, and though they had provided their worshippers with fish and vegetable food with which to sustain themselves and continue religious rites, these gods in drought, famine and epidemic had appeared to provide a less effective defence than that provided by the Christian God. Moreover, the concept of the Christian God, an import from overseas by a Mission whose representatives were highly respected, seemed to be in broad conformity with the beliefs of white men whose command of resources and political power were increasingly attractive and dominating. To the Tikopia pagans, then, who like the rest of their community wanted to take advantage of the facilities of the modern world, it seemed only reasonable to convert to the Christian system. As far as I could judge, they had changed their religious affiliation sincerely; they now believed that the One God was supreme.

But this did not mean that they felt they had to disbelieve in their old gods. These gods were regarded as still existing; but no longer summoned to concern themselves with the affairs of men, they stayed in their spirit abodes, quiescent. Indeed, they had been specifically despatched there by the thoughtful Tikopia. The priests, chiefs and ritual leaders of their people, took care to celebrate final rites in which the traditional gods were called upon, given a last feast and dismissed with placatory words which explained why they could be no longer asked to return. The new day had dawned, the One God had taken over, and they were no longer needed.

In this sense, then, the traditional gods are physically dead, but ideationally they live on, at least in the minds of the older people. A conventional view of religious conversion is that the new God is admitted as true, the old god as false. But falseness may mean only inaccuracy in prediction, and inaccuracy is not equivalent to non-existence. For people who have deserted them, pagan gods may stand for impotent and inefficient beings, not figments of the imagination. This position is reinforced by the association between traditional gods and ancestor-spirits. The line between these two categories of super-natural beings has often been tenuous. Many primitive religions, like Christianity, have had concepts of god becoming man, and man becoming god. If, as most religions proclaim, the spirit of a person survives after his bodily death, then the spirits of people's relatives and ancestors must still be extant somewhere. And if the spirits of ancestors, why not those of allied spiritual beings, the traditional gods, still surviving in some conceptual dwelling-place which does not challenge the moral destination of the faithful? For a people such as the Christian Tikopia, there is analogy too with beliefs in saints, admitted in Christian hagiology to be sometimes mythical personages, whose essential character lies in a combination of human individuality and demonstration of extra-human powers; and who are regarded as still sentient. Treated by the Tikopia as 'sacred men', and as responsive to the appeals of the faithful, saints are equivalent to traditional gods who have got on the right side of the religious fence.

It is not in memory alone that the gods survive. Presumably after a generation or so away from paganism knowledge of names and attributes of the traditional gods fades. But the themes which have given shape to the conceptualizations of the gods still may live on, in other form. In the European classical field, many of the qualities of the classical gods were absorbed into newer representations of the divine. The death and resurrection of Attis reappeared in that of Jesus; the queen of heaven, Isis, had her parallel in Mary the Mother of God. So also in a primitive pagan religion such as that of the Tikopia. Their principal god, known by such titles as the Sacred Chief, the Fear-making God, according to the accepted story had been a human being, an ancestral chief, some fifteen generations or so ago, who made his reputation as a culture hero by stabilizing relations between man and nature and instituting the major customs practised by the community. Killed by a competitor in a struggle for land, he abjured revenge and claimed supremacy in the spirit world. Death as man, rise to power as spirit, is therefore a theme which pagan Tikopia could continue to recognize and perpetuate in the story of Jesus. Of female deities the Tikopia had several, regarded as highly powerful, especially concerned with the affairs of women, and apt to be malevolent towards men, for whom they epitomized the darker forces of sex. A female deity—for such the Mother of God must be pragmatically—of benevolent habit must have been a great relief for newly converted Christian Tikopia men! Western Christian apologists have gone to great lengths to demonstrate the lack of connection, especially in the classical field, between such anterior religious themes and the more modern presentations in the form of God, Jesus, Mary and the saints. But historically, there need be no direct connection between the various named entities of the pagan and the Christian world. What is relevant, and what seems to emerge very clearly from the evidence, as many scholars from Cumont to Bultmann have shown, is the repetition of similar themes of individual and social concern at different periods of human history. What is also relevant is how these themes—'great universal ideas', as Hirn has called them—become modified and re-formulated with the passage of time, as social conditions change.

One of the most striking modifications in the religious system of ideas of the Western world was the Christian conception of God as Love. As Bultmann has put it, the basic proclamation of Jesus was that God demands the whole man, inner commitment as well as external conformity, and the demand is for love. Love had entered the religious field before Christianity but not in such selfless form, not in such highly personalized even domestic family imagery, and not with such direct and intimate application. Symbolism of the domestic family circle had been part of the pantheon of earlier religions, but with Christianity idealization of its qualities reached a new height. In the Holy Family, at a relatively earthly level, St Joseph is not much more than a kindly step-parent head of household. But at a more elevated spiritual level God the Father is not only creator and judge, he is also loving parent. Jesus, the moral analyst, teacher and ideal, personifies humanity with its imperfections and demand for understanding, forgiveness and comfort. Mary the Mother of God is the principle of womanhood and maternity, that unique sympathetic bond which, even allowing for Freudian interpretations, tradition has hallowed into the ideal of selfless affection.

In all this the Christian faith has been able to utilize some of the most powerful moral stimuli to social action. But in so doing Christianity has been saddled with two pronouncements which serve as sanctions within its bounds but, comparatively viewed, are distinct liabilities. These are the assertion of the divinity of Jesus and, backing this up, the assertion of the virginity of the mother of Jesus. The first, looked at anthropologically, is only a symbolic statement, but taken literally becomes a major sanction in giving absolute value to what are represented to be the words and ideas of the prophet and teacher, Jesus. The second is an ancillary sanction in that if Jesus is not divine his mother's virginity would be meaningless embroidery. Biologically and historically it is nonsense. But symbolically it is a statement about the supernatural quality and especially the purity of Jesus. Dogmatically its major importance is perhaps that it serves as a critical index in a test of faith.

The assertion of the divinity of Jesus is a prime stumbling block in the way of closer rapport of Christianity with its parent religion, Judaism, and its younger sibling, Islam. For orthodox Jews, conceiving of the coming of the Messiah as part of the development of God's personality, already laid down like the inevitable course of history, Jesus is a false prophet. Of more than ordinary effrontery in the personal claims made by him or on his behalf, he remains a teacher and interpreter of practical and mystical doctrines, by no means the last 'suffering servant' to see himself as the Messiah, the Christ, the Lord's Anointed. For the orthodox Muslim, assertion of the divinity of Jesus is plain heresy, an attempt to 'give God a partner' which the Koran expressly forbids. But in Islam Jesus is venerated as a major prophet, who was given clear proofs of his mission by God, strengthened by the holy spirit, and furnished with the Evangel as confirmatory of the earlier law. But just as his mission confirmed that of Moses and added to it, so that of Muhammed confirmed that of Jesus, but was final and complete. Muhammed, a man like Jesus and Moses, was the seal of the prophets and the completion of revelation. Ascription of some superhuman attributes to the messenger of good tidings, the bearer of a new revelation, is common enough in the religious field. But the concept of a prophet as God the Son, as a personal Redeemer, a Saviour who has encapsulated the divinity he proclaims, is a very odd phenomenon among the more successful religious systems, though it occurs among messianic cults in Africa and elsewhere.

The assertion of the virginity of the mother of Jesus is odder still. Mother goddesses are common in many religions, and so also are miraculous conceptions of gods. But mother goddesses normally are regarded as having gone through the physical processes leading to motherhood, while miraculous conceptions are treated as commonly followed by normal births. In neither case is virginity of the mother thought to have been preserved. The idea of a virgin giving birth to a god is spectacular, and is a flaunting of faith in the face of nature's laws, a dogmatic challenge which is intelligible as symbol, but hard indeed to accept as true of an historical person. If one believes in the birth of God from a mortal woman, there is no more reason why one should boggle at his being born of a virgin than of one whose hymen has been perforated. But it does add one step more to the height of the credibility threshold. It seems indeed that in the early centuries of the Church this concept of virgin birth caused some difficulty but was dealt with in terms of the penetrative powers of light and analogous symbolisms. But, as Yrjö Hirn has pointed out, what the successful maintenance of this dogma has done has been to present in one person the idealization of important, yet contradictory, attributes: virginity and motherhood; humanity and godhead. Moreover, the dogma of the Assumption and representations of the Coronation of the Virgin, following on her sorrowing for her Son, provide the ideal type of maternal grief and joy, as well as the sorrows of death followed by triumph over the grave. So the Madonna can serve as symbol of womanhood in all her aspects.

Judaism and Islam are monotheistic religions. Christianity is ordinarily called such, but at the level of popular faith it is very doubtful if this categorization can hold. God the Father, God the Son and Mary the Mother of God are separable conceptual entities. Leaving aside God the Holy Ghost, whose relationships are somewhat obscure to the non-theologically inclined, the other three have their parallels. It may be objected that Mary should not find place in this trio; she was human, not divine. But if the subtleties of theological defence be set aside, the Bodily Assumption of Mary and the role assigned to her in the heavenly world (including such earthly interventions as those in 1830 of ordering the striking of a Miraculous Medal) entitle her to honours equivalent to divinity. It may also be argued that God the Father and God the Son are but different facets, different symbolizations of the same unitary Being. But while this may be so at the theological level, in practical worship they are apt to be treated separately. Moreover, the phenomenon of syncretism is common in many religious systems. Christianity in this respect is like many religions which are polytheistic at the popular level but whose more sophisticated adherents, especially priests, describe them in syncretistic monotheist terms.

When we turn to the more sophisticated Christian circles,

a very interesting situation is seen. The Catholic Church may be still, as it was described fifty years ago, the Middle Ages in the twentieth century. But its more intellectual representatives, with the more advanced theologians of other Christian faiths, have been earnestly exploring the ways of adapting the tenets of the Church to modern thought and social changes.

Among the multifarious ways in which this has been occurring, two trends are of particular interest to me as an anthropologist. They are to a large extent alternatives. One is to emphasize the human aspects of religion, to show its relevance to the concerns of man, and hence to stress its up-to-dateness, its role in promoting social justice and the development of the individual personality. The worker-priests, the tentatives of Catholics and Marxists to find common ground in such subjects as workers' control of industry, or Marx's concept of alienation, illustrate this. Advocates of such points of view are apt to find dissent in their own camp, and to be marked by impatience with traditional authority. Coming to terms with the present-day problems of society means jettisoning some of the traditional attitudes towards the problems of the past—hence the pressure from within the Christian body itself for more liberal Church attitudes towards divorce, birth control and marriage of priests where celibacy has been hitherto the rule, and the yielding of authority on such matters as replacement of service of the Mass in Latin by the vernacular. In a more abstract, analytical framework of ideas attempt is made to separate the institutional trappings of religion from its essential belief core; naturally, opinion among the faithful differs on what are the essentials.

Stripping of the accretions of past centuries may be intended, however, for an alternative end, not to bring religion closer to man, but to allow him to realize more clearly its other-worldly character. The demand made upon religious belief is not then to be in terms of making the relevance of the superhuman depend upon that of the human order, but of giving credence to a superhuman order for which the human being is satellite, not focus. Hence the emphasis upon the Christian gospel as revelation; on the non-logical character of belief in virgin birth, and resurrection; on the notion of commitment; on the transcendence of God, who is not in the world even though he may be immanent in all of us.

Anthropologically speaking, the character of the idea-construct 'God' is conformable with the diverse social and intellectual currents of our time. If one regards the concept of the divine in every society as a response to social and personal needs, then one may expect such a double reaction by believers, against the challenge of modern secularist thought.

One type of reaction is to emphasize man's insufficiency and dependence on forces outside his personal control: the uncertainties of scientific generalizations; the irrational elements in human thinking; problems of the genesis of value within the human field and of cosmic origins outside it. Man alone, so the argument runs, cannot pretend to supply answers here; the only answer must be Deity. At a more concrete level the analogues with the religious concepts of primitive people here are close. They too have conceptualized and answered the problems of origins of the world and of man, the unpredictability of natural forces, the dark impulses of sex and aggression, with symbols of blood and death. But primitive peoples, confronted by external economic and political power, have for the most part conceded the temporary, contingent nature of their conceptualizations. They have acknowledged the more effective moral and intellectual scope of an alien religious ideology—even if in many cases they have re-formulated this later in terms of 'cargo cults', 'separatist churches' or other messianic movements which seem to them to fit their needs more personally and more appropriately.

Another type of reaction, perhaps more lofty, the retreat into the assertion of transcendence, has not been conceived with the aim of stifling argument, but does inhibit discussion from any contrary position. For if God *is*, but is not of this world, is not fully knowable by man even with special techniques of approach, it can always be held that objectors speak from only partial apprehension of what so far has been made available to man. Primitive peoples have not gone in much for transcendence in their characterization of their gods; they have liked the gods removed in space but ready to come when called, and accessible to some kind of approach, even to the point of providing substantial evidence of their own existence, through dream, vision and miracle.

A whole series of logical developments is linked with this assumption of transcendence, or run parallel with it. There is the flat affirmation, directly contrary to the assertion of the Maori witness years ago, that God exists, whether men believe in him or no. Belief is essential for the full existence of man, not that of God, and religious belief is idealized as the most complete form of belief, allowing man to realize his own potentialities to the highest degree. Satisfaction for the individual concerned may be explicitly rejected as the keynote here; belief may be the counsel of despair; for human dejection and ineffectiveness there may be no other resort. But to the external observer such belief does clearly represent a kind of fulfilment for the believer, if not in security, at least in hope. A position in some ways closer to that of an anthropologist, is that God is to be looked for not in the conventional notions of Creator who made the world, tutelary of the Jews, spouse to the Virgin, Real Presence in the Mass, and other personifications, but in the faculties or propensities giving rise to these notions. God is not as depicted in the myths and images, but is exemplified in what lies behind them, the creative strivings of mystic and poet, and of ordinary people, to express the ineffable, to portray in figurative, aesthetic ways the essence of human relationships. In one fashion of speaking, then, God is communication. In another, a Durkheimian retrospection, God is society divinized. Advanced theologians, speculating on what is left 'after the death of god', tend to find it in the forces of inspiration, love, imagination, for which, they argue, secularism can supply no rationale and which therefore are a fit subject for religious postulate.

To me all this offers a rich, fascinating field for anthropological enquiry. The content and structure of Jewish and Christian myths await the social analyst who will focus not upon problems of historical relationship but upon the basic themes the myths display—family, sex, status involvement, aggression, sacrifice, suffering—and upon the structural principles upon which they have been built up. One line of inquiry leads to the consideration of the particular types of social institutions and social conditions to which the myths have corresponded, at various historical periods, and the changes which they have undergone in conformity with social changes. (Where now, in popular belief, is hell?) Another line of inquiry can concentrate especially on theological exposition, and the social correlates of the different kinds of interpretation put forward of key questions of ritual and belief. Of special interest here could be an examination of theology in England before 1914; then after the First World War when neither religious ideas nor political ideas could ever be quite the same; and after the last war, which gave a new impetus to theological speculation. The trends in biblical theology, the swings away from and back towards the notion of God as truly personal—personal in himself and personal in his relations with the humanity he created—could be well set against secular intellectual movements in the natural sciences, psychology and sociology, from Darwinian evolution to communication theory. Especially interesting here is the persistence of the symbolism of the Mass—that chthonic preoccupation with ideas of victim, sacrifice, death, blood and anthropophagy, and their sacramental value.

Superficially minor, but actually far-reaching in their implications, are problems of the theory of transubstantiation in the Mass, including the distinction between the doctrine of Real Presence as veritable body and blood of Christ, who died once and for all upon the Cross, and that of the Presence as exhibiting the renewal and actual repetition of the death of Christ. This is a good instance of the intellectual compromise made between the implications of two significant but potentially dangerous principles—of commemoration and of re-enactment. Simple commemoration of the Last Supper and the death of Christ might tend, as Catholic theologians hold, to impoverish the Christian bodies which follow this plain symbolic interpretation of the Eucharist. Hence the doctrine of the Real Presence, which engages the emotional attention of the faithful. But to argue (in a 'heretical' interpretation) that the conversion of bread and wine into body and blood at the moment of elevation means that the victim is actually slain afresh strikes at the root of the notion of the uniqueness of the sacrifice of the Crucifixion—it implies that the original sacrifice was insufficient in its saving grace. Hence, rather incongruously, the elements of the sacrifice must keep on reappearing, but the act itself must not. Looked at as a total system of belief and practice, set in an elaborate institutional framework, such doctrinal controversies can be seen to have their place as regulatory mechanisms for the religious body.

In the kind of analysis I have been giving here the prime aim is not to try and demonstrate the falsity of religious belief and the superfluousness of religious ritual. It is rather to try and understand their complexity, their rationale within their own basic assumptions, their correspondence with or divergence from their own internal structure of control and the social conditions of their time. In such study, as I see it, assumptions of extra-human entities or powers are unnecessary. There are alternative and perhaps more economical assumptions—that the search for ways of coping with man's ignorance and irrationality has got to be conducted in human terms. If one accepts inadequacy, aggression, evil, suffering, as part of the endowment of man, then why should one not regard imagination, creative effort, aesthetic inspiration, love, as also part of human constitution? On such a sceptical foundation, to theo-logy succeeds anthropo-logy—the study of God is included in the study of man.

# Morality— Supernatural or Social?

MARGARET KNIGHT

Margaret Knight

Lecturer in Psychology at Aberdeen University. Vice President of the Ethical Union. Formerly on the staff of the National Institute of Industrial Psychology.

Publications include: *A Modern Introduction to Psychology* (with Rex Knight); *William James* (selected writings edited with commentary); *Morals Without Religion*; *Humanist Anthology*; *Religion and Your Child* (with others); articles in various journals.

# Morality—Supernatural or Social?

MARGARET KNIGHT

Father Ronald Knox, in a memorable phrase, once referred to 'this Something which underwrites all the dictates of conscience, hamstrings the mind with hesitations when there is a blow to be struck for self-interest, reinforces the claims of altruism and sends us back to the tail of the queue'.[1] Many believe that the existence of this Something is the strongest of all arguments for theism. In what follows, therefore, I shall try to do two things: first, to show that the Something, or something, in question needs no supernatural explanation, but can be adequately accounted for in terms of what Darwin called the social instincts—tendencies towards co-operation that have been built into us in the course of our evolutionary development, and are reinforced in each generation by training and social pressure; and, second, to argue that the ethic of Christianity is defective in that it fails to recognize the social instincts, and assumes that natural behaviour must inevitably be selfish behaviour.

The argument, like all Darwinian arguments, begins with the animals. Animal psychology in recent years has undergone a minor revolution through the growth of ethology—the study of animal species in their natural state. One result of this development has been a growing realization of the extent to which gregarious animals exhibit co-operative, altruistic behaviour, not only towards sexual partners and offspring, but towards other members of what can reasonably be called the community.

This is not a new discovery. It was fully appreciated by Darwin (as will be illustrated later) and it has since been emphasized by Kropotkin, Köhler, Allee and many others. But until recently it was an unfashionable truth, largely because behaviouristically minded psychologists preferred experimenting with animals in laboratories to observing them in their natural state; and in laboratories (and even, to a lesser extent, in zoos) the opportunities for the display of animal sociality are limited. In consequence the crucial part played by such sociality in the wild state went unrecognized. To quote Robert Ardrey:

> In zoos there are no predators and there is no fear. And all those delicate instinctual mechanisms evolved by natural selection to promote the survival of individuals or the survival of species are alike suspended. Only sex and a hearty appetite remain for us to see. But how delicate may be the instinctual social responses in a state of nature has been recorded by many an observer.[2]

The neglect of 'instinctual social responses' (or of built-in group-survival responses if a more behaviouristic term be preferred) has not been due only to the tendency just mentioned; another contributing factor has been a misunderstanding of Darwin. Most people still suppose that the Darwinian theory of evolution by natural selection implies a constant struggle for survival between individuals. If this were so, self-centred aggression would have high survival value, and co-operation would be dysgenic. But this was not in fact Darwin's view. He held that the evolutionary struggle takes place primarily between groups or communities rather than individuals; and, clearly, one of the main factors making for the survival of a community is a high degree of co-operation and mutual aid. In the fourth chapter of *The Descent of Man* Darwin accumulated examples of co-operative behaviour among social animals, and remarked very reasonably, 'It can hardly be disputed that the social feelings are instinctive or innate in the lower animals; and why should they not be so in man?' He concluded the chapter with what may be regarded as the classical statement of the humanist view on the social basis of morals.

> The social instincts—the prime principle of man's moral constitution—with the aid of active intellectual powers and the

> effects of habit, naturally lead to the golden rule, 'As ye would that men should do to you, do ye to them likewise;' and this lies at the foundation of morality.

Lest critics object that this paints an impossible rosy picture of human nature, it must be emphasized that Darwin did not deny—and no present-day humanist denies—that man, like the other social animals, has built-in tendencies towards aggression as well as co-operation. 'Natural' behaviour, both among animals and primitive man, involves co-operation within the troop, herd or kinship group (the 'in-group' in modern sociological parlance) and non-co-operation, and in some cases aggression, towards the 'out-group' (though ethologists have shown that animal aggression often involves little more than ritual combats, conducted with a maximum of noise and display and a minimum of injury).

It is arguable that the survival of *Homo sapiens* depends on widening the in-group and increasingly ritualizing aggressive behaviour towards out-groups; but this is a topic too vast to pursue here. The crucial point in the present context is that co-operation and aggression are biologically on a level. Both have survival-value; both are built-in; both manifest themselves spontaneously in appropriate circumstances. This, basically, is the humanist position, and it contrasts sharply with the traditional Christian view, as will later be shown.

But first another possible objection must be considered. The argument so far has been based on the social animals, and it has been tacitly assumed that *Homo sapiens* belongs in this category; but this could be disputed. Animal species, as everyone knows, can be classified as gregarious or non-gregarious—the gregarious, or social, species being those (such as apes, wolves or seals) who lead a communal life in troops, packs or herds, and the non-gregarious, or solitary, being those (such as foxes) for whom the basic unit is simply the family unit and who do not form wider groupings. Obviously, man now behaves as a gregarious species. But it could be argued that the tendency towards socialized behaviour is not built in to human beings as it is into apes and wolves, but that it has been laboriously superimposed by social training and/or religion on man's natural tendency to be completely selfish—

or at least to be unselfish only towards sexual partners and offspring. If this view were correct it would imply that our primitive ancestors were non-gregarious, and many people believe that this is the case—influenced, perhaps, by childhood stories about 'primitive cave men' who were visualized as solitary hunters. But anthropology gives no support to these stories. On the contrary, there is abundant evidence that our earliest human ancestors lived in communities. Indeed one can go back beyond our human ancestors to the ape-men or hominids. The earliest hominids of whom fossilized remains have been found is Australopithecus who lived not less than a million years ago. Australopithecus walked upright and used weapons, but his brain was only about one-third the size of the human brain today. Later came Pithecanthropus, whose brain was larger, but who was still considerably more ape-like than *Homo sapiens*. There is ample evidence that both types of ape-men lived in communities; and it has been suggested by Professor Le Gros Clark that 'consciously directed co-operativeness has been the major factor which determined the evolutionary origin of *Homo sapiens* as a newly emergent species'.[3]

Conceivably, the story of Adam and Eve may have done something in Christian countries to strengthen the view that man is basically non-gregarious. But whether or not this is so, the view in question would certainly seem to be primarily a Christian phenomenon. It was not held in the great pre-Christian civilizations—not in the great period of Chinese history, nor in classical Greece or Rome. The Stoics, in particular, took it for granted that man is a social animal. Thus Seneca wrote: 'We are members of one great body. Nature has made us relatives. . . . She planted in us a mutual love, and fitted us for a social life.'[4] Cicero wrote, 'Men were born for the sake of men, that each should assist the others',[5] and again, 'Nature has inclined us to love men, and this is the foundation of the law'.[6]

The traditional Christian view, by contrast, is that fallen man is by nature completely selfish, and that altruism (in the words of Professor Basil Willey) is 'theoretically indefensible except on religious presuppositions'.[7] Mr Christopher Hollis makes basically the same point: 'Nothing could be more false than the notion that something in the nature of the Christian's duty to one's neighbour is a duty universally self-evident. On the contrary, it is a derivation from the acceptance of the duty towards God, and, unless the primary duty is accepted, there is little reason to accept the secondary duty.'[8] The Bishop of Southwark has proclaimed, more briefly, that 'Christianity is the supreme reason why men and women should lead decent lives'.[9] And the Rev. Andrew Morton, Chaplain of Edinburgh University, said recently in a television programme, in the tones of one stating a truism, that 'we do not naturally act compassionately'. The widespread Christian hostility to Humanism is probably due largely to the belief that it undermines the basis of morals.

Humanists, however, are disposed to reverse the argument. They maintain that the Christian ethic is basically defective, in that it has, so to speak, stood natural morality on its head; it has denied and discouraged man's natural social tendencies, and encouraged a self-centred preoccupation with one's own virtue and one's own salvation. In the words of that great non-Christian deist, Florence Nightingale, it has been too concerned with 'smuggling a man selfishly into heaven, instead of setting him actively to regenerate the earth'.[10]

Christians, naturally, will repudiate this view, and will point to the Gospel injunctions to love one's neighbour. But if the Gospels are read as a whole, rather than in the highly selective way in which we are encouraged to read them, it is clear that they attach far greater importance to loving God than to loving one's fellow man. Furthermore, they put forward as the main motive for loving and helping one's neighbour the assurance that such conduct is pleasing to God and will earn a substantial reward in the life hereafter. To quote from the New English translation:

> The Son of Man is to come in the glory of his Father, with his angels; and then he will give each man the due reward for what he has done. (Matt. xvi, 27)
>
> Your good deed must be secret, and your Father who sees what is done in secret will reward you. (Matt. vi, 4)
>
> You must love your enemies and do good; and lend without

expecting any return; and you will have a rich reward. (Luke vi, 35)

Give, and gifts will be given you. Good measure, pressed down, shaken together, and running over. (Luke vi, 38)

The appeal to 'posthumous self-interest', in John Stuart Mill's phrase, is unmistakable in these statements as they stand. They fully justify the attitude of Mrs Fairchild in the Victorian children's classic ('"He that giveth to the poor lendeth to the Lord, and shall be repaid," said Mrs Fairchild, hastily slipping a shilling into the poor woman's hand.') Today, liberal Christians are somewhat embarrassed by the frequent references to reward in the Gospels (the word occurs nine times in the sermon on the mount) and many have tried, quite unconvincingly, to explain away some of the more disconcerting texts as 'symbolic' expressions of the view that, in Stoic parlance, the reward of virtue is virtue itself. Others have suggested that Jesus' words have been misreported.

The second argument has obvious dangers for Christians, but one may readily agree with those who use it that—since the Gospels are second or third-hand accounts written thirty years or more after the events they purport to describe—it would be unsafe to assume that any of the sayings they attribute to Jesus contain his actual words. The most that can be expected is that they give a reasonably accurate impression of the general tenor of his teaching. But if we make this assumption—and if, as already suggested, we read the Gospels as a whole and not selectively—it becomes impossible to accept the view now popular among left-wing Christians, that they show an intense concern for personal relationships. On the contrary, human ties are regarded not merely as less important than, but in some cases as a definite obstacle to, the attainment of a right relationship with God. The type of charity that is commended is a sort of impersonal self-denial based on duty rather than affection. It is admirable to give to the poor—to people one does not know and has possibly never seen—but dangerous to get too fond of one's nearest and dearest, since this may distract one from higher things. The Gospels contain some rather startling pronouncements on the latter theme, to which attention is seldom drawn by Christian moralists. For example:

> If anyone comes to me and does not hate his father and mother, wife and children, brothers and sisters, even his own life, he cannot be a disciple of mine. (Luke xiv, 26)
>
> And anyone who has left brothers or sisters, father, mother, or children, land or houses for the sake of my name will be repaid many times over, and gain eternal life. (Matt. xix, 29)

It must be granted, once again, that these sayings may have been misreported, and that it is impossible for us to know for certain what Jesus taught. We do, however, know a great deal about what the early Church taught. And there can be no doubt that in the heyday of its power, from the fall of Rome until the twelfth century, the Church taught that human ties were an obstacle to the love of God, and that we should do good to others, not from affection or spontaneous impulse, but because this was what God commanded and what God would reward. And the last people we should do good to were the members of our own family.

This doctrine was widely expressed and practised by the Early Fathers, one of whom, St Jerome (fourth-fifth century), may be quoted. (Jerome was responsible for the first Latin translation of the Bible, known as the Vulgate, and is one of the most highly-esteemed saints in the Christian calendar). His ideal of feminine excellence was embodied in one Paula, a patrician Roman lady, a widow with five children, who on her husband's death devoted herself to the ascetic life and became the head of a convent. Jerome wrote of her:

> How can I describe her far-reaching kindness even to those whom she had never seen? . . . What bedridden person was not supported with money from her purse? She would seek out such with the greatest diligence . . . and would think it her loss were any hungry or sick person to be supported by another's food. She robbed her children; and, when her relatives remonstrated with her for doing so, she declared that she was leaving to them a better inheritance in the mercy of Christ . . . 'God is my witness' she said 'that what I do I do for his sake. My prayer is that I may die a beggar, not leaving a penny to my daughter and indebted to strangers for my winding sheet . . . She obtained her wish at last, and died leaving her daughter overwhelmed with a mass of debt . . . and a crowd of brothers and

> sisters whom it is hard for her to support, but whom it would be undutiful to cast off. Could there be a more admirable instance of virtue?[11]

The phrase beginning 'and would think it her loss' is significant; it suggests that Paula was concerned less to relieve others' suffering than to enhance her own sanctity. This attitude was widespread in the Dark Ages. As Lecky remarked in his *History of European Morals*,[12] 'A form of what may be termed selfish charity arose . . . Men gave money to the poor, simply and exclusively for their own spiritual benefit, and the welfare of the sufferer was altogether foreign to their thoughts'. From this attitude it was but a short step to the view that self-sacrifice brings spiritual benefits for the sacrificer, even though it does nothing for the welfare of anyone else; and in the first centuries after the conversion of Europe, the great exemplars of Christian virtue were held to be the hermits—men who cut themselves off from all human relationships and lived alone in the desert or wilderness, starving and scourging themselves and (as they supposed) growing daily in holiness. Jerome spent some years of his life in this way and wrote an account from which the following is quoted:

> Many years ago, for the sake of the Kingdom of Heaven I cut myself off from home, parents, sister, relations, and, what was harder, from the dainty food to which I had been used. . . . But oh how often, when I was living in the desert, in that lonely waste, scorched by the burning sun, which affords to hermits a savage dwelling-place, how often did I fancy myself surrounded by the pleasures of Rome! My unkempt limbs were covered in shapeless sackcloth; my skin through neglect had become as rough and black as an Ethiopian's. Tears and groans were every day my portion; and if sleep ever overcame my resistance and fell upon my eyes, I bruised my restless bones against the naked earth. Of food and drink I will not speak. Hermits drink nothing but cold water even when they are sick, and for them it is sinful luxury to partake of cooked dishes. But though in my fear of hell I had condemned myself to this prison-house, where my only companions were scorpions and wild beasts, I often found myself surrounded by bands of dancing girls. Though my limbs were cold as ice my mind was burning with desire, and the fires of lust kept bubbling up before me when my flesh was as good as dead.[13]

Similar austerities were practised by thousands of persons of both sexes in the Dark Ages. Lecky gives an account, based on patristic literature, of the revolting excesses of self-maceration and bodily squalor in which the ascetics indulged, and concludes:

> There is perhaps no phase in the moral history of mankind of a deeper or more painful interest than this ascetic epidemic. A hideous, sordid and emaciated maniac, without knowledge, without patriotism, without natural affection, passing his life in a long routine of useless and atrocious self-torture, and quailing before the ghastly phantoms of his delirious brain, had become the ideal of the nations which had known the writings of Plato and Cicero and the lives of Socrates and Cato. For about two centuries, the hideous maceration of the body was regarded as the highest proof of excellence.[14]

Becoming a hermit meant, inevitably, breaking all ties with one's nearest and dearest, and in a letter to a young friend, Heliodorus, Jerome urged him not to shrink from this sacrifice.

> Though your little nephew hang on your neck, though your mother with dishevelled hair and torn raiment show you the breasts that gave you suck, though your father fling himself upon the threshold, trample your father underfoot and go your way, fly with tearless eyes to the standard of the cross. In these matters to be cruel is a son's duty. . . . I too have passed through all this. . . . The love of Christ and the fear of hell easily break such bonds as these.[15]

There are many stories in patristic literature about the heroic virtue with which aspirants to sainthood trampled on their natural affections. I quote (again from Lecky) a story paraphrased from one Cassian, a contemporary of Jerome.

> A man named Mutius, accompanied by his only child, a little boy of eight years old, abandoned his possessions and demanded admission into a monastery. The monks received him but they proceeded to discipline his heart. 'He had already forgotten that he was rich; he must next be taught to forget that he was a father!' His child was separated from him, clothed in dirty rags, subjected to every form of gross and wanton hardship, beaten, spurned and ill-treated. Day after day the father was compelled to look upon his boy wasting away with sorrow, his once happy countenance for ever stained with tears, distorted by sobs of anguish. But yet, says the admiring

biographer, 'though he saw this day by day, such was his love for Christ, and for the virtue of obedience, that the father's heart was rigid and unmoved. He thought little of the tears of his child. He was anxious only for his own humility and perfection in virtue!' . . . Mutius afterwards rose to a high position among the ascetics, and he was justly regarded as having displayed in great perfection the temper of a saint.[16]

Critics may be disposed to ask, 'Why drag this up? Why flog dead horses? All this has nothing to do with Christianity today.' And admittedly our official religion today is much less terrifying than the Christianity of the Dark and Middle Ages—thanks largely to the influence of sceptics. None the less, it does not seem reasonable to demand that a veil be drawn over so large a part of Christianity's history. Few people know anything of the facts set out above, just as few know much of the atrocities perpetrated by the Church against heretics at a later stage of its history. And as a result of this conspiracy of silence, the view still prevails that Christianity has been such a great force for good that it is everyone's duty at least to pay lip-service to it, and to give his children a Christian education. To quote Professor William Empson:

> Many good people still believe that support for Christianity is a public duty, however absurd it feels, because other people (though not themselves) cannot be made good without it. A great deal of whitewashing still hides from them that, until there were enough influential and well-intentioned sceptics about, the Christians could not be prevented from behaving with monstrous wickedness. It remains a tribute to the stamina of European civilization that the religion could not corrupt us even more than it did, and by this time we seem pretty well inoculated against its more virulent forms. But it is not sensible to talk about Christianity so cosily as is now usual, ignoring its theoretical evil, ignoring its consequent use of rack, boot, thumbscrew and slow fire.[17]

And there is a further reason for 'dragging up the past'. One cannot really understand an institution without knowing something of the tradition in which it developed. The epidemic of extreme asceticism lasted for some two hundred years, which is not a negligible period. But, more important, the ideals behind it—the self-centred pursuit of individual virtue, and the feeling that the endurance of useless suffering is good for the soul, and pleasing to God—these have persisted, though fortunately in diminishing strength, right through the Christian era and are by no means extinct today. Some historical examples will illustrate this.

In the Middle Ages, as distinct from the Dark Ages, the life of a hermit became less fashionable, but there was still a strong feeling that self-maceration was one of the highest forms of virtue. When, in 1170, the murdered body of St Thomas of Canterbury was undressed in the cathedral crypt, it was found to be encased from the neck to the knees in haircloth. Dean Stanley gives a description of the scene, based on various contemporary accounts.

> The haircloth encased the whole body down to the knees; the hair drawers, as well as the rest of the dress, being covered on the outside with white linen so as to escape observation; and the whole so fastened together as to admit of being readily taken off for his daily scourgings, of which yesterday's portion was still apparent in the stripes on his body. Such austerity had hitherto been unknown to English saints, and the marvel was increased by the sight of the innumerable vermin with which the haircloth abounded—boiling over with them, as one account describes it, like water in a simmering cauldron. At the dreadful sight all the enthusiasm of the previous night revived with double ardour. They looked at each other in silent wonder; then exclaimed, 'See, see what a true monk he was, and we knew it not'; and burst into alternate fits of weeping and laughter, between the sorrow of having lost such a head, and the joy of having found such a saint.[18]

Moving on from the twelfth to the fourteenth century: the blessed Henry Suso, a German Dominican mystic, wrote (in the third person) an autobiography *The Life of the Servant* in which he described the almost incredible regime of self-torment to which he subjected himself for some sixteen years. To quote:

> He was in his youth of a temperament full of fire and life; and when this began to make itself felt, it was very grievous to him; and he sought by many devices how he might bring his body into subjection. . . . He secretly caused an undergarment to be made for him; and in the undergarment he had strips of leather fixed, into which a hundred and fifty brass nails pointed and filed sharp, were driven, and the points of the nails were

always turned towards the flesh. He had this garment made very tight, and so arranged as to go round him and fasten in front, in order that it might fit the closer to his body, and the pointed nails might be driven into his flesh; and it was high enough to reach upwards to his navel. In this he used to sleep at night. . . . The nights in winter were never so long, nor was the summer so hot, as to make him leave off this exercise. . . .

In winter he suffered very much from the frost. . . . His feet were full of sores, his legs dropsical, his knees bloody and seared, his loins covered with scars from the horsehair, his body wasted, his mouth parched with intense thirst, and his hands tremulous from weakness. Amid these torments he spent his nights and days; and he endured them all out of the greatness of the love which he bore in his heart to our Lord Jesus Christ, whose agonizing sufferings he sought to imitate.

He continued his torments for about sixteen years. At the end of this time, when his blood was now chilled, and the fire of his temperament destroyed, there appeared to him in a vision on Whitsunday, a messenger from heaven, who told him that God required this of him no longer. Whereupon he discontinued it.[19]

Thereafter Suso led what was comparatively speaking a normal life, and wrote various mystical and devotional works in which he extolled the value of 'detachment'—i.e. complete inner withdrawal from human contacts and the world of the senses. Among his prescriptions for achieving detachment were—'Live as if there were no creature on earth but thee', and 'Keep thy senses closed to every image which may present itself. Be empty of everything which . . . brings earthly joy or delight into the heart.'[20]

It may be said that a movement should not be judged by its lunatic fringe. But (disregarding the adjective) Suso was by no means at the fringe of the Church's life. He was for some years the Prior of a monastery; his writings exerted considerable influence both during his lifetime and in the century after his death;[21] and he still has his admirers today. The Roman Catholic weekly *The Tablet*, on the occasion of his sixth centenary in January 1966, said that though Suso has been 'singularly neglected' in Britain 'in Germany as might be expected, he is held in great respect by Catholics and Evangelicals alike'.

To move on another two centuries: a sixteenth-century

Spanish saint who is still greatly revered today is St. John of the Cross. Self-deprivation, rather than self-torture, was his road to sainthood. In *The Ascent of Mount Carmel* he wrote:

> The radical remedy lies in the mortification of the four great natural passions, joy, hope, fear and grief. . . . Let your soul therefore turn always:
> Not to what is most easy, but to what is hardest;
> Not to what tastes best, but to what is most distasteful;
> Not to what most pleases, but to what disgusts;
> Not to matter of consolation, but to matter for desolation rather;
> Not to rest, but to labor;
> Not to desire the more, but the less;
> Not to aspire to what is highest and most precious, but to what is lowest and most contemptible;
> Not to will anything, but to will nothing;
> Not to seek the best in everything, but to seek the worst, so that you may enter for the love of Christ into a complete destitution, a perfect poverty of spirit, and an absolute renunciation of everything in this world.[22]

By the nineteenth century the intellectual climate had been transformed by the Enlightenment, and the ascetic tradition had greatly weakened. But it was still definitely alive among the leaders of the High Anglican movement. Pusey (1800–1882), for example, described in a letter to Keble his own rather half-hearted attempts at self-mortification.

> I am a great coward about inflicting pain on myself, partly I hope from derangement of my nervous system; hair cloth I know not how to make pain; it is only symbolical, except when worn to an extent which seemed to wear me out. I have it on again, by God's mercy. I would try to get some sharper sort. I think I should like to be bid to use the discipline [i.e. self-scourging]. I cannot even smite on my breast much, because the pressure on my lungs seemed bad. In short, you see, I am a mass of infirmities.[23] [24]

One cannot but feel that Pusey might have found some more worthwhile preoccupation. During the earlier part of his life, young children were working a ten-hour day in the factories, but Pusey and his fellow High Anglicans showed no interest in the campaign against child labour, just as they showed no interest in the abolition of slavery. Both these reforms were brought about largely by unbelievers—almost the only Christians who showed any interest being Quakers and Nonconformists, who were outside the main stream of the Christian tradition.[25] When the High Anglicans thought of good causes they did not think of the abolition of slavery or child labour; they thought of such things as preventing a man from marrying his deceased wife's sister. Pusey felt deeply on this subject—not from any considerations of human happiness, but because he held that certain texts in Leviticus expressly forbade such unions. But no cause, Pusey felt, must be allowed to distract him from his primary task of ensuring his own salvation. In a letter to Newman he wrote:

> I fear that often . . . the consciousness of being engaged in a good cause has engrossed me too entirely, and made me think of my existence too much in reference to what might be accomplished by my means here, instead of looking pre-eminently to the preparing of myself to meet my God.[26]

A similar concern about preparing for death has been expressed by an eminent Anglican of our own time. Mr John Betjeman. He wrote:

> When most of the poems in my latest book were written, I was the self-pitying victim of remorse, guilt and terror of death. Much as I dislike trying to conform to Christian morality . . . the only practical way to face the dreaded lonely journey into Eternity seems to me to be the Christian one. I therefore try to believe that Christ was God made Man, and gives Eternal Life, and that I may be confirmed in this belief by clinging to the Sacraments, and by prayer.[27]

This was written in 1954. Since then Mr Betjeman has become more cheerful, and the Church of England of which he is so distinguished a member has been moving progressively further from Gospel Christianity in the direction of secular Humanism. Today it is mainly the Catholic Church that preserves the traditional Christian preoccupation with the life hereafter. Thus Cardinal Heenan, Archbishop of Westminster, when he was asked by a television interviewer 'What is your chief aim in life?' replied without hesitation 'to save my immortal soul'. But even the Catholic Church is now less concerned with the next world than it formerly was. The Easter 1967 Encyclical *Populorum Progressio* showed a quite unprecedented concern for the quality of human life in this world. Pope Paul, it is true, made the customary condemnation of 'materialism', and repudiated what is described as 'isolated' (i.e. secular) Humanism. But the Encyclical went on to argue the need for 'a new humanism' which, without rejecting the supernatural, will none the less aim at 'building a world where every man, no matter what his race, religion or nationality, can live a fully human life, freed from servitude imposed on him by other men or by natural forces over which he has not sufficient control'[28]—a statement which might well have appeared in a publication of the British Humanist Association.

Cynics may suggest that the Church's increasing concern with social matters is not unconnected with the challenge of Communism in the more backward Catholic countries. And they may find confirmation for this view in an editorial on the Encyclical in *The Tablet* which referred to:

> . . . the need to convince the masses in all the poorer parts of the world that the concern of the Catholic Church for their material protests is deep and genuine, no mere lip-service, but arising naturally out of the teachings of the Christian religion, so that what needs to be explained is not the reality of such concern but why, for various historical reasons, it has so often failed to manifest itself in any at all effective form.[29]

Many older Catholics, are not in sympathy with the new approach; they argue, not without force, that otherworldliness is of the essence of Christianity, and that a Church that ceased to be otherworldly would cease to be Christian. Mr Christopher Hollis proclaimed some years ago that 'It is not the fundamental concern of religion to bring order or civilization to this world. Its fundamental concern is not with life but with death';[29] and more recently Mr Arnold Lunn has said that 'This preoccupation with economics and social problems is evidence of declining belief in the primary mission of the Church: the salvation of souls and the conversion of those who now reject the supernatural.'[30]

Whether the traditionalists or the *soi-disant* 'new humanists' will prevail remains to be seen. On the attitude of the (presumably) average Catholic today, valuable light has been shed by a Catholic psychologist from London University, Dr Monica Lawlor. In a book significantly entitled *Out of this World*[31] she describes an experimental study of the 'value-judgements' of some 300 young Catholics, most of them students. They were given a well-known standard test (the Allport–Vernon–Lindzey Study of Values) and another test specially designed to investigate their idea of the Christian ideal. The results may be given in the author's own words:

> [Their ideal was found to be] theocentric and to a less marked extent Christocentric; it embraces an emphasis on the importance of observing the Church's requirements for public worship and the observance of rules generally. 'Thou shalt love the Lord thy God', they very properly affirm, but 'thy neighbour as thyself' has an altogether weaker flavour. . . . What does emerge very clearly is the essentially private nature of the religion they hold. . . . Clearly they are in no danger of being swept into an heretical over-concern with Works. Just as private prayer has precedence over the liturgical meeting, so community responsibility and love of one's neighbour are seen as less important than personal virtue.

No comparable study has been conducted in this country with Protestant Christians, but a few investigations in the United States have been reported in psychological journals, and they give a remarkably similar picture of withdrawal from social involvement. Thus a research reported in the American Journal of Psychotherapy concludes that 'dogmatic religious preoccupation is inversely proportionate to the extent of concern with social matters'[32]

In conclusion, therefore: in view of the facts here brought forward, there seems little ground for the claim that Christianity is, and always has been, an immense force for good. Through its failure to realize that man is a social animal, it has been led throughout most of its history to proclaim, and practise, a code of morality that is in essence completely self-interested. That it does so less strenuously today is the result of its permeation by secular Humanism; and nothing but good, we suggest, can result from the continuation of this process.

## REFERENCES AND NOTES

1. *The Tablet*, October 20th, 1945.
2. *African Genesis* (1961), p. 81.
3. 'The Humanity of Man.' Presidential Address to the British Association reported in *The Times*, August 31st, 1961.
4. *Epistles*, 95.
5. *On Duties*, I, 22.
6. *On Laws*, I, 43.
7. *Christianity, Past and Present* (1952), p 81.
8. *The Tablet*, November 15th, 1958.
9. *The Daily Herald*, January 14th, 1955.
10. *Suggestions for Thoughts to the Searchers after Truth among the Artizans of England*, (1859), Vol. I, p 262.
11. Letter 108 to Eustochium trans. S. L. Greenslade, *Early Latin Theology* (Library of Christian Classics Vol. V), pp. 351, 363, 380.
12. Vol. II, Chap. 4.
13. Letter 22 to Eustochium, trans. F. A. Wright. *Select Letters of St. Jerome* (Loeb Classical Library), pp. 67–68.
14. *History of European Morals* (1877), Vol. II, Chap. 4.
15. Letter 14 to Heliodorus, trans. F. A. Wright, *op. cit.*, pp. 31–2.
16. *Op. cit.*, Vol. II, Chap. 4.
17. *Milton's God* (1961), pp. 254–5.
18. *Historical Memorials of Canterbury* (1885), pp. 75–6.
19. *The Life of Blessed Henry Suso*, trans, T. F. Knox (1865), Chaps, 17, 19, quoted by William James in *The Varieties of Religious Experience* (1903) pp. 307, 308, 309.
20. *Op. cit.*, Chap. 53.
21. Cf., for example, the chapter on Suso in J. M. Clark. *The Great German Mystics* (1949).
22. Quoted by William James in *The Varieties of Religious Experience*, p. 305. The Collected Works of St. John of the Cross have been recently translated by Kieran Kavanaugh and Otilio Rodriguez (1963).
23. H. D. Liddon *Life of Edward Bouverie Pusey* (1894), Vol. III, pp. 100–101.
24. Once again it may be well to emphasize that we are not dealing with the lunatic fringe of the Church. Pusey was an Oxford Professor, the Dean of Christ Church, and one of the leading figures in the history of Anglicanism. The Oxford University Hall of Residence for theological students is named after him, Pusey Hall.
25. Cf. G. M. Trevelyan *English Social History* (1942). 'Wilberforce confessed with chagrin that the "high-and-dry" conservative party then prevalent among the Church clergy obstructed the anti-slavery cause or were at best indifferent, while Nonconformists and godless reformers proved his staunchest allies' (p. 495).
26. *Op. cit.*, p. 95.
27. *The New Statesman*, October 8th, 1954.

28. *The Tablet*, April 8th, 1967.
29. *The Observer*, June 3rd, 1956.
30. *The Tablet*, January 28th, 1967.
31. *Out of this World: a Study of Catholic Values* (Stagbooks, 1965). The quotations are taken from pp. 16 and 130.
32. Lowe, Warner L. 'Religious Beliefs and Religious Delusions', *Amer. J. Psychotherapy*, 1955, 9, pp. 54–61.

# Mass Media and the Coming Revolution In Communications

LORD FRANCIS WILLIAMS

## Lord Francis Williams

Author, journalist and television commentator. Editor of *Daily Herald*, 1936–1940. Controller of news and censorship at the Ministry of Information, 1941–1945. Adviser on public relations to the Prime Minster, 1945–1947. Regents' Professor at the University of California, Berkeley, 1961. Governor of BBC, 1951–1952.

Publications include: *War by Revolutions*; *The Triple Challenge: The Future of Socialist Britain*; *Ernest Bevin: The Story of a Great Englishman*; *The Rise of the Trade Unions*; *Dangerous Estate: The Anatomy of Newspapers*; *A Prime Minister Remembers* (with Lord Attlee); *A Pattern of Rulers*.

# Mass Media and the Coming Revolution In Communications

LORD FRANCIS WILLIAMS

'Only connect . . .,' says E. M. Forster in his greatest novel. But how compose the unceasing rush of events and experiences that make up the human condition in the second half of the twentieth century in such a way that they will be relevant to men and women of so many different races and ages and such diverse backgrounds and aptitudes, constantly bombarded at ever greater speed and in ever increasing volume with news of the world's events.

We are in the middle of a communications revolution comparable to the invention of printing. Comparable to but by no means identical with. Rather in some ways actually antagonistic to the literate civilization of the printed word. Technological changes carry their social dynamic within themselves, their results are both quantitative and qualitative. We tremble on the edge of an era of space communication that will alter not only methods of mass communication but its content.

Already in the last four decades we have moved from a world dominated by the spoken and written word—the spoken word directly uttered in conversation or by a speaker in direct contact with his audience, the written word based on an expectation of literacy that has never been true for more than a minority of the world's population—to one in which the boundaries of distance and literacy will soon no longer exist.

The world in which the transmission of news and ideas

depended on words directly exchanged was essentially a private one. It was changed fundamentally by the printed word. But in so far as the boundaries of the printed word were set by a common language and a common literacy, it still remained private, depending on a shared culture and a shared tradition.

This was even true after the development of the mass media of the popular press. This widened the area of private communication. But although the private world extended to millions, it was still private in the sense that it embraced an audience only of those literate in the same language and sharing the same national and social backgrounds. In developed countries this meant the whole nation—or rather a series of different but inter-related groups in the nation according to their geographical situation as in the United States, or to their social and intellectual relationship, as in the division between popular and mass newspapers in Britain. But it was far from meaning this over a large part of the earth's surface where the impact of the printed word even at its most popular was restricted by mass illiteracy. The development of a mass media has always been restricted to socially and economically advanced communities. It has explored and exploited new social layers within such communities but remained essentially private to them. We talk much about the impact of the mass media but until now no such thing has ever existed on a world scale.

Radio and television further extended the frontiers of communication. Yet even so they remained essentially private, transmitted by national systems directed to national audiences and shaped and edited by producers, whether under public or commercial control, to meet the needs and satisfy the supposed tasted of private, not universal audiences.

The new space technologies now developing will, however, transcend time, space and language, all three. Even literacy has become less relevant than it was. Indeed even in some literate communities there is already a turning away from the written word, especially among the young in favour of the visual image. Even the illiterate, or semi-literate, can receive television pictures along with the literate—and soon moreover may receive them in a form owing nothing to editing but whose impact will come from the fact that the events seen are being transmitted live as they happen. The assassination of President Kennedy, the murder of his assassin, were both seen by millions as they happened without any of the processing formerly exercised by reporters and editors. The Vietnam war is not only the best reported war in history, but the only one in which immense publics thousands of miles away have been put in a position to see for themselves men fighting and dying, filmed as they fought and died. The impact of this on public opinion has been enormous. We are moving into an era where the private worlds of communication are at last becoming wholly public, the mass media truly mass on a world scale.

In a comparatively short space of time space satellites may be in orbit capable of simultaneously transmitting a volume of news some four hundred times as great as that which can be handled by the most modern trans-Atlantic cable envisaged and more than 160 times greater even than Early Bird can now handle. Three or four such satellites strategically sited may well be able to blanket the entire world with a service of quick and voluminous news.

Moreover, not only must we prepare ourselves for a situation in which it will be possible for anything happening anywhere in the world to be relayed immediately in vision via space satellites to local distribution centres and thence to television sets in millions upon millions of homes, but one in which it will eventually be technically possible to cut out local television transmitters as intermediaries altogether and service home television sets direct from space satellites.

The television set in the sitting-room could then become a window on the world in a sense far surpassing anything that has been known so far. The opportunity—technically at least—will exist for ordinary men and women of all races and cultures to participate directly as observers in every event of public importance in the world as it actually takes place and with the same sense of immediacy as if they were physically present.

It is in many ways an exhilarating prospect—especially

perhaps to those who as humanists believe profoundly in the open society, the constant movement of ideas, the continuing debate. But it is also, for reasons that will become clear, an intimidating one. We may perhaps be thankful that it is unlikely to be with us very soon, not because it is not technologically possible, for it is, or soon will be, but for other reasons. It is inconceivable for instance that at the present stage of world political development all or even the majority of national governments would be willing to abdicate their authority by agreeing to let their populations be flooded with international television programmes originating outside and quite beyond their influence, or that those involved in the immense capital and labour investment in existing communications systems, including the press, would be willing to see those systems by-passed or put aside without the strongest resistance.

Nevertheless, technology has a habit of shaping the world to its own potentialities whatever the initial resistance from political and social systems of an earlier technological age. The eruptive power of new communications systems as an agency in helping to form the conception of one world cannot be overlooked. At the very least it may help to make some barriers to the exchange of news and ideas among peoples less viable than they are now.

But the other half of the coin has also to be considered, the intimidating as well as the exhilarating side of such a technological project. At present the news that reaches the public through newspapers or radio programmes or current affairs television films is processed news. It would, you may think, be a very good thing that it should cease to be so. But do not be quite sure. If processing means propagandizing, then clearly the more of the world's news that reaches the people of the world neat and uncontaminated by intermediate handling, the better.

Yet by diminishing or actually by-passing the selective and editorial processes currently carried out by newspapers, radio and television services and international news agencies, space communications, if carried to its logical technological conclusion, could produce a system in which we would all be in some danger of becoming punch drunk with the direct impact of events. It is the editorial process that separates the important from the unimportant, transmuting into digestible form the raw material of events and translating it into terms that fall within the experience of each audience.

So necessary are such editorial processes to most people's comprehension of the world about them that the direct visual transmission of international happenings without any intermediary might lead to less understanding of the world, not more. It is by no means always enough to see for oneself. Even in the unlikely event of the political barriers to technology's advance to a truly public communications world being removed, supplementary private services beamed to particular groups and specifically adapted to their experience and needs would still be required if the public's ability to absorb and judge the significant were not to be destroyed by the sheer mass of unprocessed raw material dumped on its lap.

Awareness that the full development of space communication could bring its problems as well as its opportunities should not, however, blind us to the possibilities opened up by these new communications technologies of a far greater spread of knowledge between nations and peoples than there has ever previously been.

The current pattern of world news communication may be said to fall into two main categories.

There is first that of the movement of news between the main news centres of the world, New York, London, Moscow, Paris, each of which acts as a collecting and redistribution centre serving a wide area.

Second there is the two-way movement of news between the main news distributing centres and technologically less advanced areas of the world, which may, nevertheless, themselves be important originators of news, especially at periods of social or political transition or crisis. It is important for world understanding that the flow of news from such areas to the rest of the world shall not consist only of occasional crisis reporting.

Although technologically less advanced than the great metropolitan centres of news distribution, these developing areas often provide evidence of some of the most significant social, economic and political trends in the world. It is not only important that such trends should be adequately reported internationally, but also that those living in such areas should themselves receive an adequate, intelligible service of news from the rest of the world. Only if they do so can they relate the movements and pressures in their own societies to a world background. Those faced by inevitably rapid changes need to be able to measure what is happening in their own societies against what is taking place in other comparable societies, and in older and possibly more sophisticated ones.

There is need also to promote better means of communication within developing countries. Many at present lack adequate internal news systems because of the shortage, or in some instances, the virtual absence, of newspapers and even of radio sets, plus a still large degree of illiteracy among often widely dispersed communities.

In the present stage of space communication it is only the movement of news in the first category that has been affected. It is only within this complex of major news centres that the large ground stations required for communication with satellites exist or are likely to exist. Such ground stations are at present in operation in the United States and Canada on the one side of the Atlantic, and in Britain, France, Western Germany and Italy on the other.

Except in the transmission of live television programmes, for which the satellite system is already being used on occasion, space satellites, therefore, at this stage of development complement, rather than add to, existing mass communication systems. Even in television the high cost—$5,400 an hour—restricts their use to the live transmission of news and news events of such urgent world-wide interest or prestige importance as to make it worth while to avoid the short delay—in most cases of a few hours only—if the alternative of ferrying video tape by jet plane is employed.

Although nineteen governments are parties to an agreement urging that 'satellite communications should be organized in such a way as to permit all States to have access to the global system' (the original objective was to achieve basic global coverage in the latter part of 1967) it seems unlikely for cost and other reasons that we shall for the present see the extension of the system of space communication far beyond areas where existing communication systems already operate at maximum density and efficiency.

However, even at this present stage there is one factor of great significance that deserves careful consideration. Satellites have one great advantage over ground systems: because of the absence of intermediate handling the cost of transmitting messages is unaffected by distance—it is the same irrespective of the number of hundreds or thousands of miles between the points of origin and receipt. Once a communication satellite system is established on a global basis there is, therefore, no good reason why a flat transmission rate should not be established, or at any rate the present big differentials in cable rates be ended.

The very wide differentials that exist in the cost of transmitting press messages often without relevance to distance have a distorting effect on the movement of news. The high cost of sending messages from some parts of the world, as, for example, many Middle Eastern countries, leads to the under-reporting of developments in such areas, compared with elsewhere, and particularly affects that continuing coverage of trends against which 'hot' news should be seen.

The opportunity provided by satellite communication for a basic flat rate throughout the world could represent a practical advance of immense importance in securing a full exchange of news and information between peoples, and in helping to remove current distortions in world news coverage.

Even when basic global coverage by space satellites is achieved, the full integration of the less developed areas into a space communication system will, however, depend upon the economic ability of such areas to build the necessary land stations. The cost of these may well for many years be too high to be carried in their national budgets by many countries already grappling with urgent social and economic priorities. International aid is needed if the communications revolution is to have its full effect in making possible a more adequate flow of news between all areas of the world, whether they are at an advanced stage of capital development or not.

Meanwhile until the economic problem of building ground stations in economically underdeveloped territories is overcome, a network of local telecommunication services, based on currently existing radio or cable links, might be devised to feed satellite ground stations much as local road or rail services feed the major trunk networks in road and rail. A comparatively few well-sited ground stations could in such circumstances act as distributing centres for the servicing of wide areas. It might also be appropriate not only for the owners and controllers of space satellites but for the great world news agencies who wish to use them, to consider how far they might be able financially to assist in the construction of ground stations or ground service station-linking systems to ensure that news services transmitted by space satellite adequately cover the world.

In many underdeveloped territories the current problem of news distribution is only partially one of lack of communication networks. It comes also from the absence of physical means of producing newspapers in all but a very few centres, and the lack of television and even radio transmitters capable of covering more than a few metropolitan centres.

Where there is a high degree of illiteracy, television or radio provides the easiest means of mass communication. It is sensible in such areas to concentrate in the first instance on improving broadcasting facilities. But both radio and television programmes suffer from a lack of durability. Newspapers which can, where necessary, be read and re-read at leisure, studied and discussed, are as essential to social and political advance in underdeveloped communities as in more sophisticated ones. Until illiteracy is overcome the initial potential audience for such newspapers cannot, of course, be large. It will consist only of numerically small and often widely scattered groups of the better educated—official and commercial administrators, doctors, teachers, students and the like. Their importance, however, is much greater than their numbers because they are opinion formers in their societies.

Such men and women need newspapers, for newspapers are an essential part of the apparatus of increased information and understanding even where initial circulations can only be small. The absence of newspaper printing plants and their high capital cost where only very limited circulations can for some time be expected stand in the way of this.

Space communication, however, is technologically particularly suitable as a link in the production of facsimile newspapers—newspapers, that is, produced in much the same way as a photograph is transmitted by wireless and without the need of a printing press. Facsimile newspapers receivable by comparatively low cost receiving stations could help to overcome the difficulty of providing adequate newspapers in scattered low income societies.

Is it too much to ask that the major world news services consider the possibility of co-operating in the provision of facsimile newspapers transmitted via space communication to meet the needs of underdeveloped communities? Such facsimile newspapers would need to be internationally sponsored and the basic material provided by international news agencies edited and co-ordinated by an international editorial group. This might very suitably be provided by UNESCO.

In the long term it seems technologically well within the bounds of possibility that most of the normal links in the communication chain as we now know it may be by-passed. Live television programmes covering events taking place in any part of the world may be channelled direct to individual viewers all over the world without the intervention of local or national television organizations; facsimile newspapers may be available to individuals through small photo-production units attached to their television sets without any of the present processes of printing and distribution.

Although technically conceivable, it is however hardly possible that such developments will move into the area of the practical, without changes in national and international attitudes which may be remote. It is possible, however, that agreement might be reached for direct-to-consumer television transmissions in particular areas of news activity under the supervision of an international agency as a complement to the services provided by national braodcasting and press services. There would be advantage, for example, in the direct transmission by space satellite of live television programmes covering the activities of the United Nations, particularly at periods of crisis, and the constructive efforts of other world agencies in attacking poverty and ill health. By such means we might begin to move towards a new conception of the mass media in latest technological form as a servant of mass understanding throughout the world.

Technological development is one of the major influences on civilization. But if technological advance is to be wisely used, it must at each stage be measured against, and if necessary amended by, consideration of the ends which civilization properly sets before us.

The movement of news and the international acceptance of ourselves as members of one human family is, to the humanist certainly, but also surely to very many believers in traditional religious faiths, fundamental to civilized progress. We must do all we can to see to it that the technological opportunities now opening before us as firmly and constantly developed against this background of principle.

# Against Indoctrination

ANTONY FLEW

## Antony Flew

Professor of Philosophy in the University of Keele. Visiting Professor at New York University (1958); Swarthmore College (1961); Universities of Adelaide and Melbourne (1963); University of Pittsburgh (1965); University of Malawi (1967).

Publications include: *A New Approach to Physical Research*; *Logic and Language* (editor); *Essays in Conceptual Analysis* (editor); *New Essays in Philosophical Theology* (joint editor), *Hume's Philosophy of Belief*; *God and Philosophy*; *Evolutionary Ethics*; and articles in philosophical journals.

# Against Indoctrination

ANTONY FLEW

*'Give me a child until it is seven.' A Church of England (aided) infant school, in Midlands, three hundred children, excellent church teaching, needs new building. No diocesan funds available. Will anyone who realizes the importance of Church Schools please communicate. Write Box C. 705 The Times, E.C.4.*

Advertisement in the Personal Columns of *The Times* for August 26th, 1965.

In this paper I first propose, explain and defend a definition of the term *indoctrination*. After that I begin to put this notion to work. The first Part is long, and the practically-minded may well become impatient with these philosophical preliminaries. They do nevertheless have a practical point. For it is in this Part that I shape the framework within which the whole discussion ought to take place. Once given this right framework clearly appreciated it becomes easy to realize, what I try briskly to indicate in the second Part, where the onus of proof really lies, what has to be proved, and what hinges upon success or failure in the attempt to prove it.

In this second Part I argue, generally, that indoctrination is presumptively, although not for that reason necessarily also categorically, always wrong; and, in particular, I urge that parents (and others) have no moral right to indoctrinate (or to arrange for other people to indoctrinate), their (or any) children in a religious (or political) creed of the parents' (or anyone else's) choice. From the general conclusion I draw out the general corollary that the onus of proof must lie on the indoctrinator to justify his practices, if he can; and I then indicate how the recognition of this corollary must underline the importance of the sometimes underrated issues of theological epistemology. From the particular conclusion I extract the particular corollary that states—whatever their duties of toleration—have no right, much less any duty, to provide—as ours most lavishly does—positive support for indoctrination.

In the first Part, and to a lesser extent in the second also, I draw on materials which I have already presented within my contributions to a discussion started by Professor R. M. Hare and Mr John Wilson in a book on *Aims in Education: the Philosophic Approach*, and continued in the journal *Studies in Philosophy and Education*.[1] But the manner in which these materials are arranged is totally different, and they are here employed for quite explicitly practical purposes.

I

(*a*) Indoctrination consists in implanting, with the backing of some sort of special authority, of a firm conviction of the truth of doctrines either not known to be true or even known to be false. The classical, albeit imaginary, instance is found in Plato's sponsorship of his 'noble lie . . . a sort of Phoenician tale . . . demanding no little persuasion to make it believable'. Plato proposed that the whole power and authority of his supposedly ideal state—*The Republic*—should be deployed 'to persuade first the rulers themselves and the soldiers and then the rest of the population . . .' of the truth of his own deliberately made up Myth of the Earthborn. Plato's 'Socrates' and his interlocutor despair of so indoctrinating the first generation, but believe that it would be possible to persuade 'their sons and successors and other men who come after'.

The object of the exercise is to instil an acceptable, though false, account of the origins of *The Republic*. This is an account of origins which is supposed at the same time to provide an acceptable, though nevertheless strictly unwarranted, justification of the peculiar institutions of that allegedly ideal state. The final comment here of Plato's 'Socrates' is that, allowing that you could only reasonably hope thus to indoctrinate the successors, still 'even that would have a good effect in making them more inclined to care for the state and one another'.[2]

We must not, however, even as we consider this classical example, overlook that in the completely typical case the indoctrinator does believe that his doctrine is true. This is so even where he might reasonably hesitate to claim that, by ordinary and non-sectarian standards, it constitutes an item of knowledge. This does not, of course, even begin to show that such indoctrination is morally unobjectionable. Yet it is, equally obviously, importantly relevant to the entirely different question of the goodness or badness of the intentions of the indoctrinator. For, notoriously, a man may from the best of motives unfortunately do the wrong thing; just as he may chance to do the right thing despite the most evil of intentions.

(*b*) In explaining and defending the definition proposed we shall be appealing both to the present accepted usage of the term *indoctrination* and to considerations of economy, clarity and utility. Usage seems in this case to be somewhat untidy and even inconsistent; this is only to be expected with a term so emotionally charged and so much a focus of conflict. In so far as there is any such untidiness and inconsistency in the present usage any definition determining a philosophically satisfactory concept of indoctrination must be to some extent prescriptive (or stipulative), as opposed to purely descriptive (or lexical).

Nevertheless, even where and in so far as our definition is intended to prescribe for an improved concept of indoctrination, we have to attend to previous usage: first, because a reformed concept can only be any sort of concept of indoctrination in so far as there really is some substantial overlap between the new and the old use of the term; second, because examination of the existing usage may well reveal subtleties of which the wise reformer will wish to take account; and, third, because—since speech habits are as difficult to break as other habits—it is foolish unnecessarily to try to go against the grain of well-established verbal habits.

(*c*) The first thing to explain and to justify is the employment in our definition of the word *implanting*, and the inclusion of the clause *with the backing of some sort of special authority*.

The point is to exclude from the scope of the concept of indoctrination all cases where one man persuades another of the truth of some doctrine by the straightforward presentation of arguments as man to man. The indoctrinator has always to be in some sort of privileged situation as against those who are being indoctrinated, usually that of teacher to pupil; and certainly not that of one man carrying on a frank, give-and-take, discussion with an equal. Thus Plato's 'Socrates' is the Founder–Teacher–Legislator of *The Republic*, notwithstanding that his role is to be concealed behind his self-made Myth of the Earthborn. Typically it is an educational system which indoctrinates; and the teacher as such is obviously the bearer of a special authority over the pupil. Or, again, a state or private propaganda machine may—and all too probably will—attempt to indoctrinate; and any such machine is necessarily in a privileged position as compared with the individual exposed to its efforts to persuade.

This first restriction of the scope of the concept of indoctrination seems, as we have suggested, to accord with present ordinary usage. Even if it did not, there would be very good reason to prescribe that it should. For without some such limitation the word *indoctrination* is left with no peculiar and useful job to do. It becomes either a ponderous and offensive synonym for *persuasion*, or at best an unnecessary word for persuasion of the truth of a particular class of propositions. But what we want—and have here got—is a special word for such persuasion, backed by advantages which might be—and at least by me are—thought to be improper and unfair.

(*d*) The second thing is our definition requiring explanation and comment in the word *doctrines*. The employment of this particular word is again quite deliberately restrictive. Not every proposition constitutes a doctrine, although it would be hard if not impossible to specify precisely what propositions do and what do not. In so far as this is so our concept of indoctrination must necessarily be in this direction and to this extent vague. Yet it would be entirely wrong to think that a concept which is in any way imprecise, unspecific or indeterminate must therefore be rejected as useless—or worse than useless. It is, as Aristotle long since insisted, a mark of the educated man to demand only that degree of precision and specification which the particular subject permits and requires.[3]

Although the term *doctrine* is thus admittedly imprecise, the point of using it, and of confining the word *indoctrination* to the implanting of doctrines, can be brought out sufficiently by considering the misuse of the latter term in a very characteristic piece of apologetic for *The Catholic Way in Education:*

> Every educational institution makes use of indoctrination. Children are indoctrinated with the multiplication table; they are indoctrinated with love of country; they are indoctrinated with the principles of chemistry and physics and mathematics and biology, and nobody finds fault with indoctrination in these fields. Yet these are of small concern in the great business of life by contrast with ideas concerning God and man's relation to God . . . the Catholic educator makes no apology for indoctrinating his students in these essential matters.[4]

This is a remarkable and instructive passage. Every statement in it except those of the final sentence is false, and of these the first is most importantly misleading. In effect the author is denying that there is any difference between teaching and indoctrination. For only if this were true would it be correct to say that every educational institution is involved in indoctrination. But there is a difference, and what makes the term *indoctrination* useful is that it is employed to make the distinction. Certainly children are taught the multiplication table. But that twelve twelves are one hundred and forty-four is not a doctrine. Hence to teach this necessary truth cannot be to indoctrinate. Again, children in many other countries are studiously taught to be patriotic. But patriotic affections and inclinations as such, precisely as affections and inclinations, do not presuppose or contain any beliefs. Hence to encourage these affections and inclinations is not essentially and necessarily to implant false or disputatious doctrines. And where the teaching of patriotism is as a matter of contingent fact tied up with the implantation of such doctrines some people do—in my view rightly—find fault with the indoctrination so involved.

What makes a proposition a doctrine is its being in some

way ideological, a possible candidate for inclusion in a creed: 'The principles of chemistry and physics and mathematics and biology' do not qualify, whereas assertions 'concerning God and man's relation to God' obviously and paradigmatically do. Some may perhaps find it significant that the author of the passage under discussion temporarily stops employing the word *indoctrination* at precisely the point in his list where for the first time it becomes apt. Certainly we must notice the use which he wants to make of his very proper insistence on the enormous importance of 'ideas concerning God and man's relations to God'. For he proceeds to slide, easily but illegitimately, from this innocuous and noncontroversial general premise to an obnoxious and highly particular conclusion—that it must be perfectly all right for 'the Catholic educator' to indoctrinate his pupils with his own particular doctrines about 'these essential matters'.

The crucial, but constantly neglected, difference here can best be brought out in terms of the distinction between two totally different, yet too often confounded senses of the curriculum cliché *religious knowledge* ('RK'). In the first interpretation religious knowledge is knowledge about the religious beliefs which have been, and are, in fact held; and about the religious practices which have been, and are, actually pursued. In this interpretation to allow that there truly is religious knowledge carries no necessary commitment to the highly disputatious proposition that certain religious beliefs are indeed (not merely true but) known to be true; nor does it carry any implications about adopting any of these practices. There is, therefore, nothing in the least incongruous about an atheist humanist claiming to possess religious knowledge in this first sense; and, furthermore, most of us do in fact and consistently support the demand that 'RK' in this sense is so important that it must have a place in the most basic school curriculum, as well as some representation in all universities.

It is the second, totally other, interpretation which is the focus of conflict. In this second interpretation 'RK' consists in some particular set of religious propositions which are taken to be, and are taught as if they were, themselves knowledge; on which assumption it seems appropriate to teach the corresponding practices, not as facts about what some people do, but as practices which the pupil is himself to adopt. It is one thing—and obviously desirable—to know what Roman Catholics, qua Roman Catholics, believe, and do. But it is another and totally different thing to claim and to teach that these beliefs are themselves items of knowledge; and to train your pupils to follow the corresponding practices.

(*e*) The third and last clause requiring explanation and defence is, *either not known to be true or even known to be false*. To know it is necessary, but it is not sufficient, to believe and to be right. There is, of course, no doubt but that these are both necessary, indeed constitutive, conditions of knowledge. Thus it would be contradictory to claim to know what you also at the same time claim to believe to be false. More interestingly, it is also contradictory to say, without reservation, that someone knew something while you are also maintaining that what he claimed to know was false. Certainly we do intelligibly and pointedly say such things as 'He knew that his horse would win the Two Thousand Guineas, but he knew wrong'. But this genuinely is a rule-proving exception. For had he really known he must necessarily have been right: the whole paradoxical point of saying 'He knew, but he knew wrong', lies precisely in the fact that it is strictly self-contradictory. If he was wrong then he did not really know, but only 'knew' (in inverted commas): just as, if there were no pink rats really there to be seen, the dipsomaniac on his lost weekend can only be said to have 'seen' (in inverted commas), and not truly to have seen, such creatures.

In addition to these first two necessary, constitutive, conditions there is also a third. Properly to know you have to be in a position to know, you must possess sufficient reason for believing. Consider how, when we are exercising the fastidious caution appropriate to a statement upon which a great deal hinges, we may admit to believing that someone is a thief while nevertheless insisting that we are not (yet) in a position to know: 'it is only a hunch, a suspicion'; 'there is no (real) evidence'; and so on. It follows, therefore, that a claim to know may be rebutted, not only by challenging the sincerity of the claimant's belief in what he claims to know, or by showing that the content of his belief is in fact false, but also by showing that he has not got sufficient reason to justify him in claiming to know. If any one of these objections can be sustained then what we have is simply not a full standard case of knowledge proper.

## II

(*a*) There can now, after the elucidations of Part I, be little doubt but that indoctrination must be presumptively—and hence whenever the presumption cannot be defeated also categorically—wrong. For to try to implant a firm conviction of the truth of some doctrine is to teach this doctrine as if it were known truth, whereas it is a constitutive condition of indoctrination that the doctrines involved are either not known to be true or known to be false; and this is misrepresentation. Again, to indoctrinate a child is to deprive it, or at least to try to deprive it, of the possibility of developing into a person with the capacity and the duty of making such fundamental life-shaping judgements for himself, and according to his own conscience; and if anything is an assault on the autonomy and integrity of the human person this is it. (One might say that it was paradoxical were it not so much what one wryly expects, that, just as the Plato who elsewhere in *The Republic* insists that a high value must be placed on truth advocates the implantation of a 'noble lie', so those who are hot for Christian indoctrination commend their own God on other occasions for his desire to create not automata but free creatures.)

To say that something is presumptively wrong is to say that it is always categorically wrong, unless some overriding consideration makes it all right in the particular circumstances. To say that something is categorically wrong is to say that it just is wrong, either absolutely in all circumstances, or at any rate in the circumstances in question. Take lying for example. This is always at least presumptively wrong. But it may—and by most moralists would—be allowed that there are other still more urgent moral claims, which may sometimes override the obligation not knowingly to assert what is false. Hence there may be—and surely are—some circumstances where to tell a lie not merely is not categorically wrong but even is positively obligatory.

Thus the first thing which now, thanks to our long preparations, comes out very clearly is that the indoctrinator—like the liar—has a presumption to defeat. It is up to him to vindicate himself by showing: either that the doctrines in question are known to be true, and hence that strictly he is not indoctrinating at all; or that there are overriding moral reasons why those beliefs should be so implanted notwithstanding that they cannot be rated as actually known truths. That this initial framework conclusion is indeed worth establishing begins to become clear when we notice how common and how respected is the assumption that parents (or alternatively states) have a moral right to arrange for the indoctrination of their (or the nation's) children in whatever religious (or political) doctrine they as parents (or states)—or as parents to be—may choose.

If once it is appreciated that indoctrination must be presumptively wrong, any such assumption becomes very hard to defend. For unless it is in some way drastically qualified it is surely impossible to appeal to the goodness of the ends achievable by these presumptively evil means: it would be ridiculous to suggest that good results would follow from indoctrination in any set of doctrines which any parent (or any state) might happen to favour!

The only apparent alternative would be to argue that parents (or states) are indefeasibly entitled to do what they like with their own; and that it is for this reason that indoctrination, though always presumptively wrong, is not categorically wrong when sponsored by parents (or states). Such servile notions of absolute property rights in human beings certainly are found in, and are perhaps essential to, theist religions: it is, for instance, urged that God, because He is our Creator, has not just total power over but unlimited legitimate claims upon us; and Christian theologians have frequently endorsed the objection to suicide of certain slave-holding Greek philosophers, that it is wrong because it violates God's property rights in his creatures. But this is not a line of argument which we are likely to meet in the present context. Hence it can safely be left to condemn itself.

(*b*) It is, therefore, clear: both that it must be presumptively wrong to (try to) implant in children a firm conviction of the truth of doctrines either not known to be true or known to be false; and that, if this presumption is ever to be defeated, it will have to be defeated, not by any general appeal to the rights of parents (or states), but by arguments referring to particular cases or to one particular case. So let us come to cases.

There can be no doubt, though there often is an extreme reluctance frankly to acknowledge, what is overwhelmingly the most extensive and important case in Britain—and indeed generally in the English-speaking world. It is, obviously, religious indoctrination—especially that most whole-hearted and successful form effected in Roman Catholic schools. These schools were of course determinedly founded, and are stubbornly maintained, precisely and only in order to produce indoctrinated Roman Catholics. Since nowadays it seems to be thought to be bad form for any non-Catholic to assert this manifest fact I quote a statement from a Catholic source: 'Our basic philosophy must not only be a part of education but must be the core and centre of it, and every subject in the curriculum must be considered expressly as an instrument for making that philosophy prevail in the formation of children's character and beliefs'.[4] (The word *philosophy* here can be taken as being synonymous with our *ideology*.)

If the indoctrinator is to vindicate himself against the presumption that his activities are morally wrong, then—as we suggested in the first section of the present Part—he will have to show one or both of two things: either that the doctrines which he is implanting are in fact known to be true, and hence that he is not properly speaking indoctrinating; or that the effects of believing these doctrines are so excellent as to defeat any presumption that it is wrong thus to implant them. Confronted by this challenge many apologists—at any rate in Britain—will wish to respond in both ways. Thus it will be argued, or—more likely—simply assumed, that the content of the proposed religious instruction actually is religious knowledge: the employment of the ambiguous and question-begging cliche 'RK' can here be helpfully confusing. But appeal will probably also be made to a piece of the established British conventional wisdom, the falsism that religion is the essential foundation of morality.

(*c*) Consider now the first of these two contentions in the light of what we have said about the two senses of *religious knowledge* and about the constitutive conditions of knowledge (in I(*d*) and I(*e*), above). Obviously we are concerned here only with the second and disputatious sense: the question of indoctrination can hardly arise where—as must often be the case nowadays within the ordinary state schools—Religious Instruction ('RI') consists only in the presentation of religious knowledge in the first sense. The constitutive condition which is crucial here is the third: for a full standard case of knowledge proper the claimant has to be in a position to know, has to have sufficient reasons to justify his claim.

No one who wants to say—as perhaps most contemporary Protestant Christians do—that the fundamentals of his religion belong to the sphere of faith, and who then wants to contrast faith with reason, can at the same time consistently claim that his belief in these fundamentals, by ordinarily exacting standards, rates as knowledge. Nor again will it do—notwithstanding that it is all too often done—for a believer to claim, and for others to allow, that the incorrigible intensity of his conviction is by itself sufficient reason for describing his beliefs, whatever these may happen to be, as knowledge. It is, again by the ordinarily exacting standards of everyday life, plain false to concede that he knows unless it is the case his beliefs are in fact true and that he has sufficient reason to warrant his claim to know. We ought surely to be shocked, even if we are too old to be surprised, to see how often people see fit to lower their standards in precisely those areas which are on their own showing the most vital: whether this lowering is a matter of allowing as knowledge what fails to satisfy the constitutive conditions upon which they themselves would elsewhere insist; or whether it is a matter of accepting as sufficient reasons which in a less privileged context certainly would not pass.

If, therefore, this first contention is to be made good it must be by spokesmen who are prepared to maintain that the fundamentals of their religion are indeed known truths, and hence that there are sufficient good reasons to warrant claims to know. Traditionally Roman Catholics have been inclined to claim exactly this. Indeed decrees of the First Vatican Council define as essential and constitutive elements of the Roman Catholic religion the dogmas that it is possible to know of the existence of God by the natural light of human reason, and that it is possible similarly by recognizing the occurrence of endorsing and constitutive miracles to authenticate the genuineness of the Christian revelation.[5] Cardinal Newman was, therefore, exactly 'on the party line' when in his *The Idea of a University* he wrote: 'Religious doctrine is knowledge, in as full a sense as Newton's doctrine is knowledge. University teaching without theology is simply unphilosophical. Theology has at least as good a right to claim a place there as astronomy.'[6]

This is not the place for a thorough examination of this bold, not to say brazen, thesis; and we disclaim the task here with a better conscience for having ourselves undertaken it elsewhere.[7] Two very relevant points must however be made, briefly. The first is that the upshot of the whole argument of the present paper is to underline the practical import of such issues of philosophical theology: the question whether or not Newman's contention can be made good is seen to bear directly upon major educational decisions.

The second is that such a contention about the epistemological status of the basic doctrines of (Roman Catholic) theology cohabits most incongruously with the famous zeal to catch them young: 'Give me a child until it is seven'. If these doctrines really were epistemologically on all fours with the fundamentals of astronomy, then surely believing parents could afford—as they ought—to wait until their children become of an age to consider the evidence for themselves. But the fact is, of course, that while we need have little fear that if we introduce a mature adult to astronomy he will reject the conclusions of the astronomers as unwarranted or false, everyone—and most especially the indoctrinator—is very well aware that with religion unless you catch them young you are nowadays most unlikely to catch them at all.

Notoriously, it is the exception rather than the rule for adults who without benefit of earlier teaching as juveniles set themselves to examine the evidence for (any set of) religious doctrines to become persuaded that the evidence really is adequate to justify belief; and even of those few who do thus as adults 'see the light', most seem to be converted at periods when there is good independent reason to think that the balance of their minds is disturbed. Of course, this actual unpersuasiveness of the (particular favoured) religious case may—albeit somewhat arrogantly—be attributed to the bigotry and the inbred sin of those who are not persuaded. Nevertheless at the very least it has to be admitted that this absence of actual consensus constitutes a striking negative analogy between the basic propositions of (any positive) theology and the fundamentals of astronomy.

(*d*) The second possible response, that religion is the essential foundation of morality, often is, and consistently may be, combined with the first. Sometimes, however, it is instead disreputably but equally consistently supported by the cynical claim that, since—as every sensible person is supposed to know—in the sphere of religious belief knowledge is impossible, we are free to believe, and to teach our children to believe, whatever may be most convenient to us, or whatever may be thought most beneficial to society. To this shabby suggestion it should be sufficient to reply: first, that where knowledge is impossible the reasonable man must be convinced of nothing at all, save perhaps that knowledge is indeed impossible, rather than convinced of anything whatever that he or his tutors may have chosen for his credence; and, second, that it reveals a frivolous indifference to truth which I for one would not wish my children to learn—least of all from any example of mine.

By contrast there is nothing similarly shabby about the position of those who, while believing that their own particular religious beliefs do constitute knowledge, then offer as a further reason for instilling them into their wards the statement that, happily, these convictions do also tend to produce morally excellent fruit. What and all that can be said against this further thesis is: first, that in the particular and locally important case of Roman Catholicism the utterly inadequate evidence available points, if anywhere, in exactly the opposite direction; and, second, that any suggestion that religion (any religion?) is essential to morality is certainly wrong.

Again, as with the first response (considered in II(*c*), above), it is impossible to provide an adequate treatment here. And again we can disclaim the attempt with a better conscience for having ourselves traversed some of this well-trodden ground on another occasion.[8] A very few remarks will have to suffice now. On the first point it ought to be a familiar fact that there seems to be a statistically highly significant positive correlation between delinquency and Roman Catholicism: every study of the religious affiliation of those in prison or in approved schools has revealed that the proportion of Roman Catholics inside is two or three times that in the population as a whole.[9] Nor will it do to say that these delinquent Catholics are those who have been deprived of the peculiar benefits of Catholic schools. For, to quote from a Catholic source, 'At the annual meeting of the Catholic Moral Welfare Council, Fr. McCormack said many Catholics tended to shrug off the high percentage of Catholic delinquents by saying these were only nominal Catholics. But . . . figures he had obtained from Catholic approved schools showed that more than 90 per cent of the boys in them had spent from 3 to 10 years in Catholic schools.[10] The proportion of all Catholic children in Catholic schools is about 66 per cent.

Of course, in the present wretched state of the evidence the possibility is certainly not precluded that the real connection is not between delinquency and Roman Catholicism but between delinquency and something else which in Britain—and in the several other countries yielding similar data—just happens to correlate with Catholicism. Yet this is scarcely a promising line for the apologist, since the most obvious alternative suggestions—such as the poverty and the size of the families from which so many delinquents come—are certainly themselves really connected with Catholicism: he can scarcely afford to boast of the practical effectiveness of Catholic behavioural teaching while at the same time denying that it tends in fact to encourage (at least relatively) large families and hence (at least relative) poverty!

Suppose that we concede—as no doubt we should—that all this is a controversial matter of the interpretation of admittedly insufficient evidence. Still what at least does emerge quite clearly is that it must be utterly outrageous for spokesmen of the immensely successful Roman Catholic education lobby blandly to take it that the salutary effectiveness of their behavioural teaching as a bulwark against delinquency and bad citizenship is so much a plumb obvious established fact as to constitute a major reason why the state should continue, and continually increase, its enormous grants to Roman Catholic schools. For these are schools which, as we have insisted already, are established and maintained as separate institutions precisely and only for the purpose of Roman Catholic indoctrination (II(*b*), above.).[11]

The general suggestion that religion is essential to morality can be construed in two ways, either as a proposition about a supposed logically necessary connection, or as a claim about some contingent causal relation. As the former, the contention will presumably be that moral concepts logically presupposed the idea of God (presumably because the moral law is taken to be essentially the positive law of a Divine Legislator) and/or that obedience to the demands and precepts or morality somehow does not make sense unless God provides for suitable rewards and punishments for compliance and defiance, respectively. In the latter construction the contention would presumably be that it is contingently impossible for an atheist or an agnostic to be anything but a scoundrel.

This last is not a contention of which in this day and age we need to take account. But the former theses are still popular misconceptions. To the idea that the moral law is essentially the positive law of a Divine Legislator the most direct and decisive reply is that, on the contrary, it actually is of the essence of morality that it must always make sense to ask of any edict of positive law—the putative positive law of any supposed God not excluded—the further and different question: 'Yes, I know that it is the law. But is it right? Is it a good law?' The different idea that morality somehow can not make sense unless there are rewards and punishments no doubt arises partly from the same mistaken equation of morality with a (rather special) system of positive law. But partly too it arises from a gross confusion of morality with prudence: while prudence cannot dictate any course which conflicts with my own long-term self-interest, morality may; and, notoriously, often does.[12] The conventional wisdom which assumes that morality logically presupposes the idea of God thus exposes itself to the charge of just not knowing what morality is.

(*e*) Earlier in the present Part we drew out some general conclusions about the presumptive wrongness of indoctrination; and then applied these to what is in Britain the most important particular case—religious indoctrination, above all that effected in the Roman Catholic schools (II(*a*) and (*b*), above). We then proceeded in the next two sections to consider and dismiss the two sorts of attempt which might be made to defeat this presumption (II(*c*) and (*d*), above). The upshot therefore seems to be that such indoctrination is not merely presumptively but also categorically wrong. Hence we cannot allow that parents have any moral right to so indoctrinate their children: those who do this or arrange to have this done are doing something which—however pure their intentions and however clear their consciences—is in fact morally wrong. And furthermore, though it might be as wrong as it would certainly be imprudent for the state to try to prevent parents making private arrangements for the indoctrination of their children, it must also follow that the state can have neither a moral duty nor even a moral right either to subsidize such efforts from public funds or in any other way to give positive support to the indoctrinators.

It would be elegant and apt to end there, with a final recapitulation of clear-cut conclusions. Unfortunately experience teaches that the protagonists of indoctrination, and particularly Roman Catholics, when confronted with objections such as we have presented, usually respond by accusing their opponents of being, whether openly or covertly, simply advocates of some rival brand of indoctrination.[13] Really it ought not to be difficult to appreciate the difference between: on the one hand, going all out to persuade children that—say—Roman Catholicism is true, or going all out to persuade them that it is false; and, on the other hand, presenting these or other disputatious doctrines to children as disputatious, as issues, that is, about which equally well-informed, honourable, and reasonable men do sincerely disagree, and hence as issues about which they will in due course need to make up their own minds.

Both of the first two alternatives are kinds of indoctrination; and as such I—along with most British humanists—reject both as morally wrong. The second option is an eschewal of all indoctrination; and it is this course which I am advocating, and which my wife and I try to follow in our own home with our own children. (As one result our five-year-old daughter recently announced: 'Mummy and Daddy don't believe in God, but Granny and I do; and that's all right!').

The difficulty which so many Roman Catholics seem to find in grasping this surely quite easy distinction, and in appreciating that it refers to a vital difference, may be instructively, and at the time of writing topically, compared with the apparent inability, commonly displayed in the same quarter, to recognize that the Abortion Law Reform Association is working to relax a law which at present (almost always) forbids abortion, not to impose another which would make it (even sometimes) compulsory; and hence the apparent inability to see that all talk of compelling Roman Catholic doctors, mothers-to-be, and so on to act against their consciences is altogether beside the point. It would, I'm afraid, be more charitable than realistic to refuse to recognize in all this any element of unscrupulous and calculating misrepresentation. But another and much larger part of the explanation surely lies in other damaging facts: that an authoritarian Roman Catholic upbringing does little to make the essential concepts of a liberal and 'open society' familiar;[14] and hence that Roman Catholics are apt to attribute to others their own zeals, both to indoctrinate the young with favoured doctrines, and to enforce their own particular morality with the sanctions of the criminal law.

## REFERENCES AND NOTES

1. The book was edited by H. B. Hollins, and published by Manchester University Press in 1964. The relevant issues of the journal, which is sponsored and published by Southern Illinois University at Edwardsville and Carbondale, Illinois, are Vol. IV, No. 3, of 1966 and Vol. V, No. 2, of 1967.
2. §§ 414B-415D.
3. *Nicomachean Ethics*, 1094B12–28.
4. A. C. F. Beales, Reader in Education in King's College, University of London in *Looking Forward in Education* (ed. A. V. Judges: Faber and Faber, London, 1955), p. 84.
5. H. Denzinger, *Encheiridion Symbolorum* (29th Revised Edition: Herder, Freiburg in Breisgau, 1953), §§ 1806 and 1813.
6. Ed. G. N. Schuster (New York: Image Books, Doubleday, 1959), p. 80.
7. *God and Philosophy* (Hutchinson, 1966).
8. *Ibid.*, Chap. V.
9. The Home Office, which should of course supply complete statistics, is in fact extremely reticent about religious affiliations; for reasons which we can only, but may easily, guess. But, for instance, A. G. Rose in his *Five Hundred Borstal Boys* (Blackwell, 1964), found 23 per cent Roman Catholics, compared with 8·9 per cent in the population as a whole. Mrs Margaret Knight tells me that she extracted figures for 1957 from the Scottish Home Department, showing that in that year about 40 per cent of all prison and 36 per cent of all Borstal admissions were of Roman Catholics; compared with about 15 per cent Roman Catholics for the whole population of Scotland.
10. *Catholic Herald*, for November 20th, 1964: again my attention was drawn to this passage by my friend and fellow contributor Mrs Margaret Knight. She also supplied the motto for the whole article.
11. See, for instance, Mrs Margaret Knight's 'Should the State back Religious Education?', in *New Society* for July 21st, 1966.

12. See, for instance, my 'Must Morality Pay?', in *The Listener* for October 13th, 1966.
13. See, for instance, the correspondence following Mrs Knight's article in *New Society* for July 28th, 1966 and August 4th, 1966.
14. K. R. Popper *The Open Society and its Enemies* (Routledge and Kegan Paul, 1945), especially Vol. I.

# Children with Problems

PETER HENDERSON

Peter Henderson

CB, MD, QHP. Senior Principal Medical Officer at the Department of Science and Education. Milroy Lecturer, 1968.

Publications include: various papers on health and disabilities of children in *The British Medical Journal*, *Lancet* and *Practitioner*.

# Children with Problems

## PETER HENDERSON

Those who assert that life on earth has no meaning or purpose without the spur of belief in life after death, and in a God who watches our every action and who will sit in judgement on us, are, I believe, professing a barren and, indeed, socially destructive creed. They make much of man's cruelties and injustices over the centuries, of his ghastly wars that destroyed and mutilated vast numbers, and that poisoned the minds of many of those who survived—wars that so often were supported by one or other church or creed. They ignore, however, the other side of man's story: of his struggle for liberty of speech and of conscience; of his seeking into his own nature and that of the world around him; of his efforts to improve his physical conditions and, increasingly, though all too slowly, his relations with his fellows. And no chapter of this story is more revealing of man's quest to improve the quality of human life than that which tells of his untiring struggles against disease and infirmity.

At first it was a struggle against evil spirits; indeed, this 'belief' still lingers in backward, and some not so backward, communities. Then came the wearing of charms, and still there are some who cling to them as talismans. Next came the utilization of plants and inorganic substances. Aconite, opium and rhubarb, iron and arsenic were used as medicines in China 5,000 years ago, and sheep's thyroid was given to cretins. More remarkable still was that dried crusts from the pustules of patients with smallpox were sniffed up the nose as a prophylactic against the disease by those exposed to it.

About 400 BC, on the Island of Cos, off the coast of Greece, Hippocrates was urging the necessity for accurate observation of the signs and symptoms of illness, careful prognosis and an ethical relationship between physician and patient: 'Into whatsoever houses I enter, I will enter to help the sick, and I will abstain from all intentional wrong-doing and harm, especially from abusing the bodies of man or woman, bond or free.'

It is from such beginnings that the whole complicated apparatus of modern medicine was built up, often against apathy, prejudice or outright opposition. Oliver Wendell Holmes, in 1843, was reviled by some of his fellow practitioners in Boston for advocating that doctors should wash their hands and change their clothes before delivering a woman in labour. Semmelweiss had to resign from the maternity hospital in Vienna about the same time for expressing a similar opinion. Simpson, when professor of midwifery at Edinburgh, introduced chloroform as an anaesthetic in 1847, and was bitterly attacked for interfering with the will of God: one clergyman wrote: '. . . chloroform was a decoy of Satan, apparently offering itself to bless woman; but in the end it will harden society, and rob God of the deep earnest cries which arise in time of trouble for help.'

Those who promoted the Abortion Bill of 1967 faced much the same opposition, and endured the same intemperate language, as Holmes, Semmelweiss and Simpson had to contend with 100 years ago.

Following Pasteur's discovery that putrefaction was caused by micro-organisms which could be air-borne, Lister, in 1865, in the Royal Infirmary, Glasgow, introduced the antiseptic system, his first patient was a boy with a compound fracture of leg. Thus was modern surgery born; anaesthesia made it painless and antisepsis (later asepsis) made it relatively safe. Later advances in surgical and nursing techniques, in anaesthesia, and particularly in chemotherapy, made it safer still.

Successful vaccination against smallpox was first demonstrated by Jenner in 1796 and has since saved millions of lives throughout the world; but, it is still endemic in remoter parts. Smallpox was also a serious cause of blindness; of the 1,456 children admitted to the school for the blind in

Liverpool—the first such school to be opened in England—between 1791 and 1860, no fewer than 250 were blinded by the disease.

The nineteenth century witnessed not only the introduction of anaesthesia and antiseptic surgery but also revolutionary discoveries in bacteriology: the tubercle bacillus was discovered by Koch in 1882, the diphtheria bacillus by Klebs in 1883, and diphtheria antitoxin by von Behring in 1890. Other discoveries followed rapidly: X-rays by Roentgen in 1895 and radium by the Curies in 1898. In 1909, Ehrlich, after over 600 attempts, discovered salversan for the successful treatment of syphilis. In 1922, in Toronto general hospital, Banting and Best used insulin for the first time to treat a boy gravely ill with diabetes. In 1923, Ramon, in the Pasteur Institute in Paris, found that diphtheria toxin could be modified by formaldehyde without interfering with its antigenic action and so made possible the virtual elimination of diphtheria by immunization. In 1929, Fleming observed, by sheer chance, the action of the mould penicillium on the staphylococcus, and by 1938 Florey and Chain had elaborated a method of making a concentrated solution of penicillin. Sulphanilamide, the active principle of prontosil, was discovered by Domagk in 1932; by 1947 streptomycin was in general use in the treatment of tuberculosis. In 1958, the Salk type poliomyelitis vaccine was introduced for general use in this country and was followed by the Sabin type oral vaccine in 1962.

These and other discoveries were made by men and women of different races and nationalities, professing different religious beliefs or none. They have revolutionized the practice of medicine, have saved millions of lives and prevented much disability and suffering, particularly in children in whom the whole pattern of disease has changed in the lifetime of many of us.

These great advances in medicine were accompanied by equally important improvements in economic and social conditions, in child care generally, and in educational provision.

The condition of most of the people in the eighteenth and

nineteenth centuries was deplorable: 'In every town, beside the prosperous masters, journeymen and apprentices, lived a mass of beings, physically and morally corrupt for whose bodies no one and for whose souls only the Methodists had a thought to spare', wrote Professor Trevelyan.

The children of the poor were treated barbarously. In 1814, a fourteen-year-old boy was hanged at Newport, Monmouthshire, for stealing a sheep. Many children were in the care of the parish authorities who sent a considerable number, from the age of seven years, to work in the cotton mills of Lancashire. One mill owner agreed with a London parish '. . . to take one idiot with every 20 sound children supplied'; J. L. and Barbara Hammond wrote that '. . . their young lives were spent at best in monotonous toil, at worst in a hell of human cruelty'. Francis Place, in a letter to Harriet Martineau, in 1832, said that '. . . girls are willingly debauched at 12 years of age; . . . almost every young man considers girls of any grade below his own fair game for debauchery'.

Slowly housing was improved; water supplies made safe; drainage and sewerage provided; dispensaries and hospitals established; and educational services expanded. The first Census was taken in 1801. Lord Shaftesbury's Mines Act of 1842 forbade the employment underground in coal mines of children under ten years of age and of women. The first Public Health Act was passed in 1848; and in the same year the first medical officer of health was appointed, in the City of London, who in 1855 became the first medical officer of the General Board of Health, the forerunner of the Ministry of Health. The first school doctor was appointed in 1890, in London.

In 1839, the Education Committee of the Privy Council was established with an annual vote of £30,000 (in 1966 the public cost of the educational services of the United Kingdom amounted almost to £1,800 million). This direct intervention by the state in the education of its children was fiercely opposed. Kay Shuttleworth, from first-hand experience, commented: 'The Church in defence of her traditional privileges assumed the responsibility of resisting, by the utmost exercise of her authority . . . the first great plan ever proposed by any government for the education of the humblest classes in Great Britain'.

The Education Act of 1870 required the provision of a public elementary school in every district without a church school; but elementary education became compulsory only in 1880. It was not until 1893 that the state accepted responsibility for the education of handicapped children although a number of special schools had already been opened by religious and voluntary organizations; the first, in fact, was established 100 years earlier in Liverpool. In 1893 an Act was passed making provision for blind and deaf children, and in 1899 another Act was passed for the education of mentally defective, physically defective and epileptic children. In 1906, local education authorities were given powers to provide necessitous elementary school children with school meals; and in 1907 they were given the duty to provide for the medical examination of elementary school children. In 1908 the school medical service was established on a national basis. The Ministry of Health was formed in 1919 and the National Health Service came into force in 1948. (In the financial year ending in March, 1965, the cost of the National Health Service exceeded £1,100 million.)

What have been the achievements of all this human endeavour, both individual and corporate? The facts speak for themselves. Of every 1,000 children born alive 153 died in the first year of life between 1841 and 1900; 19 died in 1966. The death rate 100 years ago was 23 times greater in children aged 5–9 years, and 16 times greater among those aged 10–14 years, than today. Between 1861 and 1870 almost 6,000 children of every million under 15 years of age died annually from the four common infectious diseases, scarlet fever, diphtheria, measles and whooping cough; in 1965 only 11 died.

Before immunization was generally introduced diphtheria was widespread; as recently as 1938 about 65,000 persons contracted the disease and almost 3,000 died; in 1965 there were only 23 notifications among children and no deaths.

The largest outbreak of poliomyelitis in this country was

in 1947 when 2,720 children, aged 5–14 years, were affected and 168 died; in 1965 there were 11 notifications and no deaths.

Although tuberculosis has not yet been eliminated it is no longer the scourge it once was; 60 years ago three times as many school children died from it as now develop it. In 1907 it killed over 3,000 children aged 5–14 years; in 1965 it killed 5. Tuberculosis not only destroyed life but severely disabled many thousands of children. In 1910 there were 863 boys and girls severely crippled by tuberculosis of bones and joints in the day special schools for physically handicapped children in London alone; in 1964, in all these schools in England and Wales there were 31.

Much the same story can be told about rheumatic fever and rheumatic heart disease; over 900 children, aged 5–14 years, died from them in 1938; 31 died in 1965. Even 20 years ago rheumatic heart disease was one of the major causes of children's admission to the special schools for the physically handicapped; by 1964 there were only 76 with chronic rheumatic heart disease in all these schools in England and Wales.

If the death rates of 100 years ago from all the infectious diseases, tuberculosis, and acute rheumatism among children under 15 years of age prevailed today over 70,000 boys and girls would die annually whereas the actual number is about 400. This immense saving of life from infectious diseases and rheumatism has been dramatic, but there has also been a substantial reduction in child deaths from other diseases, due largely to chemotherapy and the better distribution of specialist medical care following the introduction of the National Health Service in 1948. Between 1938 and 1965 the number of children, aged 5–14 years, dying annually from diseases of the ear and mastoid process fell from 230 to 4; from osteomyelitis from 150 to none; from appendicitis from 370 to 31; from epilepsy from 129 to 48 and from diabetes from 69 to 16.

The chief causes of death among children under 5 years of age, in 1965, were congenital defects and respiratory diseases (mainly pneumonia), each group accounting for 19 per cent of the total of 19,000; accidents claimed 7 per cent but infectious diseases and enteritis only 2 per cent each. Among children aged 5–14 years accidents are now far and away the chief cause of death, being responsible for 36 per cent of the total of about 2,500 in 1965. Cancer (including leukaemia) is the second largest cause, about 20 per cent; followed by congenital defects, 10 per cent; respiratory disease, 8 per cent; and infectious disease only 3 per cent.

Deaths from respiratory disease, particularly in young children, can be still further reduced; research will, in time, conquer cancer; congenital defects present a tough problem but they can no longer be thought of as an 'act of God'. In 1941, in Australia, it was found for the first time that German measles (rubella) if contracted by a woman in the early weeks of her pregnancy might produce defects of the eye, ear, heart or intelligence, or a combination of these defects, in her baby. If rubella can do this why not other infections? We simply don't know. It was not until 1961, in Germany, that a relationship was first suspected between the taking of a drug, in this case thalidomide, by a woman in the early weeks of her pregnancy and the occurrence of limb or other deformities in her baby. And if one chemical substance can do this why not others? Again, we simply do not know. But these two recent findings about rubella and thalidomide have opened doors to new fields of research.

Yet another door to research was opened in 1959 when, for the first time, a technique was elaborated for the examination of human chromosomes that has already led to surprising and promising discoveries. It has now been found that those mentally retarded children described as mongols have an extra chromosome although the parents of most of them have a normal chromosome pattern. It has also recently been found that certain criminals have abnormal chromosomes. The practical significance of these findings is as yet unknown but they give us reason to hope that, in time, congenital and hereditary defects and disabilities that now destroy so many young children, and are a major cause of physical and mental handicap in tens of thousands of others, will be reduced.

But what about the children—2,300 in 1965—killed in

accidents in their homes or on the roads? More than half of those over, and almost a fifth of those under, 5 years of age died in motor vehicle accidents. Many who survived accidents were severely injured or gravely ill. An investigation of the records of in-patients discharged from hospitals in 1962 showed that there were over 20,000 children, aged 5–14 years, with head injuries; they exceeded the combined total of those with tuberculosis, all other infectious diseases, mental illness, epilepsy, diabetes, asthma and rheumatic fever. One way or another the prevention of accidents is the direct concern of every one of us; at least in this respect we are our brother's keeper.

Although most children are now well nourished, healthy and without handicaps there are still many with disabilities and defects of various types and degree of severity. In 1966, almost 100,000 boys and girls received special education or were waiting admission to special schools; over 50,000 attended child guidance clinics; about 30,000 were severely mentally retarded and outside the educational system and in the care of local health or hospital services; and almost 70,000 were in the care of local authorities. In 1962, over 66,000 boys and girls under 17 years of age were convicted of indictable offences (mainly larcency and breaking and entering), compared with 28,000 in 1938.

Almost 30,000 of the 70,000 in care were in temporary care for a few weeks during their mother's confinement or illness; it seems incredible that not one of these women had a relative or friendly neighbour able and willing to look after her children when she was in hospital. And what can life hold for the 5,000 children in care because they were homeless or had unsatisfactory home conditions; or for the 6,000 and more who had been deserted by their mother or whose parents were in prison; or for the 500 who had been abandoned or lost?

What about children brought up in poverty? In 1966, over 300,000 school children lived in homes where the net family income was so low that they were given free school dinners; that same year a British household with three or more children spent 11s a week per head less on food than a family with one child; and almost $\frac{3}{4}$ million houses were unfit to live in.

Thus, although the health, social circumstances and education of children have greatly improved over the years there is still much to do. What has been accomplished has been due to sustained individual and co-operative human effort, often against severe discouragement, scorn or outright opposition, and seldom at the first attempt. This record of human progress is strong encouragement to those who believe that man will progress by his own endeavours, and that the Kingdom of Heaven is in himself, and the key to it is in his own keeping. It stimulates and sustains those who believe that just as man, by painstakingly exploring his physical world, has reduced the ravages of disease and increased the material circumstances of the lives of many, and will yet do so for the multitude in Africa, Asia and elsewhere who are still shackled by poverty and disease, so will he by exploring his own nature yet come to recognize that although he is not his brother's keeper he is his brother; that mankind is not divided into 'us' and 'them', either by colour, class or creed. The reduction of disease and defect, and the conquest of poverty, are relatively easy compared with the subtly elusive, difficult task of convincing men, not only across the world but in their immediate community, that they are brothers one with the other.

We live in a mysterious, exciting and beautiful world. Those of us who are robust in health and engaged on work of our choice, and paid for doing what we like, are the world's elect; and if we are honest with ourselves we will acknowledge that we shall leave it with regret. But what of the host of our fellows who are less fortunate? Those born so disabled that they will need community care for the whole of their life; those less severely afflicted in body or mind who yearn to live a full life but know that they cannot—'Like anyone else, a handicapped person not only likes to feel wanted, but also to feel needed . . . we want to live useful lives in spite of the barriers which confront us', wrote Miss Mona Younis, a contributor to *Stigma*; those born into families that are a mockery of the name, where there is no sense of family solidarity—'the only good thing', wrote Marie Curie after the death of her beloved husband and partner in life, 'I have been deprived of it so I know'—those born in Western poverty, or in the more terrible degradation of the teeming Eastern slums and streets such as those in Old Delhi, Bombay or Calcutta; those born in countries where preventible diseases decimate children by the hundred thousand, where medical and educational services are meagre or non-existent, and where there is not even such an elementary necessity of civilized life as a pure water supply.

In the large province of Bamiyan, high up among the austere beauty of the Hindu Kush, where the hillsides are studded with long-empty caves in which Buddhist monks taught more than 2,000 years ago, and where the deep, still, cobalt-blue lakes of Band-i-Amir lie in the silence of the hills—a scene of matchless beauty in the clear light of early morning—live about a quarter of a million people for whom, when I was there two years ago, there was only one hospital of ten beds for men only, one doctor, one male nurse, no midwife and no ambulance.

Two years earlier, in the rapidly developing and lively city of Accra, the children's hospital had over 500 out-patients a day, all under five years of age; babies and young children acutely ill with diseases such as malaria, pneumonia, and measles, or extreme marasmus, sat or lay on the floor, cheek by jowl. The hospital had only thirty-five beds; three whole-time and two part-time women doctors attended this mass of ill children; they were an admirable team but their task was almost superhuman.

None of these children, whether in this or any other country, was responsible for his plight. It is hard, too hard for me, to reconcile the circumstances of their lives with belief in an Almighty Creator, the source of all knowledge, all wisdom, all goodness, who created man in His own image. There is only one certain answer to the question: What is Life, how did it begin, what is its purpose? We don't know. The answer has eluded philosopher, theologian and scientist alike. Whether or not there is another, or more than one, life after death, or whether there is personal immortality, the only 'faith' that seems to make sense in this uncertain world is the belief that man is still at the early stage of his development, and that improving the quality of human life in all its aspects is a task that concerns us all. Those who bewail man's 'sinfulness' and assert that this cannot be changed by men themselves, 'human nature being what it is', have precious little belief in the validity of the faith they themselves espouse: that men are fashioned in the image of God. Irrespective of religious belief, Christian or otherwise, or the lack of it, there is little hope for mankind until men everywhere practice what Confucius taught 500 years before the birth of Jesus—'Do not do to others what you would not like yourself'—and what Jesus himself said in almost identical words, as reported by Luke, 'as ye would that men should do to you, do ye also to them likewise'.

REFERENCES

Guthrie, D. (1945). *Hist. of Medicine*, London.
Garrison, F. H. (1929), *Hist. of Medicine*, London.
Bettany, G. T. (1885), *Eminent Doctors*, Vol. 11, London.
Trevelyan, G. M. (1944). *British History in 19th Century and After*, London.
Hammond, J. L. and Barbara (1941). *The Town Labourer*. London.
Himes, N. E. (1930). *Place on Population*, London.
Adamson, J. W. (1919). *Short History of Education*, Cambridge.
Shuttleworth, J. K. (1853). *Public Education*, London.
Stigma. *The Experience of Disability* (1966), ed. P. Hunt, London.
Curie, Eve (1938), *Madame Curie*, London.
*Monthly Digest of Statistics*, HMSO, London.
*Rpt. Sub. Committee on Standards of Housing Fitness* (1966), HMSO, London.
*Rpt. Hosp. In-patient Enquiry*, 1962, Pt. 1, HMSO, London.
*Child. In Care in E. & W. in 1966*, HMSO, London.
*Rpt. on Work of Child Dept.*, Home Office, 1961–1963, HMSO, London.
*Stats. Education*, 1965, Pt. 1, HMSO, London.
*Reg. Gen. Stat. Review for E. & W. for Each Year up to 1965* Pt. I, Tables Med, HMSO, London.
*Annual Reports C.M.O., Dept. Ed. & Science*, HMSO, London.
*Annual Report of Min. of Health for 1965*, HMSO, London.
*The Analects of Confucius*, translated by W. E. Soothill (1947), OUP.

# Moral Education

JAMES HEMMING

James Hemming

PhD. Educational Psychologist. Chairman of the British Humanist Association Education Committee

Publications include *The Psychology of Adolescence* (with others); *Problems of Adolescent Girls.*

# Moral Education

JAMES HEMMING

Education is a process of guided personal development. The infant clashing his toy cymbals or tinkling his miniature xylophone on the sitting-room floor will one day, if given the right encouragement, stimulation and opportunities, attain his full musical stature, whatever that may be: at most a composer; at least someone who knows how to enjoy music. The young child in the infant school playing with materials—sorting, weighing, measuring, matching—is embarking upon the road that, so long as his confidence and interest are sustained, will enable him, in course of time, to participate to the limit of his potentialities in that area of social behaviour we call mathematics. (Adults who jib at the mere sight of a graph or a formula are unlikely to lack endowment for mathematics; it is much more likely that their capacity has been blocked and ruined somewhere along the line by rigid authoritarian instruction.)

The relationship between potentiality and encouragement in the learning process is particularly well shown in what has happened to school art during the last half century. Formerly children, if taught art at all, were set to copy models and practise perspective in a way that petrified their potentialities. Over the years art teaching has been transformed. Instead of having irksome tasks imposed upon him, the child today is encouraged to explore his own powers by using the materials made available to him. By this means he finds out what his powers are, constantly challenges himself to overcome difficulties, and, at the same time, *he discovers the discipline of the medium*. The astounding results of this revolution in art teaching can be seen at any exhibition of children's painting. The modern generation could almost say 'we are all artists now'.

Moral education is basically no different from any other form of education. At the start we have the baby—a bundle of energies and potentialities. By the time the child has attained adulthood we hope he will have developed his moral powers to the full. Whether he does or does not depends on what kind of opportunities and guidance for his moral growth we provide in between. Traditional moral teaching was—and is—rigid and authoritarian, imposed and unrelated to personal development. Many of those subjected to such teaching become blocked, resentful and antagonistic to the whole thing. So we find a good deal of moral illiteracy in society just as we find a good deal of mathematical illiteracy, and for the same reasons—bad education.

Today we need changes in the content and approach of moral education at least as far-reaching as those occurring in mathematics, science and languages. We have to start with the developing child and work through the dynamics of individual development. The baby is born wholly dependent and, therefore, wholly self-centred. He soon begins to be socialized in his relationships with his mother, his father and, later, with others. If his personal and social potentialities are nourished by the right experiences, he will gradually acquire the personal capacities of the mature adult: to love and receive love, to be aware of others and their needs, to know how to co-operate with others, to accept responsibility for himself and his actions, to be concerned to acquire knowledge relevant to the moral decisions he will have to make, to live through reality rather than fantasy, to be involved in purposes that transcend immediate personal advantage. Fostering this growth is what moral education is about.

To read significant records of struggle and search, like the Bible, and to learn about patterns of belief, like Christianity or Buddhism, may well be part of the informational *content* of moral education; they can no longer be regarded as the *means* to it. Education by inculcation is now a thing of the past on all fronts. One cannot attempt to implant on top of a society founded in, and sustained by, experimental science and non-authoritarian relationships an absolute dogma of belief and expect the outcome to be morally healthy.

Nevertheless, all education is a selective process. In moral education, as in all other education, we have three main questions to answer: What are we going to teach? Why are we going to teach it? How are we going to teach it? The first question leads straight to another—What are moral values? This we must look at for a start. We may say that moral values are those values which are especially venerated in a society because they are regarded as essential to the good conduct of personal and social life—they provide the dependable structure within which the affairs of the society and its members may be carried on. In part such values are universals for humanity; in part they vary from society to society and from age to age. To be honest in your dealings with your neighbours is virtually a universal; to be unquestioningly obedient to those in authority is not.

The values which an educational system will seek to foster will, therefore, be partly what might be called 'the values of interpersonal relationships' and partly the values by which the particular society maintains itself. A third group of moral values are the *intra*-personal values, without which individual life can only limp along or be driven purposelessly about by random compulsions. Such values include courage in facing the problems of personal life and a capacity for self-discipline. All effective human action, from playing table tennis to writing a symphony, from hop-scotch to climbing Everest, involves a combination of spontaneity and control. Both people who are too rigid to release their spontaneity and those who are too chaotic inwardly to provide sufficient control are morally handicapped.

In some societies the three groups of values—the interpersonal, the societal and the intra-personal—conflict with one another. For example, in an authoritarian culture, you are expected to be kind to those who support the culture but not to the nonconformists; you are expected to show courage in the face of the enemy but not in standing up to your superiors. In a democracy, however, these sharp ambivalences need not occur. By definition, a democracy exists to carry out the wishes and serve the developmental needs of its citizens. To the extent that a democracy lives up to its principles, personal, interpersonal and social development can go along together without unresolvable conflict. Since moral education in a democracy should clearly be working towards a more complete fulfilment of democratic principles, the values it develops should be those very values upon which personal and social development mutally depend. We can, without difficulty, identify the obvious ones. For example:

Reverence for individual personality.
Respect for truth.
Honesty in dealings and relationships.
Consideration for others.
Responsibility for one's own actions.
Love of justice.
Courage and pertinacity in the face of difficulties.
Care for the weak and needy.
Open-mindedness to new ideas.
Responsible involvement in the betterment of mankind.

This list of values is not to be regarded as complete or exclusive. Some people would wish to alter the items, or extend the list. But such values—give or take an item here and there—embrace the basic principles of living, and of living together.

If the purpose of life is development and growth—personal and social and world fulfilment—then such values set a framework for moral truth. For growth depends on formative interaction between the individual and his environment—between person and person; between organization and organization; between nation and nation—and the listed values are the ones upon which creative interaction is founded.

The second question—Why should we teach any particular set of values?—has been answered in dealing with the first question: What values? We can now turn, therefore, to the third question: How are we going to conduct moral education?

We have seen that moral education is to be regarded as an aspect of personal education. This means that it is not an intellectual content only, or even primarily, but a carefully planned combination of formative experience and valid information, each aspect being matched to the maturation of the child, so that moral insight and understanding gradually deepen and extend as the child grows. What we have to do is to promote not only knowledge of moral values but the will and the capacity to live morally, founded on a personal moral insight. To know that stealing is wrong is ineffective as a guide to action if unsupported by a motivation to resist temptation or if overridden by a compulsion to steal rooted in a psycho-pathological condition which in its turn arises from impeded personal development. The consideration of moral education, in fact, takes us right to the core of the psychodynamics of growing up. As Piaget and others have shown, children conceptualize moral issues differently at different stages of maturation. They also relate to one another in different ways. We must always be careful to move with the child, and not impose adult concepts and behaviour upon him, if we are to make moral insight *valid for the child*.

For the sake of simplicity the two main aspects of moral education—experience and information—will be considered separately, although in the life of the child they react constantly upon one another. Formative experience starts with birth, and the absorption of morally relevant information from the time the child begins to ask questions. We are, therefore, concerned with a wide span of development. Indeed moral education need, and should, never stop. The changing circumstances of adult life constantly bring with them the stimulation to re-assess and refine the principles on which we conduct our lives.

Incidentally, all people *do* have principles, at least of self-justification: cynics, nihilists, thieves, traitors, everyone. Man is an ethical animal and must have some frame of reference in terms of which to make decisions. Life is not possible otherwise. The idea that everything is a fiddle and that the logic of life is to grab for yourself without regard to others offers a principle for living even though it is an ignorant one. The difference between moral and immoral behaviour is not that the one is subject to principles and the other is not, but that the principles of the one are valid in personal and social terms and the principles of the other are founded in error.

To return, formative experience begins at birth. The way the child is loved or denied love, encouraged or denied encouragement, helped to achieve things for himself or over-protected, made to feel of value as a person or made to feel inadequate, will determine how far a young child gets in laying foundations of self-respect and personal confidence—of fundamental importance for continuing moral development. Two other pre-school experiences are also vital. One is early lessons in mixing and sharing with others—particularly important for children of the 2½–5 years age-range. The other is the understanding that acceptable behaviour takes place within limits. Healthy children—particularly boys—are self-assertive. This is a thoroughly wholesome trend. We grow by expressing, not by submerging, our own personality. But the young child needs to know what the limits to his self-assertion are and he probes to find them. Established limits give a structure and security for his personal freedom. If his freedom is too curtailed, he lacks space for exploration and growth; if no limits at all are set, his world becomes formless and frightening.

The skill of parenthood is to define limits at every stage of the child's development so that both freedom and limits are matched to the constantly extending capacities of the growing child. The area of freedom, let it be noted, is also the area of responsibility, because it is the area of self-determination. Both the over-protected and the under-controlled children are denied the milieu in which the nature of responsibility can most readily be discovered.

A child equipped before he reaches school age with these four essentials—self-respect, confidence, an experience of sharing and an understanding of limits—is well prepared for the next stage of formative moral experience: the more intensive interpersonal and group interaction of the infant classroom. Unfortunately, not all children have been provided with adequate early experience so that the infant school—and indeed any school—has two tasks in the continuing socialization of the child: to provide further formative experience for those who are functioning as individuals well up to their capacity, and to seek to rehabilitate those who, through inadequate experience, are lagging behind in personal development. The decisive factors for both tasks are the level of stimulation and the quality of interpersonal and community life that the school offers. The principles are basically the same for all schools, whether infant, primary or secondary. They are now well-known and well-founded, and may be summarized as follows:

1. The school should be a warm, friendly, purposeful community of which every child can feel he is a valued member with a contribution of his own to make.

2. The school should strive to reach a common ethos which the staff—and, where older children are concerned, the pupils also—have worked out and agreed together, and of which the accruing values are manifest in the day-to-day life and relationships of the school.

3. The school should be so organized socially that all children have the experience of regular participation in small groups.

4. The net of responsibility should be widely spread so that the *modus vivendi* of the school brings home to all children:

   i. Their responsibility for themselves and their own actions.
   ii. Their responsibility for a contribution to the community life of the school.
   iii. Their responsibility for helping one another.
   iv. Their responsibility for participating in solving the problems of the community.

The further commitment of service beyond the school should also be available and encouraged.

5. The curriculum should be designed to draw on the curiosity and creative powers of the children and develop self-confidence along with self-discipline.

6. Success as the reward of effort should be secured for every child.

7. Adolescents should be given opportunities, within the curriculum, for discussing their personal problems together with a sympathetic member of the staff.

8. The school should maintain a system of guidance and counselling through which children under stress or in difficulties will be quickly noticed and given the support and help they need.

For the over-worked headmaster and staff such principles may sound like unrealistic idealism. But the truth they represent has to be faced if we are to be serious about the moral development of our children. The Victorians imagined that children could be sped along the road to virtue by copying out moral maxims in a writing book. Those who produced the 1944 Education Act appear to have thought that regular exposure to Christian belief would do the trick. We now know that behaviour is largely the outcome of relationships and community life. Ideas are important too, but the interpersonal milieu as such—including the ideas it represents—is a very powerful influence in moral education. We also know that isolation, alienation, low attainment, delinquency and maladjustment tend to be found together. In a confused, atomized, often overcrowded society such as ours, the school may be the only source of dependable community life for the child. As such, the school has within its control the opportunity to provide confused and stressed children with support, warmth and *moral clarity through experience*, or it can become too absorbed with other things and neglect to do so. Many schools are, of course, fully aware of this and exemplify community principles in action in a magnificent way. But others are still putting second things first and leaving the formative personal experience of the children far too much to chance.

The informational aspect of moral education falls under three headings: content that gives an orientation on life and the universe from which the individual can draw a sense of significance and dignity; morally relevant information and ideas derived from the traditional content of the curriculum; and direct information about man's religious and moral striving. All three aspects should be approached in an exploratory way with ample opportunity for questions and discussion.

The importance of orientation for moral education has only recently been grasped. We now realize that to feel lost and unrelated is an alienating, demoralizing, disintegrating experience. Simpler societies had the edge on us here because every individual knew his place within the social order, itself set in a cosmological framework which made sense, even if founded on mythology rather than fact. As the social and ideological framework crumbles, so does it become harder and harder for people to hang on to a sense of relatedness and value. But an answer is not to be found in seeking to stick together the already broken structure; the solution is to reinterpret cosmology and society in terms of changed knowledge and changed circumstances.

At present we are subjecting children to a hopelessly confused cosmological picture. The small-scale one-world cosmology of traditional Christianity, or the remains of it, is constantly presented to children while the immense exciting reality is only taught by the occasional teacher, if at all. The wonderful new cosmology, and man's evolutionary adventures and responsibilities within it, are all but withheld from the children in our schools. Children are instead left to pick up a phoney, inaccurate and mainly unchallenging distortion of the truth from comic strips, grotesque films and space fiction. Indeed, if they read the best space fiction they might well gain some grasp of cosmic reality, but only the more literate do.

What is the picture that we should be offering all our children? First the wonder of the infinitely dynamic universe, with its thousands of millions of galaxies and thousands of millions of stars within each galaxy, linked to all the exciting explorations of modern astronomy. Then, the place of our world in this immensity, not as an inconsequential speck in the ocean of space but as of great significance because on our planet—no doubt along with other planets attached to other stars—life exists. Then the story of the evolution of life on this planet, man's recent appearance and struggles, his impressive achievements in learning to control his environment, and now his first tentative adventures beyond the protective sphere of the earth's atmosphere. Finally, man's great responsibilities as the custodian of life on this planet, whose future is inescapably in his hands. Children are heartened and enthralled by such a picture as they can never be by a patched-up mythological cosmology that breaks down *under five minutes of their own questioning*, as every teacher of RI knows.

Social orientation involves recent history, current struggles, the way one's own society operates, the responsibility of one's own country in world affairs. This too—essential to a sense of belonging and personal involvement and commitment—is very largely left to chance in our schools. Some schools make a first-class job of it, but whether a particular child receives a sound social orientation is, as things are now arranged, a matter of chance. But to give a child a frame-work within which to understand his own life is a top educational priority for personal and moral development.

Schools often accept the need for such orientation but complain that they lack the staff to put it across in an informed and interesting way. This may well be so. If it is, then Schools Television should take on the responsibility of supplying co-ordinated orientation courses that *all* secondary schools could take. One way or another it has to be done in order to provide children with a common corpus of information and understanding, clarified by their own questions and discussion. It is vain to hope to build a morally mature nation without providing a factual common ground that can put individual life in a valid, significant perspective.

The ordinary school subjects are rich with possibilities for developing and deepening moral insight. Through English literature children can be given greater understanding of themselves and others and be confronted, in their imagination, with a variety of moral situations. Literature is about people and their relationships, their behaviour and the consequences of their behaviour—the very stuff of morality. Literature ranges over feeling from lyrical delight to darkest foreboding. In all moods it can stir wonder, excitement and curiosity about the human condition.

At the other extreme, mathematics should not be taught only as hard fact and rigid process. It too has its moral component, and not only as reverence for a particular kind of truth. The history of mathematics is the story of how man has become more and more aware of the complexities of his environment and has struggled to find ways of ordering and understanding it. The infant can experience this at his level just as the higher mathematician can experience it at his. The wonder of discovery, the satisfaction of control through discovery, and the discipline of precision are equally open to both. Similarly, science offers a continuous story of unremitting courage, effort and achievement in the struggle against ignorance, full of wonder and excitement whether we look at it in terms of the scientist as a person, the nature of his work, or the social consequences of his discoveries. And with every new discovery comes the moral issue of how it should be used.

History and geography are about the behaviour and habitat of people. Unless reduced to stagnant facts by the academic strait-jacket, they bring the children naturally into the arena of human and moral issues. The arts, in their turn, develop sensitivity, a *sine qua non* of the moral life. All subjects offer splendid examples of noble lives with which children may identify their aspirations for themselves—children long to be admirable and need the reassurance that human beings, in spite of frailties and incompleteness, can attain greatness. The educational habit of the past has been to compartmentalize knowledge and to hive-off moral education into yet another compartment. We are now beginning to see the need to unify and interrelate all knowledge by teaching each part of it vivified by its personal and social references—which also means in its moral context.

There is, all the same, a place for more specific study of man's moral and religious striving. Children are not sufficiently mature for this before adolescence but, thereafter, they are themselves deeply concerned about what is right and wrong behaviour in the conduct of their own lives and are capable of discussing situational problems, including their own and one another's, with sensitivity and insight. This provides an opportunity to deal with religious belief and comparative religions, with the insights of the great moral teachers, with the elementary psychology of human nature, motivation, relationships and behaviour, with a little sociology and with some comparative anthropology. The precise course such specific moral education takes should be sensitive to the particular concerns and capacities of the young people themselves. No adolescent was ever improved morally by being bored.

Sex education is an important aspect of specific moral education, not because it is to be regarded as something separate and tabu as in the days of prudish morality, but because young people are deeply concerned about how to deal with their own sexuality and how to conduct their relationships with the other sex. Much of sex education can, and should, come in through other subjects: English, history, art, biology, health education, homecraft. But experience has shown that gaps will be left, curiosities left unsatisfied and, often, ignorance left uncorrected if young people are not given definite opportunities to learn and question about sex, in its physical, emotional and social aspects. Schools that lack the resources to deal effectively with this important aspect of personal and moral development can supplement what they can offer internally by drawing from outside in personnel who have been trained to talk to adolescents about sex and to discuss their doubts and uncertainties with them. It should be noted that schools that fail to provide adolescents with the information and guidance they need in the conduct of their relationships with the other sex are, in effect, rejecting the adolescents themselves, and that this will be picked up by the adolescents as a rejection so that their relationships with the school itself will be impaired in consequence. One cannot reject or undervalue the central reality of the adolescents' lives—the attainment of physical maturity—and expect, at the same time, to retain their trust. This is why frank, positive, sex education is such a crucial component in moral education as a whole—because, once trust has gone, no moral education will count for anything. A vital point, which applies not only to sex education.

The many strands of moral education, each important in itself, need drawing together in the life of the school. This is to be attained mainly in two ways. One is through the establishment of a network of care within, and beyond, the school, which provides immediate succour and support for all children who are suffering difficulties or stress which are too much for them to handle alone. The school should be, and should be felt to be, a *caring* community. The network of care should draw in every member of the teaching staff in his or her pastoral role. In addition, every considerable establishment in secondary and tertiary education needs, *as a member of its own staff*, an adequately trained counsellor who can assist in the support and personal guidance of adolescents in need of help. The network of care, of course, also includes parents, the school psychological service, the youth employment service, and others concerned with young people. Its existence, and the relationships between its members, provide an enduring object lesson in the nature of human responsibility.

The other principal means of focusing a school's ethos is through the assembly. The role of assembly in a secondary school is to celebrate the civilized and civilizing values for which the school should be seen to stand. The themes of assembly should be the great human themes: courage, achievement, love, compassion, wonder, imagination, joy, tragedy, endurance, hope, responsibility, humanitarian endeavour, and the challenge and mystery of existence. Children should leave assembly reinforced in their sense of value and responsibility as human beings. The Christian contribution to human thought and striving has a place in the total of experience offered, but the daily reiteration of Christian belief, however carefully arranged, is plainly inadequate as an inspiring, integrative influence for a community of young people today.

# Moral Progress: A Reappraisal

MORRIS GINSBERG

## Morris Ginsberg

DLitt, LLD, FBA. Professor of Sociology at the London School of Economics, 1929–1954, and now Emeritus Professor. President of the Aristotelian Society 1942–1943 and past editor of the *British Journal of Sociology and Sociology Review.*

Publications include: *The Psychology of Society*; *Studies in Sociology*; *Sociology*; *Essays in Sociology and Social Philosophy*: Vol I, *On the Diversity of Morals*; Vol II *Reason and Unreason in Society*; Vol III *Evolution and Progress*; *Nationalism: a Reappraisal*; *On Justice in Society*; (and with others) *The Material Culture and Social Institutions of the Simpler Peoples*; *Law and Opinion in England in the 20th Century*; and a biography of L. T. Hobhouse.

# Moral Progress: A Reappraisal[1]

MORRIS GINSBERG

In approaching the problem of moral progress we must note that all progress, as distinguished from evolution or development, is in a sense moral progress. In other words, it is a movement towards a better state of affairs. Here, however, I am concerned with the narrower problem of progress in morality. Our first task is to find out what is to be included in morality.

Philosophers influenced by the more fully developed forms of morality are apt to consider morality from the point of view of the individual and, therefore, to stress the personal or inner side of moral conduct. For example, F. H. Bradley says 'morality is the identification of the individual will with his own idea of perfection. The moral man is the man who tries to do the best which he knows.' If the best he knows is not the best as judged by other standards, or if in fact he fails to achieve it, that is, speaking morally, irrelevant. He has done what is best as he sees it.[2] It is easy to see that on this view it would be impossible to compare or grade the morals of different epochs or peoples.

Bradley's approach is highly individualistic. Other philosophers recognize that the individual's moral attitudes are socially conditioned. 'No individual can make a conscience for himself. He always needs a society to make it for him.'[3] From this angle moral goodness might be regarded as consisting in loyalty to the recognized or accepted code. Moral goodness would then be identified with conformity. But this is an identification which developed forms of morality would certainly not accept.

Combining these two approaches we may perhaps say that an individual's morality consists of that part of the moral beliefs of the community in which he has been instructed and which he has adopted through authority and suggestion, but also of his own modifications and rejections which his own insight and experience have taught him.

For purposes of comparative study the approach through the analysis of the individual conscience is not practicable. We have no means of estimating the degree in which people live up to the rules and ideals of their society. All we can do is to inquire what sort of conduct society expects of the individual and what ideals or standards of perfection are put before him as models to emulate. We can also study heresies and prophetic criticisms of current moralities.

The reality of moral progress has frequently been denied or doubted. An early form of this is to be found in the writings of Buckle:

> 'There is, unquestionably, nothing to be found in the world which has undergone so little change as those great dogmas of which moral systems are composed. To do good to others; to sacrifice for their benefit your own wishes; to love your neighbour as yourself; to forgive your enemies; to restrain your passions; to honour your parents; to respect those who are set over you; these and a few others are the sole essentials of morals; but they have been known for thousands of years and not one jot or tittle has been added to them by all the sermons, homilies and textbooks which moralists and theologians have been able to produce.'[4]

This view is echoed by some modern anthropologists. Thus Boas maintains: 'It may safely be said that the code of primitive ethics, so far as relations between members of a group are concerned, does not differ from ours. It is the duty of every person to respect life, well-being and property of his fellows and to refrain from any action that may harm the group as a whole. All breaches of this code are threatened with social or supernatural punishment.' There has been in Boas' view no evolution of moral ideas. There has been progress in ethical conduct, but this has been due to the enlargement of the groups and therefore of the number of the members who share in the rights enjoined within the closed society.[5]

It will be seen that this conclusion is not based on anything like a comprehensive survey of the elements of constancy and variance in moral ideas. Elsewhere in the same chapter Boas stresses the variability of standards. 'The social ideals of the central African negro, of the Australian, Eskimo and Chinese are so different from our own that the valuations given by them of human behaviour are not comparable'.[6]

The critics of the belief in moral progress fall into two groups. There are those who maintain that the fundamental principles of morals are simple and have always been known —that we should wish well and do well to others, that hatred is evil, that we should rid ourselves of envy and greed. Others think that the principles of conduct vary indefinitely and that there are no reliable criteria for evaluating or grading them. Neither of these views seems to me acceptable. The constancy of morals is illusory, unless we are to write off the whole history of reflection on human nature and its possibilities as of no significance. Those who believe that the principles of morals are well known might be invited to try their hand at some of the problems of our own day—the legitimacy and limits of the use of force, the principles of the equitable distribution of the means of life within states and between them or, more generally, how the line is to be drawn between the sphere of law and the sphere of morals. On the other hand, although moral codes differ in important respects, the variations are far from arbitrary and they do not rule out the possibility that behind the diversity general principles are discoverable which in the course of development come increasingly to be accepted as universally binding. I have examined this problem at length in my book *On the Diversity of Morals*. Here I confine myself to some points of special importance. In its advanced forms morality consists of a body of judgements and attitudes applied impartially to purposive acts of responsible individuals, or on their character as tending to issue in such acts, in so far as they affect (*a*) the general conditions of social life and (*b*) so far as they affect other individuals, including the individual acting.

If there is such a thing as moral progress it must consist in: (i) growing knowledge of the nature of purposive acts, of responsibility, of the ends of action and of the order of social relations most likely to be conducive to their fulfilment; (ii) the progressive use of the knowledge thus attained in the criticism and reconstruction of social, political and economic institutions; (iii) the building up of cognitive, emotional or affective systems needed to sustain the sense of moral obligation, to extend the range of imaginative sympathy and to provide the energy and drive required for the pursuits of ideals.

Before proceeding to inquire whether there is any evidence for moral progress in this sense there are certain preliminary observations which it is necessary to make.

First, as has already been stated above, we have no direct access to the inner or personal side of morality. We cannot measure conscientiousness, that is, steadiness in acting in accordance with one's sense of duty. Second, we cannot even estimate with any accuracy the extent to which in our own time practice corresponds to precept. For earlier times the evidence would completely fail us. Third, we have no reason for believing that there has been any improvement in genetic make-up. Men are not born with a better moral equipment than in earlier times. There are those who believe that improvement in institutions make men appear better than they are, that, for example, the custom of forming queues or driving on one side of the road may diminish the opportunity for aggressive behaviour but leave inborn aggressiveness untouched. It would follow that bad institutions would tend to make men appear worse than they are. But this conclusion is not generally drawn. In my view neither the belief in 'original sin' nor the belief in the fundamental goodness of man can be accepted. Both rest on too abstract a view of human nature, separating it too sharply from its manifestations in behaviour. The concept of an 'original' human nature, sinful or otherwise, has little meaning.

The history of conduct, as I have said, cannot be studied directly, since there are no reliable criteria for assessing how far conduct follows the rules. We can only ask what conduct is enjoined on the individual and what ideals he is expected to strive for.

The vast data available were examined by Hobhouse and Westermarck in the beginning of this century.[7] Since then no survey on a comparable scale has been attempted. On the evidence before us now a number of trends in the history of morals can, I think, be discerned which are in the line of progress.

1. *Universalization.* There has been an extension of the range of persons within which common rules have come to be applied and a growing insistence on impartiality involving a firmer grasp of principles and a widening of the range of sympathy. As we have seen, Boas denied that this involved any change of moral ideas and argued that it was due to the increasing size of political units to be attributed to non-moral factors, for example, war and technological advances. Westermarck, from another point of view, argued that the extension of range was due mainly to emotional factors, especially to a widening of the scope of sympathy and the growth of altruistic sentiments brought about by the widening of social units and increasing contacts between them.[8] Sympathy, however, is not a matter of feeling only, but requires imagination and the power of seeing oneself in the place of the other and recognizing that the other is a person. The quantitative extension of moral rules must therefore be regarded as correlated with a qualitative change in the conception of the human person. Moral universalism, in short, goes beyond kindliness and benevolence which, psychologically, must always be limited and discriminatory. One cannot love anybody and everybody with the same intensity, but one can come to recognize that there are certain things to which men are entitled, whether we love them or not. This is a matter of moral intuition involving both thought and feeling and both can be deepened by enlargement of experience and increased insight into the essentials of human relations.

The part played by the spiritual religions in the growth of universalism has been much stressed. It should be noted that the doctrine of universalism is not confined to monotheistic religions. It was taught also by Buddhism and Confucianism and the Stoics based their cosmopolitan ideas on the identity of reason in all men. As a doctrine universalism is generally stated without qualifications. 'Love all men,' say the Rabbis. 'Whoever hateth any man hateth Him who spoke and the world came into existence,' we are told in the *Talmud*. The stoically trained Roman lawyers came to look at the *jus gentium* as based on natural law applicable to all men. As an operative belief, however, universalism has limitations. In Christianity and Islam the unity of mankind has often meant the unity of the faithful. Confucian writers speak of mankind in general, but in view of China's history it is doubtful whether they reached the conception of humanity as a whole. In the West this conception begins to emerge as an idea with the discovery of a new world, the revival of learning and the rise of new knowledge. In the eighteenth century there came into being a literature devoted to the study of 'human nature', of human societies. The French writers of the Revolution declare that the *genre humain* forms *une seule et même societé*.

Limited in theory, universalism is even more restricted in practice. Group morality persists; it survives in race discrimination, in war and the precarious rules supposed to govern its conduct, in chauvinistic nationalism. Nevertheless, on the whole, universalism has grown; the scope of common principles and the impartiality shown in their application have expanded, despite set-backs or reversals.

2. *Growth of inwardness and individual responsibility*. This is a phase of the process of differentiation whereby morals become distinct from custom, law and religion and moral attitudes emerge, recognizing value and obligation as self sustained and independent of external sanctions. Movements in this direction can be traced in the history of different civilizations. Stress comes to be laid on purity of motive as distinct from outward conformity, on inward acceptance as distinguished from external and prudential sanctions. Witness also the growth of individual responsibility in the criminal law. These developments can be clearly traced in Greek

ethics, in Judaism and Christianity, in Buddhism and Confucianism.

3. *Rationalization.* I follow Kant in thinking that it is in becoming rational that man becomes moral. By this I mean that the development of morality has consisted in the growing power of reason to relate the instincts and emotions to general and permanent needs, and, with the aid of the imagination, to construct ideals going beyond what is to what might be if the obstacles to human fulfilment could be removed. This, however, is not to say that intellectual and moral development coincide. Moral codes are affected by the institutions within which they are embodied, which they slowly pervade and in varying degrees modify. Institutions may be conceived as: 'experiments in living', that is, in adjusting human relations to the needs of life. In the earlier stages they proceed by trial and error and changes are not guided by conscious purpose. The rational element gains in strength as men begin to pose the problems of human relations consciously and seek to discover the conditions of progress or deterioration. In the course of this development the ethical element proper, that is, the distinctively moral attitude is differentiated from other factors shaping or regulating human life, such as law and religion. Moral progress on this view has consisted in the deeper appreciation of human needs, the clarification of moral ideals and the widening of human sympathies, leading slowly to the recognition that moral principles are universal in scope, applicable to man as man.

I cannot here attempt to trace the process of rationalisation in any detail. It can be seen (*a*) in the distinction that the religions come to draw between ritual rules, prescribing acts due to God and moral rules, that is, rules necessary to human well-being; (*b*) in the gradual elimination of the magical and taboo elements in morals and (*c*) the growing criticism of customary morality, of law and other social institutions and the attempts to reconstruct them on a rationally defensible basis.

Perhaps the clearest evidence of moral progress is provided by the moralization of religion and the rationalization of law. The spirits of animism and even the gods of polytheism reflect the morality of the blood feud and even when they reach the notion of a god administering justice, the standards do not rise above those current in the group life of the time. The ethical codes of the spiritual religions make higher demands. They set up an ideal of conduct going beyond the requirements of current morality and the practical wisdom of the worldly-wise. In doing so, however, they subordinate ethics to religion. In later development this relation tends, in varying ways, to be reversed. Ethics is taken as fundamental and to provide a test to which religions must conform. These generalizations are no doubt subject to important qualifications, but on the whole they are widely accepted. To cite only one authority, Dean Inge tells us: 'The moralizing of religion is in the true line of progress.'[9]

The relations between law and morals have varied greatly in the course of history. The influence of law on morals is so great that some have thought law to be the sole source of morality. In fact both law and morals are derived from custom and as they diverge in development they come in different ways to influence each other. The complicated relations thus arising have not been adequately studied, but there can be no doubt that in modern times persistent efforts are made to base legislation on some conception of well-being and to use law as an instrument of social policy. Witness the movements for the reform of the criminal law, of the laws of divorce and, in recent times, the effort to come to grips with the problems of distributive justice. The case for moral progress rests among other facts on the persistence of the quest for justice in the history of mankind, spurred on by the sense of injustice. Of this quest we can say with greater confidence than of the religious quest, that it persistently shows upward trends. This does not mean that the movement is not fitful or irregular or that it is not liable to retrogression. But it does mean that despite set-backs there is some continuity of advance towards greater clarity of purpose, the elimination of inconsistencies and anomalies, accompanied by efforts to reform legal procedure so as to make it more conformable to the underlying purposes of the law.

Granted the great advances that have been made in the clarification of ethical ideas, the question arises whether we ought not to expect greater improvements in the behaviour of men and in social institutions. How are we to account for the failure to benefit from such knowledge and wisdom as there is?

In dealing with this difficult question it must be admitted at once that the early theories of progress were at their weakest in the view they formed of the part played by reason in morals. They took it for granted that 'enlightenment' would bring virtue and with it happiness. It is strange that it was not realized that the simple identification of virtue with knowledge and vice with ignorance had been shown to be untenable by the post-Socratic philosophers of ancient Greece and again and again by religious thinkers. As far as the individual is concerned the problem of behaviour contrary to reason was handled by Aristotle in a masterly manner in his discussion of the 'incontinent man', that is the man who knows what is good and does what is bad. He showed that knowledge of principles was not enough. The knowledge acquired has to be integrated into the character and, indeed, in the field of morals full knowledge is only possible for the fully formed character. Even when the principles are accepted as binding, the application to particular cases may easily go astray under the influence of passion or self-interest. That the resources of self-deception or sophistication are well nigh endless has been shown again and again by moralists and novelists of all ages. Modern psychology has deepened this explanation by revealing the strength of unconscious drives and their imperviousness to the influence of reason and by showing how in various ways cognition and emotion may be dissociated, producing a sort of apathy which robs knowledge of its power to initiate or control action.

Next, we must notice that there is a certain vagueness in the principles enunciated by the great moralists. They are often expressed in terms of beautiful simplicity but high generality. 'Love your neighbour as yourself'; 'Hatred does not cease by hatred, but by love alone'; 'What is hateful to you do not do to your fellow creatures'; 'Treat humanity in your own person and in others as an end in itself and not as a means merely'—these are all noble maxims but they inculcate a general attitude rather than a detailed scheme of conduct. To apply them in practice and to base institutions on them requires more wisdom than is generally available. You can love men as much as you like and yet make them miserable if you do not understand their needs and difficulties and their complex and conflicting relations to each other. It is a fine thing to treat men as ends in themselves, but how decide what conditions of employment would satisfy this requirement? To translate the principles of personal ethics into principles of social ethics requires a combination of 'mediating' principles of morals with factual knowledge both of needs and possibilities which in the present stage of development is sadly lacking.

It may be added that the very highest ideals owing partly to their vagueness are exposed to a process of distortion or confusion. Couched in lofty terms they are apt to give a glow of satisfaction without inducing action. They tend to be kept in the safe atmosphere of abstractions, not to be taken seriously by practical men, or else to be used to provide spiritual boost for policies which stated nakedly would make no appeal. Their failure when put to the test is very readily exploited by the 'realists'. Examples should easily suggest themselves to anyone who considers the use made of ideals of 'justice', of 'making the world safe for democracy'; 'national self-determination' during the First World War, or the nauseating mixture of power politics and moralizing in the period following the Second World War.

It is now clear that we must not exaggerate the influence of moral forces in the development of mankind. They have frequently been overborne by other forces, economic, political, religious and even intellectual. It is not surprising that Marxist writers have argued that each stage of economic development generates its own morality. Yet even Marxist writers believe that when class antagonisms have been overcome, 'a truly human morality' as Engels has said, will become possible, and it can hardly be doubted that the socialist movement owes a good deal to the moral passion and idealism of the few who have transcended class morality without waiting for the millennium of the classless society and to the many who followed their inspiration out of a vaguer, but none the less powerful, sense of injustice. On the whole, it seems probable that the influence exerted by social and economic changes on morals is greater than the converse influence of changes in moral outlook on the forms of social life. But we must avoid the error of ascribing social decay to moral deterioration, while at the same time denying to moral factors the power of influencing society for good. In either direction the power of morality may not be great, but it is not insignificant. On the whole, the evidence suggests, I think, that while morality is still far from dominant in human affairs it is gaining in strength.

Among other indications in this direction I should like, in conclusion, to lay stress on the following points:

1. The influence of the scientific spirit. The intrinsic value of truth was of course recognized by the Greeks, but the virtues of truth seeking, the cultivation of detachment, disinterestedness, the readiness to abide by the evidence, in T. H. Huxley's phrase: 'veracity in thought and action and the resolute facing of the world as it is' have only entered fully into the moral consciousness with the growth of modern science. These are virtues much more difficult to practise in the sphere of social investigation than in other branches of inquiry. But even in the social sciences very considerable advances have been made. Witness the efforts to get behind 'ideologies', to distinguish judgements of value and judgements of fact and to require workers in this field to make their hidden value assumptions explicit.

2. The growth of social responsibility. In democratic societies the sense of responsibility is now more widely diffused. People are growing impatient of being told what they want or ought to want. The problem of individual responsibility for collective action is raised and debated. It is coming to be recognized that men acting in concert

do not on that account lose their responsibility, though the precise incidence of responsibility in group action may depend on the structure of the group, the genuineness of the control which the members can exercise over those who act in their name, the opportunities for sharing information, active consultation, effective protest or repudiation. In practice we recognize differences in degree of responsibility. The responsibility of an ordinary citizen who refrains from protesting against, or merely acquiesces in, an unjust war is real though not so great as that of those who actively participate in it or of the statesmen directly concerned in bringing it about. From this angle moral progress consists partly in increasing participation in the shaping of social policy, the sharpening of the sense of responsibility for common action and its wider diffusion.

3. Fact finding and critical inquiry into ends as a basis for legislation and public policy. Compare the following statement by an eminent lawyer:

> 'Law is not an end in itself . . . it has to justify itself by its ability to serve the government, that is, to help to promote the ordered existence of the nation and the good life of the people.' (Lord Wright in the University of Toronto Legal Journal 1941, p. 71–2, cited Friedmann, *Legal Theory*, 1944, p. 275).

That this is more than a pious wish can be seen from the growing number of commissions set up by governmental and non-governmental agencies in this and other countries to inquire into the factual and moral basis of the criminal law, the law relating to divorce, homosexuality and abortion, and the regulation of industrial relations.

4. Growing recognition of a duty to posterity and to mankind as a whole. This can be seen in the importance attached to the study of population problems and the recognition of the duty of economically advanced countries to come to the aid of underdeveloped nations in their efforts to raise their standards of life.

To all this the sceptic might reply that even if it be granted that we now have fuller insight into the nature of moral ideals and of the conditions in which they can be realized, it does not follow that there has been any improvement in the behaviour of men. Though no detailed comparison with former ages may be possible, it is clear none the less that the clash between what is and what should be is more violent in our time than in any other. Witness the horror and savagery of the Nazi period, all the more terrible for its cold-blooded and systematic ruthlessness. Yet on a fuller appraisal of the facts, is there not much to be said on the other side? As against the acts of senseless brutality and destructiveness may we not set the countless examples from all over the world of heroism, endurance and the readiness to give one's life in the service of a great cause? Is it not fair to say, despite the difficulty of balancing gains and losses, that in no previous age has so much been done to relieve suffering, and to abolish poverty, disease and ignorance in all parts of the world? It is clear enough that virtue and knowledge do not necessarily go together, that knowledge may be used for evil as for good and that the power conferred by knowledge may produce situations that moral wisdom at its best cannot encompass. These failures rule out any law of necessary or certain progress. We cannot assume that the ethical element will prevail. But it does not follow that we are committed to unrelieved pessimism. Taking into account the successes as well as the failures, we may reasonably hope that as moral ideals gain in rational coherence, through growing insight into human nature and its possibilities, they will also gain in their power to inspire and control social action as well as individual effort.

REFERENCES

1. See my earlier discussion in the Frazer lecture on *Moral Progress*, Glasgow University Press, 1944, reprinted in *Reason and Unreason in Society*, Chap. XVI.
2. *Appearance and Reality*, p. 431–432.
3. T. H. Green, *Prolegomena to Ethics*, p. 351.
4. H. T. Buckle, *Introduction to the History of Civilisation in England*, I, Chap. IV, pp. 102–103.

# Putting Ethics to Work

LORD RITCHIE-CALDER

## Lord Ritchie-Calder

CBE, MA. Author, scientific, political and social journalist. Science editor of *News Chronicle*, 1945–1956, and on the staff of other papers, notably *Daily Herald* and *New Statesman*. Montague Burton Professor of International Relations at Edinburgh University, 1961–1967. Member of the Council of British Association. Fellow of the American Association of Advancement of Science. Fabian Executive. British delegate to UNESCO 1946, 47, 67, 68, special adviser at UN Famine Conference, 1946, Chief of the first UN Special Mission to S-E Asia, 1951. UN mission to the Arctic and a second one to S-E Asia in 1962. Member of the UN Secretariat at the Peaceful Uses of Atomic Energy Conferences, 1955 and 1958, and member of the WHO group on Mental Aspects of Atomic Energy, 1957. Consultant to OXFAM, and to the California Centre for Study of Democratic Institutions. Chairman of the Chicago University Study Group on Radiation in the Environment, 1960. Kalinga award for Science writing, 1960.

Publications include: *Conquest of Suffering*; *Men Against the Desert*; *Science Makes Sense*; *Science in Your Life*; *Commonsense About a Starving World*; *Agony of the Congo*; *Living With the Atom*; *World of Opportunity*; *The Evolution of the Machine; Man and The Cosmos.*

# Putting Ethics to Work

LORD RITCHIE-CALDER

The story is told of a Scottish clergyman whose sermon on the miracle of the loaves and fishes was interrupted by a voice from the congregation which said 'Minister, I could do that!'. The preacher ignored the intervention and when he got home he said to his wife, 'Did you hear that dreadful fellow, Willie McGillivary, who said he could do the miracle of the loaves and fishes?' To which she replied 'Yes, but it was your fault. You said 2,000 loaves and 5,000 small fishes'. The minister was a conscientious fellow and on the next Sunday, returned to the subject, got the figures right, leaned over the pulpit and said 'Now, Willie McGillivary, could you do that?' And the same voice replied 'Aye, minister, fine, I could do that'. The minister thundered 'You blasphemer! How could you feed a multitude with two small loaves and five small fishes?' And the voice answered, 'With what was left over from last Sabbath.'

There is nothing 'left over from last Sabbath'. There is no miracle of the loaves and fishes. The devout do the praying and the hungry do the fasting. In the 1966 Report of the Food and Agriculture Organization the wishful-thinking which had smugly obscured the desperate predicament of mankind was finally dispelled. It was shown that while the world population in that year had increased by 70 million, the world food supply had not increased at all. If all the calories in the world had been put together and rationed out, no one would have had enough to eat. Of course, there were plenty of 'I'm-alright-Jacks'. In the highly developed countries there was 'death on the expense account', the malnutrition of over-eating, the occupational hazard of the executive class. (Two-thirds of all the papers at the Sixth

International Conference on Nutrition held in Edinburgh in 1963 were concerned with the malnutrition of the well-to-do).

The United States, with only 7 per cent of its labour force now engaged in agriculture, produced enough food to supply the minimal calorie requirements of 1,000 million people, five times the United States' population. Canada and Australia and New Zealand had surpluses. Britain was feeding about half its population from its own farms and war-ravaged Europe had made a remarkable recovery and was roughly keeping pace with its requirements. But this food-affluence made nonsense of the figures for global calories. It always had. When we were told over the years (and Pope John believed it) that food production converted into calories *per capita*, was in fact keeping pace with the population increase, this ignored the fact that it was not *per stomach*—if there were adequate food it was not getting into the bellies which needed it.

Some of us, including myself, can put names and faces to statistics. When we see the figures in official reports we can identify them as actual human beings. I have seen the Face of Hunger in Latin-America, in Africa and in Asia. Furthermore, I saw it on the Hunger Marches of my own country in the 1930s—something which is too often forgotten as having happened, and may happen again. We know what hunger means: *kwashiorkor* 'the sickness the first baby dies of when the next baby is born'; *marasmus*, the gross calorie-deficiency of walking skeletons; *hunger oedema*, the swollen belly of the famine baby; *xeropthalmia*, 'dried-out eye' of children blinded by vitamin deficiency; and dehydration of starving infants, robbed of their body fluids.

No amount of prayer can abolish the nightmare of those who have actually seen famine. But there is also the chronic hunger of those who have never had a square meal, who have never had food adequate to well-being. There are some people, like Professor Colin Clark, who, justifying population increase on religious grounds, say that the figures of food shortages are exaggerated. Colin Clark actually alleges that Lord Boyd Orr, when Director-General of the FAO, misrepresented the protein requirements and screwed up the figures from then on. He is prepared to concede that something like 300 million people may be suffering from calorie deficiency. I say that there are at least 500 million in that category of chronic famine but I would maintain that at least two-thirds of our fellow human beings are malnourished—lacking the food factors which the body and brain need for proper functioning.

In this running-down food situation, the world population is increasing. The figures are out-of-date as soon as they are uttered and they are always worse than they appear to be because on every review the UN demographers have to correct them upwards: emergent countries, as they improve their censuses always find that their populations are much bigger than they had guessed. In 1967, one could say that every time the pulse beats there were three more mouths to be fed; 8,000 an hour; 200,000 a day and over 70 million a year.

*Homo sapiens*, Thinking Man, took a million years (from the prosimians) to reach 3,500 million, it would take *Homo insapiens*, Unthinking Man, only thirty years to double that figure. Estimates of how many the world could ultimately sustain include Colin Clark's 47,000 million which he assumed possible merely by expanding and improving conventional agriculture; Harrison Brown's 50,000 million who would in effect be 'eating rocks' in the sense that nutrients would be artifacted from elements; or J. H. Fremlin's sardonic prediction of 100 people to the square yard, stacked in hutches 2,000 storeys high. Such projections are not fearful fantasies—Harrison Brown's figure on present trends could be reached in 150 years, no further ahead than the Battle of Waterloo is behind. What matters now is the rate of growth, the survival rate, which is cancelling out the rate of development of resources. It is like running up a down-escalator, moving fast even to stand still, and not succeeding.

For instance, Central Java was, before the Second World War, a rice bowl, exporting to other peoples in S.E. Asia. Today there is chronic famine, redeemed only by relief supplies. Yet the peasants there were, and still are, intelligent and industrious farmers tilling the 'living pyramids', the window-ledge rice terraces right up to the top of the mountains, and expert in fish-farming. After the war, the UN and other international agencies were encouraged by the response of the Javanese farmers to the improvement of methods, better seeds, better irrigation, manuring, new breeds of fish and so on. They intensified their already intensive farming at a rate of 2½ per cent per annum. But the population increased at 3 per cent per annum. In India, adding every year the equivalent of the population of the Australian continent, all the hundreds of millions invested in modern textile industries did not add half an inch to the tail of the average Indian's shirt; there were millions and millions more shirts but millions and millions more Indians needing them.

Of course, there is a simple answer to the population problem—*Homo sapiens* can veto the evolution of his own and every other species in a nuclear holocaust, unleashing the nuclear stockpiles which represent 100 tons of TNT-equivalent for every man, woman and child on earth and turning his planet into a radioactive desert. Or he can let loose the Doomsday Bug, man-made pestilence for which there would be no natural immunity. Short of such indiscriminate non-selection, restraint on the rate of population increase is imperative and measures, far beyond anything so far employed, are needed to increase the food supplies. The race is between production and reproduction. We shall have at least to treble the production of food in the next thirty years, even if we slow down the momentum of population increase. If family planning were successful even on a world-wide scale and as effectively as it has been done in Japan where the birth rate was more than halved in ten years, we would still be coping with the survival rate, the extension of the span of life. People who are saved from premature death have to be fed. And, as has been pointed out, two-thirds of the people we have are not properly fed. Food therefore has to be increased in quantity and quality. It can be done if the equation $C = B:E$ (first defined by

William Vogt in *Road to Survival*) can be brought into balance. *C* means the carrying capacity of any area—from a window-box to the world itself—and what it 'carries' may be people or herds of flocks etc.; *B*, biotic potential, means the ability of the land to produce plants, especially for food; and *E* means environmental resistance, or the limitations that any environment, including the follies of man, places on the biotic potential.

The equation can be brought into balance by reducing the environmental resistance and increasing the biotic potential, (in other words you might recover deserts) so that a given area can carry more. Or you can restrict the numbers you expect the area to carry. In other words, it is possible to improve the biotic potential and, at the same time, to restrict the population. Both ought to be done together so that the capacity is not over-taxed. At the present moment the population has exceeded the biotic potential.

The food and population problem is the most serious that confronts the world—short, that is, of the ultimate and definitive insanity of a nuclear war. The population explosion is not the result of an orgy of procreation. It is the result of man's ingenuity and of medical science. Any schoolboy can date to the last count-down second the moment of the nuclear explosion—5.30 a.m. on July 16th, 1945, when the first device was exploded in the deserts of New Mexico. The fuse of the population explosion was started ten years before. In February 1935 a young girl was dying of generalized septicaemia. The doctors could give no hope. Her desperate father injected into her veins a red dye. The girl survived. The father was Gerhard Domagk. The red dye was sulphanilamide, the dyestuff which he had demonstrated to be effective against streptococci in mice but had never used until then in a human case. That was the beginning of the new age of pharmaceuticals, the advent of the modern age in medicine—because, while penicillin was later to make an even greater impact on infectious diseases, without the sulpha-drugs of which this was the first, the antibiotics in spectacular terms which we know them today might not have happened. Fleming had already observed the 'penicillin effect' in 1928 but no useful drug had emerged. There were many reasons—side-steps of history—but the main reason was that the climate of medical thought was not right. The doctors, the medical scientists and pharmacologists had forgotten the Ehrlich principle that germs could be attacked *within the living body*. They had a built-in caution, that a chemical, toxic to a germ, would, taken internally, be toxic to human beings. Domagk had shown, as Ehrlich had previously done in 1911, with salversan for syphilis, that a specific germ could be attacked internally by a specific drug. When Florey and Chain took another look at Fleming's penicillin-papers in 1938 they recognized it for what it was—a powerful inhibitor of germs *within the living body*. The sulpha-drugs, the antibiotics, and DDT insecticide were mass produced during the war to treat battle-casualties and avert the camp-diseases. As a result there were large stocks and large manufacturing potential of pharmaceuticals available at the end of the war. They were used in the war-ravaged countries to prevent the pestilences which, in the past, have followed broken armies and displaced people. But they were also available to the humanitarian services of the United Nations and international agencies for use in the underdeveloped countries where epidemics were rife and death-rates were high. BCG vaccinations could prevent tuberculosis and the new drugs could treat it. Antibiotics could cure contagious and infectious diseases and insecticides could control insect-borne disease.

In the advanced countries death-rates had been reduced by extensive and expensive public health services and by health education. The disease-ridden poor countries had not been able to afford such elaborate services—and disease (and the poverty it caused) was one of the reasons why they could not afford them. And now, with international help and with new scientific means it was possible, by direct intervention and merely with the co-operation of illiterate peoples, to control disease. A thousand million people could be protected against malaria. Tens of millions of people could be treated for that dreadful disease yaws. Pestilential diseases could be checked. The puerperal infections of childbirth, which had killed so many mothers, could be abated. More lives have been saved by penicillin than have been lost in all the wars of all human history.

The effects were dramatic. They were significant enough in the improvements in treatment of disease in the advanced countries, but in countries with a high death rate the cutting off of the peaks due to mass-diseases changed the curves of mortality statistics. Mothers who did not die in childbed lived to have more children. In 1946 the expectation of life of a girl baby born in India was 27 years. Today the expectation of life of a girl baby born in India is 46 years. That means that the average girl can live out her entire reproductive life span. She can go on having babies. Children survive to marry and to multiply. Adults live longer.

Traditionally, the limiting factors in the increase of human population have been famine, pestilence and war. 'War,' Sir Arthur Keith once said, 'is nature's pruning hook.' We can now control pestilences and we are trying to avoid wars, knowing that the next total war with nuclear weapons will not 'prune' but annihilate the human race. So we are left with famine, as the likely ruthless form of population control. Over 160 years ago, the Rev. Thomas Malthus insisted that reproductive capacity encouraged population growth far in excess of the likely increase in the means of subsistence. He pointed out that population increases in geometrical progression and the extension of food supplies in arithmetical progression. Thus he argued that unless there was a voluntary means of control of numbers (he was thinking of continence) mankind would run into the disasters of famine. There was nothing wrong with his mathematics, nor can his basic thesis be disproved by showing that in the past we have 'got by'. But, as the Hammonds pointed out in *The Town and Country Labourer*, 'Malthus put a cushion under the conscience of the upper classes'. During the nineteenth century all the social abuses—bad housing, bad sanitation, bad working conditions—could always be justified: if you did anything to improve the conditions of the poor, they would just have more children and, poor things, they would die of hunger!

This leads intelligent and humane men to look at this

problem in the abstract, without putting names and faces to people, and to what Professor A. E. Hill called the 'ethical dilemma'. As president of the British Association in 1952 this Nobel prizewinner for medicine expressed himself thus:

> Had it been possible to foresee the enormous success of this application of the benefits of science, would humane people have agreed that he could better have been held back, to keep in step with other parallel progress so that development could be planned and orderly? Some might say 'Yes', taking the purely biological view that if men will breed like rabbits they must be allowed to die like rabbits, until gradually improving education and the demand for a better standard of life teach them better. Most people will still say 'No', but suppose that it were now certain that increasing population, uncontrolled by disease, would lead not only to a widespread exhaustion of the soil and of other capital resources, but also to continuing international tension and disorder, making it hard for civilization itself to survive: would the majority of humane and reasonable people go and change their minds? If ethical principles deny our right to do evil in order that good may come, are we justified in doing good when the foreseeable consequences are evil?

That was the rhetorical problem posed by an-eminently humane man. But consider the implications: they are nothing short of genocide. The ignorant, biologically improvident peoples of the backward races are to be denied the advance which science has made. All the humanitarian work which has gone on since the Second World War, offsetting so much that is squalid and cynical in world politics, has been 'doing good when the foreseeable consequences are evil'.

But putting the problem this way also ignores the essential truth, which takes no account of mathematics and scientific abstractions. The people who would thus be left in limbo are those of the emerging nations whose governments at their certain peril will deny them the benefits, the *known* benefits, of modern science, because science which has deployed such benefits has also provided the means of communications which have made people aware of them.

Knowledge, once given, can never be taken away. That is the essence of The Revolution of Rising Expectations—the awareness everywhere in the world that the problems of mankind can be solved by the wit of man. And at the root of much of the disenchantment with impoverished 'freedom' and of the disturbances all over the world is the sense of being deprived of the advantages of which the technologically endowed countries so consistently boast and of being denied their basic wants.

Just as indefensible as the Catholic resistance to birth control is the professed Marxist doctrine of 'free demographic expansion'. One notices that the Soviet intellectuals and better off people limit their own families and apparently have means to do so. One notices that in China, when the food situation becomes difficult, parents with more than three children are frowned upon. Academician E. K. Fedorov, at the United Nations Conference on Science and Technology, blandly suggested that space research would find the answer to this problem: that before the pressures on this planet became impossible the other planets would come to the rescue. This, of course, was on the analogy of what happened in the nineteenth century when the opening up of the great open spaces of the western hemisphere, of South Africa, of Australia and New Zealand, provided not only food, by import, for the multiplying populations of industrial Europe, but a spillover by emigration of the surplus population. What Fedorov had not calculated was the actual figures. The total emigration in the world was 50 million in a century and a half, but that is 20 million less than the *annual* increase of population today. The space analogy of the coffin-ships which took the starving Irish to the United States would be a space vehicle carrying 8,000 people every hour. If he were thinking of a milkround bringing the produce of H. G. Wells' 'moon-pastures' to supply the earth or if he was thinking of bringing the raw materials of Venus to supply the terrestrial factories, the freight charges would be pretty prohibitive! No, we cannot escape into space from the problems of this planet.

Emphatically, it is not a question of denying essential humanity; it is a question of balancing death control with birth control. Professor Hill was right in another of his statements: 'There is no possibility of widespread family planning and control if women remain ignorant and illiterate'. But as he also pointed out the problem cannot await the processes of formal education.

There is, however, another process of women's emancipation and education which has been consistently frustrated throughout the world until recent years by the veto of the Catholic Church, and it comes through humanitarian processes. Throughout the world tens of thousands of mother and child health clinics have been established largely through the United Nations' Children's Fund. Even in the countries of purdah and zenana and the Hidden Women, they have succeeded in reaching the women. Through a mother's anxiety for her child, she is attracted to such clinics. She meets women doctors and women nurses. She finds that women are respected and, professionally do the work of men. She finds that they care for her as much as for her child, and through their respect for her as a human being she learns her own self-respect. She finds that she is something more than a breeding-machine, or a chattel. And presently, almost without fail, she is asking for birth control. Oh, no, she does not put it that way. She puts it more tragically: 'Why should I have babies who die?' And more tragic still, international doctors and nurses have been denied, until recently, the right to give her the right answer. All they could say is 'Your babies need not die.' They could not tell her that she need not have babies to risk death. They could not teach her birth control.

For years, under veto of the Roman Catholic Church, the United Nations and the WHO were not allowed even to examine the problems of human reproduction. As far as WHO is concerned, this was circumvented by John F. Kennedy, the late president of the United States. 'Why,' he asked, 'place so much emphasis on fertility? Why not examine the problems of sterility?' What he meant was that if you examine the problems of sterility you must also examine the problems of fertility. Thus, as far as the medical aspects were concerned, human reproduction was no longer a banned subject.

This, however, does not take us very far, except that it

may lead to the discovery of more effective methods of biological control than we at present have. In the poor countries, the Pill is too sophisticated and too expensive. The intra-uterine devices may be cheap and easy to make but they have to be clinically inserted and this means, in India for example, that clinics as well as information have to be got into some 800,000 villages.

It was suggested by Professor Homi J. Bhabha, the famous Indian scientist, that since we were dealing with an epidemic of children we should treat it like an epidemic. He proposed that contraceptives should be introduced into the water supply for given periods of the year. This would, statistically, take care of the abnormal rate of increase. This, like compulsory sterilization, is a draconian or Nuremberg way of dealing with an intimate human problem. People should not be deprived of the means of having children but should have the children they choose to have. They might lose their children; they might get married again. Some way must be found of making contraceptives available in a form which is simply accessible, like putting iodine into salt or 'fortifying' bread or rice. And, as long as it was cheap enough, people could choose when, and if, they want to limit their families. This is very different from the religious compulsions which would condemn them to have the children they do not want. And, remember, science has given them 'too many children'. When it was necessary to beget perhaps fifteen children in order that four or five might survive, people went on having children. While it was necessary to have so many pairs of hands in the fields parents had as many children as they could to ensure that some would survive. If medical science can guarantee that the babies they want will live they will not want to have so many babies.

Pope John (for whom one learnt to have a degree of respect) while he maintained that birth control was not yet necessary because the world could provide for so many people, did speak of parental responsibility and bringing children up 'in human dignity'. The answer to that is quite simple: if people breed like animals, they will live like animals. Too many children reduce a family to degradation and to squalor. The children cannot be adequately fed; they cannot be adequately educated; they cannot escape from poverty, they cannot have human dignity.

The religious opposition to birth control, or family limitation, can be exposed as a cruel hypocrisy. When they talk about 'interfering with the will of God' they should remember, by their own argument, that death-control is also 'interfering with the will of God'. When a mother died in childbirth or was sacrificed to the child she bore, that was 'the will of God'. If that mother is saved by antibiotics, that must be interference. The ethics of simple humanity as well as the mathematics of hunger demands that if we have death control we must have birth control.

Humanist ethics, as I understand them, are concerned with mankind. As humanists we believe in reason, but we also believe that knowledge is not just a hedonistic luxury in which privileged individuals can indulge, but which must be put to work for the benefit of humanity. This raises the interesting question of space research. One recalls that it all began with that most interesting exercise in international co-operation, the International Geophysical Year, in which the scientists of over a hundred nations combined to study the nature of planet earth, of its atmospheric envelope and the forces which impinge upon it from space. It included in the programme a worthy proposal for modest satellites in orbit which by instruments could extend the senses of man to the threshold of space to observe the earth from outside and to measure external influences. The United States and the USSR offered to build such satellites. It was generally assumed (probably by the Russians themselves) that the US with its enormous technological capacity would get its satellite into space first. One fine morning, in October 1957, Sputnik was discovered in orbit. This was a remarkable achievement, not only because the Soviet satellite was first up, but because of the particular orbit in which it was circling. It was the kind of orbit which the Americans were not preparing to attempt. They were proposing to use the 'sling-shot'. This meant 'borrowing' 1,000 miles per hour, the rotatory speed of the earth, to contribute it to the escape velocity of the rocket. This west-to-east orbit was to be at the equator. The USSR, however, put their Sputnik into an orbit circling from latitude 60° N. to 60° S. Thus every inhabited place on earth would be scanned within that orbit. And they did not borrow any speed. The result was consternation. The technological supremacy of the United States had been dramatically challenged and also it was obvious that the USSR had pretty powerful rockets for launching, and to spare. This led to the yelp about the 'missile gap' and the clamour of the Defence Departments of America for bigger and bigger appropriations. The world was well and truly launched into the space race. By 1967 the American civilian Space Agency (NASA) was spending 5,000 million dollars a year, but with the military programme for missiles, etc., the figure was possibly ten times as great. The USSR was probably spending as much and even those nations who were not in the race were spending hundreds of millions. A certain amount of scientific knowledge was required but few, even the most zealous protagonists, could pretend that the 'man into space' part of the programme had much to do with science, except through the technology of getting someone into space, and a man on the moon by 1970. It was frankly a prestigious, albeit adventurous, operation.

It disturbed many people and particularly nations which saw their own brains being drained into the American space programme. This was a fantastic diversion, not only of money but, much more seriously, of human ingenuity, to space and away from the urgent problems of planet earth.

The Civilian Space Administration in the US directly employed 40,000 people and had available to it the efforts of 400,000 workers spread over 20,000 firms. The cost of the civilian operations amounted to 1 per cent of the US gross national product and employed 5 per cent of American engineers and scientists. But the space cult was also distorting the educational system all over the world. And more talented men and women were being attracted into the American space programme. It is true that the kind of technology, in the engineering sense, which was going into the space programme, could not be directly transferred to the feeding of the people of the world but while the 'hardware' might not be transferable, scientific talent, otherwise directed, might have found many of the answers for which the world was desperately looking. This was scientific and technological bombast. The ancients squandered their material success by creating pyramids which stand as the gravestones of civilizations which died out of the neglect of their own backyard. But modern man was throwing his pyramids into space, and there they might orbit eternally round a planet which could die of his neglect.

Moreover, humanist ethics must look with grave concern at the destruction of man's environment by poisons and pollutions of the air, the water and the land. This is not just the concern of the sentimental nature-lover lamenting (and rightly) the drowning of some beauty spot, the detergent-frothing of some trout stream and the hedgerows lost in the asphalt jungle. This is the measurable destruction of man's family estate with immeasurable consequences. At the rate at which we are squandering and destroying our water resources we shall presently be having a 'Freedom from Thirst' as well as a 'Freedom from Hunger' campaign. In humanist ethics we should accept the trusteeship for future generations.

Putting ethics to work means sharing knowledge and skills for the common advancement of mankind. The operative word is 'sharing' because we should learn in all humility that the science and technology of our so-called civilization does not have all the answers. Science, unfortunately, is not wisdom. Wisdom is knowledge tempered by judgement. Experience is often a good substitute for experiment. In the one and three quarter millions miles which I have travelled for the UN and its agencies to see how science and technology can be best applied to the problems of the developing countries, I have seen mistakes writ large because we did not learn before we started to teach. We did not know what we were changing before we started to change. I have come to realise that in appreciating the cultural values of the civilizations older than our own, one does not have to accept the trappings of a religion or the abuses of superstition in acknowledging the value of traditional practices which we so often dismiss as primitive. I have learned enough from native wisdom to be tentative about textbook answers which are over-glib, and experts who are arrogant in the confidence of their methods. You have only to fly over the Indus plain in West Pakistan to see what misplaced technical enthusiasm can do. There, one acre of land is being lost to cultivation every five minutes by salination and water-logging. In the last twenty-five years barrage-engineers have done their job efficiently; canal-builders have capably spread the irrigation waters over the land; the soil-chemists and the soil physicists have done their job to the best of their knowledge; the peasants have moved in and cultivated what was a desert. But one decisive factor was ignored: the whole system depended on 'inland delta drainage' which meant that the surplus water would drain back into the Indus; but the incline is 700 feet in 700 miles so that the natural drainage was ineffective. The water table rose to within inches of the surface, drowning the roots of the crops, bringing up salt from below. The surface irrigation water evaporated and deposited more salt until the whole landscape shimmered with crystals. It will take another twenty-five years and 2,500 million dollars to restore the damage.

As Professor P. M. S. Blackett has said, the developing countries should shop cautiously in the super-market of science.

# The Undeveloped Countries

LORD BOYD ORR

## Lord Boyd Orr

DSO, MC, FRS, LLD. Director-General of the United Nations Food and Agricultural Organisation, 1945–1948. Nobel Peace Prize, 1949. Chairman of the Scottish Scientific Advisory Committee and joint-editor of *Nutrition Abstracts and Reviews.*

Publications include: *Minerals in Pastures and Their Relation to Animal Nutrition*; *Food, Health and Income*; *Food and the People*; *The White Man's Dilemma*; *Feast and Famine*; *As I Recall.*

# The Undeveloped Countries

LORD BOYD ORR

The problem of the widening gap between the poverty of the undeveloped countries and the wealth of the countries where industries have been developed is a part of the effect of the impact of modern science on human society. In the last few decades the tremendous new powers produced by modern science have brought about the biggest revolution in the evolution of human society since the discovery of food production with settled communities about 8,000 years ago, which was the beginning of the growth of civilization.

*Science and Wealth*

The main source of wealth is science which gives the 'know how' and technology which applies it to industries. It is important to remember that modern science did not originate in the now wealthy countries and that they may not continue indefinitely to have almost a monopoly of the physical sciences, the source of money power and military power. It originated in the now poor countries of Asia and in Egypt. Mathematics was well advanced in the second millennium BC and was applied to the study of astronomy to foretell the flooding of the Nile and the coming of the monsoons which was needed to decide the best time for the sowing of crops. Technology was developed for irrigation projects and other means of increasing food production and for its storage and distribution. In these old civilizations it was known that the sun and not the earth was the centre of the then known universe and that the earth was round and its circumference was 2,400 miles. These old civilizations also made the greatest advances in religion and ethics. All the great religions of today, the Jewish, the Christian and the Mohammedan, originated in Asia Minor, and further East in Asia, Buddhism and Confucianism which, at first, were rationalist. Thus, in Egypt and parts of Asia, civilization had reached a relatively high level when the Europeans, who are now the wealthy nations, were as backward and ignorant as the Hottentots of today.

Apart from the great contribution to art, philosophy and politics made by the ancient Greeks, and to war and the administration of conquered countries by the Romans, it is only within the last four hundred years that modern science began to be developed in Europe. During the thousand years of the Dark Ages the Roman Catholic Church which had inherited much of the political power and authority of the Roman Empire, discouraged free thought, an essential for the advance of science. Any expression of ideas which conflicted with the teaching of the Church was regarded as heresy liable to incur the death penalty. There was, therefore, no advance in science until the Renaissance in the fourteenth century. This was the re-birth of the science of the East which was carried by the Mohammedans to the part of Spain they had conquered, and from there it filtered through to Italy and other European countries. It was followed by a breakaway of part of the Church to become the Protestant religion which allowed freedom of thought in the study of the natural sciences.

*Exploitation of Coloured Races*

As so often happens the first fruits of science were applied to the improvement of weapons of war. In the fourteenth century gunpowder which had been invented by the Chinese and used for pyrotechnic displays was applied to a crude form of cannon. It was later applied to hand firearms. With these weapons the Spaniards were able to conquer the Aztecs and the Mayas of Latin America, and exploit them, seizing their gold and other treasures, and using the natives as serfs. Other European nations followed suit, taking possession of whatever part of the world they could grab first. The control of the coloured races enabled the Europeans to get vegetable and mineral raw materials for their industries which, with the advance of science and technology, increased the output of wealth at an accelerating rate.

This exploitation of coloured nations has increased since they gained their freedom and independence. The late Dag Hammarskjold calculated that, since the last war the fall in the price of their exports to the industrialized countries—their only market—caused a bigger fall in their income than all the aid received, including loans from the World Bank. Cheaper exports of primary products from the coloured nations and dearer imports of industrial products needed for their development make the poor countries poorer and the rich countries richer.

*Wealth and its Distribution*

The total wealth of the world and the capacity for producing wealth is now so great that it is now possible for the first time in the history of man to produce in abundance everything needed for the physical necessities of life for all mankind if it were devoted to that end. It can also produce lethal weapons which, if applied in a third world war would destroy our civilization and probably add the human race to the long list of species which have become extinct, because they could not become adjusted to new conditions. Almost all the wealth surplus to what is needed for a low level of subsistence is now in the hands of the Europeans, the white race, which includes the British Dominions, the United States of America and the minority of whites in South Africa and Rhodesia.

The United States has 40 per cent of the total wealth of the world and consumes 50 per cent of the raw materials used in the world. This is due not to any superior ability of the Americans but to the fact that they took over the rich sparsely populated continent of North America and during the last two world wars developed their industries because there was a market for everything that could be produced while, during the war, the European countries were destroying their industries.

While the European countries and the countries in America, Australasia and South Africa which the Europeans conquered and occupied have so much wealth with such a high standard of living that the well-to-do working class have luxuries that the wealthy did not enjoy a hundred or even fifty years ago, the people of the undeveloped countries are so poor that they suffer premature death for the lack of adequate food and hygienic housing. The expectation of life at birth in the undeveloped countries is only about 40 years compared with about 70 in the industrialized countries.

The following table giving the income per head illustrates the gap between the industrialized and the undeveloped countries of Latin America in 1947.

| | *Dollars* |
|---|---|
| United States | 550 |
| Switzerland | 450 |
| Colombia | 68 |
| Brazil | 49 |
| Bolivia | 67 |
| Haiti | 15 |
| Costa Rica | 84 |

*Aid to Undeveloped Countries*

Nearly all the industrialized countries including Russia and China have given aid. Britain has given financial aid to India and to her former colonies; in 1966 it spent £210 million on this aid. Germany has this year given Ghana £3,200,000 free of interest for seven years and then at a low rate of interest of 3 per cent per annum thereafter. Russia has given aid in food and armaments to Egypt and the Arab countries. China has given aid to the African countries, including this year an interest free loan of £100 million to build a railway from the coast to Zambia. Canada and Australia have given gifts of wheat to relieve famine in India. All this aid, however, has been far surpassed by American aid. From the end of the last war till 1960 it gave 50,000 million dollars. In 1948–1952 under the Marshall Plan it gave 13,150 million dollars to the Western countries of Europe to repair the damage of the Second World War, and from 1962–1964 gave 13,500 million tons of wheat to relieve famine in India and is still supplying a million tons a month.

It is difficult, however, to find out how much of this aid

was given solely for the benefit of the people in the poor countries. Financial aid to get allies and armaments to get their military aid in wars to stop the spread of Communism did little or nothing to alleviate the poverty. Some of the financial aid like that given by the Russians for the Aswan Dam was a direct benefit, as was some of the American aid for similar constructive projects, but the recent armaments and food from Russia to the Arab countries seemed designed to oust American political and economic power from the Middle East.

*Are Coloured Races Inferior?*

Before considering the kind of aid needed by the undeveloped countries it is necessary to decide whether the coloured races are inferior and fit only to supply cheap labour in industries and servants to the superior white race. That view was held by the English in the late nineteenth century when Britain was the most powerful nation in the world. To rule 'men of lesser breed' was the 'White man's burden'. That is still believed by a few with the 'Colonel Blimp' mentality and by some whose financial interests would be affected by giving equal wages to coloured workers with the same ability as white workers. It is now acknowledged by those who have studied the subject that, with equal education and equal environment including food and housing, there is no evidence of any difference in ability of the different races. This has been proved in recent years. Many coloured men, including two Negroes, are Nobel prizemen. At Glasgow University, from among two thousand medical students, a Negro from Ghana was the most distinguished graduate in 1963. The Japanese showed, in the war with Russia, and in the more recent war with America, that they are not inferior as fighting men, and since the last war have shown that in the development of industry they are not inferior to any white nation.

China, which in 1948, when it drove out the invaders, was possibly the poorest and most disease-ridden country in the world, has developed its industries faster than Japan did. About ten years ago General Montgomery after a visit to

China said that within fifty years it would be the most powerful military country in the world. Since then it has produced nuclear weapons.

The coloured races are now being rapidly educated, most of them at their own universities and are adopting Western science and technology. They are now on the march, with a grievance about being exploited in the past, and nothing except war will stop them until they have political and economic equality with the white race. All the white nations must either do as the European nations did, give them their independence and allow their governments to try out any political or economic ideology they choose, or fight for world supremacy in a series of wars like that in Vietnam. The revolt of the coloured races, which has already begun, has a profound effect on the kind of aid which should be given to the undeveloped countries.

*Kind of Aid Needed*

Their poverty is due to the exploitation referred to above. It has been increased by the explosion of world population. This began in Europe in the eighteenth century with the increase in the food supply from North America. In the later part of the nineteenth century the rate of increase accelerated by preventive medicine which reduced the death rate. In England and Wales the population, including the emigrants to North America and Australia, increased from about 10 million to nearly 40 million, an increase by about 400 per cent, while the total world population during the century increased by only about 8 per cent.

Since the beginning of the present century preventive medicine began to be applied to the coloured nations with resulting fall in the death rate and no corresponding fall in the birth rate. By 1946 when the World Health Organization was established the population was increasing at 22 million a year. Since then the rate of increase has reached 70 million a year. In the European nations the birth rate has fallen. The slow increase consists largely of old people. It looks as if the population may soon become stabilized. Nearly the whole of the increase in the coloured nations which are now growing at a rate which will double the population in about twenty-five years.

Food production is increasing in the food deficit countries, but not at a rate to make any reduction in malnutrition and starvation. In former years the growth of population would have been arrested by famines. Now food is sent from industrialized countries. Apart from the United States food aid to India mentioned above, Russia and China have sent food to Egypt. Canada and Australia have sent gifts of wheat to food deficit countries.

The author of an American book published this year, *Famine 1975*, says that nothing can stop the explosion of population in the hungry countries, the granaries of the world are empty and by 1975 the only country with food to export will be America which must decide which countries will be given food to survive and which allowed to perish.[1] This is in my opinion an exaggeration. The population growth can be arrested. Japan, by legalizing abortion and making 'the Pill' available for every woman willing to take it, has reduced the number of births from 2,677,000 in 1949 to 1,070,000 in 1962. Population growth has been arrested, the number of children born being only about sufficient to replace the people who die. The government of India is considering sterilizing all fathers with more than three children and offering rewards to unmarried men to be sterilized.

If birth control could be applied in all countries the growth of population could be arrested. The Catholic Church prohibits it. In a recent meeting of the World Health Organization delegates from Catholic countries declared they would leave the Organization if the subject were even considered. There is some hope that the Vatican may reconsider this ban. Fortunately, Japan and India are not within the sphere of influence of the church.

The growth of population can be arrested and with modern engineering and agricultural science the earth can be made to produce sufficient food for several times its human population. But the increased food needed must be produced

[1] '*Famine 1975. America's Decision—Who Will Survive*, by William and Paul Paddock. Little, Brown & Co., Boston, Toronto. 1s 6d. 50c.

in the deficit countries. That is the most important need of the coloured nations. Otherwise they will never become independent members of the world community of nations. They cannot do it themselves because they do not have the fertilizers, the modern agricultural equipment, the pumps for irrigation and other industrial products needed, nor the foreign exchange to import them. It can only be done by the co-operation of all governments in a world project, which will double food production to eliminate malnutrition and starvation in the present population and provide for the increase in population before birth control can be applied in all the coloured nations.

Two attempts have been made to do this. The first was by the League of Nations in 1935. Delegates of the principal countries including America and Russia outlined a plan to double world food production as a means of providing a market for the enormous amounts, of industrial goods produced, and so reducing the number of unemployed in the industrialized countries. The outbreak of war in 1939 put an end to that project. Then, during the last war the plan was revived at an international conference called by the late President Roosevelt. It was designed to prevent a post-war slump such as occurred after the first war, and also even more important to get the nations to begin to co-operate in a world plan for their mutual advantage, as a contribution to permanent world peace.

Out of that conference arose the Food and Agriculture Organization. It was able to get the nations to co-operate to deal with the post-war food crisis. It failed, however, to get co-operation in a permanent world food board because though all the other member nations of FAO were willing to co-operate, Britain and then America refused to join. Without these two, at that time the wealthiest nations, it was impossible to form an international authority designed to abolish hunger, stabilize prices in the world market, provide a world reserve of food which could be drawn upon by any country after a bad harvest, bring about a great expansion of industry to replace armaments and be an important step to a world of economic prosperity and peace, which were the purposes of FAO. Roosevelt had died and America probably thought that as it would need to provide half the funds needed, it might as well do the job itself by bilateral agreement with the hungry countries and promote its own political and economic interests. Since then the world-food position has grown worse. Increase in production is failing to keep pace with rise in population. There is now less food per head of the world population than there was a few years ago, and as the American authors referred to above stated, the granaries of the world, having been drained by export of food to prevent famine in the deficit countries, are empty.[1]

If these views be right, what the undeveloped countries need is a world food authority which will increase their food production to provide a diet adequate for health, and an international agency free from control of the Catholic Church to get humane methods like the pill applied to reduce the birth rate as Japan has done. If these objects were achieved they would be able to increase their wealth and be able to introduce modern sanitation and the things necessary to raise their standard of living.

### *Undeveloped Countries in World Affairs*

Arnold Toynbee in his recent book *The Challenge of our Time*[2] after a survey of world affairs reaches the conclusion that our civilization cannot survive unless there is a world authority able to bring about disarmament and prevent war between nuclear powers, and a world food authority to deal with the world food shortage. That would prevent a war between the coloured nations led by China and the white nations led by America.

In the present inflamed political atmosphere there is little hope of the nuclear powers disarming and giving the United Nations Organization power to prevent war. Further, the production of armaments for home defence and for export is, next to the production and distribution of food, one of the

[1] '*Famine 1957. America's Decision—Who Will Survive*, by William and Paul Paddock. Little, Brown & Co., Boston, Toronto. 1s 6d. 50c.

[2] *Change and Habit—The Challenge of Our Time*, by Arnold J. Toynbee. Oxford University Press, London. 25s.

biggest industries. Including the attempt to put a man in the moon, the governments of the world are spending on it about the equivalent of about 200,000 million dollars a year. A sudden stoppage of that expenditure would bring about an economic crisis greater than the one in 1929. When the war in Korea looked like ending an American newspaper article had the heading 'Peace threat slump in Wall Street'.

A world food authority could bring about a change in international affairs enabling the development of an international authority which could prevent war. The nuclear powers say they are in favour of disarmament. If they would begin gradual and equal disarmament by reducing their military budgets by say 10 per cent; devoting half of the savings, which would amount to about 10,000 million dollars in the first year, to an international food Authority, managed by business men representing all areas in the world; and retaining the other half to reduce taxation and to subsidize the gradual change over from armament production to the enormous quantity of industrial goods needed to double world food production in the immediate future, with a further increase to provide for the growth of population until birth control is established—the wheels of industry would be kept turning without an economic crisis. The co-operation of all governments in such a plan for their mutual advantage would bring about a better atmosphere in international politics which would facilitate the establishment of a world authority able to prevent war.

There is now the possibility of governments adopting this policy. The writer had a long talk with the late President Kennedy. He was a man with the vision and good will of Woodrow Wilson who founded the League of Nations to prevent war and get the nations to co-operate in the abolition of hunger, slavery, the traffic in drugs and other evils, and the vision and goodwill of President Roosevelt, the real author of the United Nations, designed for the same ends. A few weeks after the interview Kennedy said, in a speech to the Assembly of the United Nations, that America would support a world food policy which would provide a good diet for every child in the world. A similar change has taken place in Britain which opposed the setting up of a world food authority. Harold Wilson the present Prime Minister put on his election programme the establishment of a world food board. Russia has said that it would join if America and Britain did. The hungry nations would welcome it, as would the food exporting countries which would get a world market for all they could produce.

Thus there is hope that the abolition of hunger in the coloured nations can become part of the world plan of political and economic reconstruction which would be the beginning of a wonderful new era free from the intolerable evils of war and poverty.

# Humanism and the Arts

KATHLEEN NOTT

Kathleen Nott

Poet, novelist, critic.

Publications include: *Mile End*; *The Dry Deluge*; *Private Fires*; *An Elderly Retired Man*; *Landscapes and Departures*; *Poems from the North*; *The Emperor's Clothes*; *A Clean Well-Lighted Place*; *Creatures and Emblems*; various articles and reviews in literary journals and newspapers.

# Humanism and the Arts

KATHLEEN NOTT

What I am going to say should be taken as referring to the literary arts. I am not qualified to make generalizations about any others.

I think that humanists of our time are not as strong as they should be on the meaning and value of art and the artist. I do not mean of course that individual (and leading) humanists may not keenly appreciate one, some or all of the arts, or even practice one of them. And the point is not so much that humanists don't *do* anything about the arts as that they don't fully grasp the significance of art-language.

In *The Humanist Frame*, a symposium published a few years ago, we have, out of twenty-six essays, only two which are about an art or artists—Michael Tippett ('Towards the Condition of Music'); Stephen Spender ('Social Purpose and the Integrity of the Artist'). Spender's attitude, out of the whole book, seemed to me to be the most relevant to my own beliefs; artistic integrity, he implies, may not only be anti-social in any given state of society, but even anti- what many humanists believe to be Humanism.

However, Sir Julian Huxley in his introductory essay devoted a fair, indeed a fairly high, proportion of his space to a discussion of the arts and of their human significance. Whether he brought the arts and Humanism very much closer together is arguable.

Before I go any further I had better admit that as soon as I begin to write about Humanism or speak from a Humanist platform I find myself in full retreat towards square nought. If someone does not ask me what or who is a humanist—I find I am asking myself—or the audience. Perhaps it's a bit less like Ludo than darts: one is always trying to throw a double, to get started on a meaningful definition, and then get somewhere. (I feel that many of the writers in *The Humanist Frame* felt something similar: some may have found the Frame an odd trucklebed to be in and may even have been surprised in a jourdainesque way to find that they have been humanists all their lives without knowing it.)

I don't think this is all just *folie de doute*: rather that there is a great deal of emotional hypostasis about our idea of Humanism and even that a great many of us don't altogether want to make it too precise and to get pinned down. One part of the question is: where did the modern movement really begin, and where has it perhaps stuck?

Many humanists seem to be just non-Godists. All they seriously worry about is the mid-Victorian controversy and it is here that they seem irremovably stuck. 'Stuck' is the word, because the large mass of contemporary literature has made at least one thing clear: that on the subject of God's existence and of the supernatural there is no longer any possibility of reasoned communication. Not only will the non-Godists never convert the Godists; it cannot even be said of the Godists that, like the Cabots, 'they speak only to God'. A surprising number of them—to mention only Anglican Woolwich and Catholic Haughton—suggest to one that they have decided that God's existence is only Pickwickian. *Don't look now and He will be there.* They behave as if after all they had really succeeded in inventing Him. But in fact they have the metaphysical splits—and speak only to themselves. *Credo quia impossibile.*

But perhaps the humanists too might give up their secret and possibly unconscious worries about God and the supernatural and the 'God-shaped hole' and spend less time arguing to the non-convertible. Perhaps they have the first opportunity in history to *invent the human being* and to establish Humanism as what it has been in glimpses and moments—an examination of the real possibilities of the real concrete human being.

This is where art and artists come in. If they are any good, it is just this concrete entity which they try to precipitate or to make visible: whereas practically everybody else, including humanists, finds it much easier to generalize about 'Man' and the 'Species.'

It is a sad thing to have to bring into the discussion, so early if at all, that weary and fraudulent old cliché, the Two Cultures, but I see no help for it. For humanists have not only climbed out on the wrong limb of this bifurcated monster, but since their mid-nineteenth-century Anno-non-Domini, have encouraged it to go on doing the splits. The real antithesis is not between science and the 'humanities', not even between science and arts or arts, but rather between the idea of one kind of human being who might be called a scientist or scientific technician, and that of another who might be called an artist. And the conflict is not really about their relative value, either aesthetic, moral or social, but about who is going to run the show and to be the future representative of the human species.

Since the cliché as we have it was the invention of a boffinized politician, it clothes, if lightly, this claim to naked power with some frills of moral superiority—the boffins ought to run the show which they *are* going to run, because of some preferential virtue (caring about the future, about hunger, war, etc., and also having a much purer, more raptly contemplative kind of 'aesthetic' vision, which is also—for the species—more hygienic).

Snow deplored the 'existential' character of the typical artist, meaning—so far as one can make out—that art-work entails thinking about the real, live, suffering, enjoying, often far from hygienic and even bloody-minded human being, in some or all of his aspects.

I do not know whether Snow calls himself a humanist or not, but I feel sure that humanists are seldom 'existential' in the sense he rejects, and that, on the contrary, they are 'future-minded' in a way which should win his highest awards. They are committed to the species and to man, and if they are not by any means one hundred per cent confident about our future that is often because they are afraid that certain unnatural causes may intervene before the scientists and the technicians succeed in making us over to be fit to survive (indefinitely).

Now art, certainly literary art, *is* 'existential' and has to be so. It is, if nothing else, about the real concrete human being as he is and as he is becoming in a real present. And this is what Humanism also ought to be. So that we can invert Sartre's question (to which he gave no very satisfactory answer)—and propose instead: *Is Humanism an Existentialism?* A typical fault of the Sartrean (and no doubt the Kierkegaardian) existentialist is to be so overwhelmed by the Death of God that (like many humanists) he fails to extract from it the true humanist profit. Sartre certainly proclaims that because gods (with all the 'theologies') are no more, then we are out on our own (and a limb)—we are completely 'free' and self-responsible.

What he means by freedom is not much more than 'the key of the street': there is no one to care about us or to tell us what to do.

The significant error is that Sartre has thrown out the baby with the font. The job for the humanist is to try and extract the *human* values of religion, to separate them out from the theological languages in which they disguise themselves.

One essential human value of the world-religions is their realistic tragic sense: that they have not parted company with the awareness that a human being is limited, if by nothing else, by his mortality: and that his values as well as his suffering spring from the tension created by this awareness. This basic human-existential fact tends to express itself in poetry. Art-language, said Lawrence, in a moment of lucidity, is the only language. Arnold talking of religion and literature meant something similar.

Partial and exaggerated, yes—for, if we want to exchange information as we do and must, particularly of a specialized kind, circumscribed by definitions, agreements and conventions, we also need a rigidly referential and scientific language.

But a humanist must not lightly part with the 'humanities'. I don't mean particularly Latin and Greek: or if I do, I also mean Sanscrit and Chinese. The point is the same: a tradition is important, not because it is the past, but in so far as it is the present. It remains valuable because it teaches us about *us*, and if we break with it in an arbitrary fashion, we may to some extent lose the thread of our evolutionary identity and even our actual location today. All this was foreseen by the American humanist Irving Babbitt about fifty years ago. He had not only a vast range of literary knowledge but also of philosophies and religions: he saw that science could instruct us in power and its uses, but not in values, not therefore in the human being.

Many humanists, both professing and among those who would clearly not object to the label (Waddington, Bronowski, as 'scientific' humanists are specially significant) have an almost mystical devotion to poetry. But I suspect that, humanistically, this may be fishy. It sidesteps the fact that poetry is trying to be a real language of perception and makes the old 'emotivistic' confusion. (Freud with his 'oceanic feeling' made the same confusion about religious insight—which, freed of its accretions of theology, has often been *human* insight expressed in the best language available at the time.) With some distinguished humanists, well-disposed towards the 'humanities', one might think that 'sensibility' still belonged to the eighteenth- or nineteenth-century drawing-room and called for the smelling-bottle and the unloosening of stays. (There is that famous story, told by Huxley with awe, about Bertrand Russell fainting on the stairs at a first hearing of Blake's 'Tiger, tiger——')

Any scientific humanist would say, I am sure, if challenged, that he is deeply if not primarily concerned with the individual man and woman; and that if he talks too much of 'Man' the 'species', and uses a number of other abstract terms such as 'progress' or the 'future', it is in full awareness that these are only linguistic conveniences, necessary generalizations. He might also say that he has to rely on 'experts' in various fields (including perhaps artists) to clear some sort of a path and try to get something, anything, done at all.

But about the human being there are no true 'experts'—not even artists, certainly not psychologists. The first job of a humanist is to learn about him, in himself and in other real people he comes across (beginning of course in marriage and the home, which is enough to frighten anybody). Of course this needs a change of attitude, a kind of conversion, which very few people are able or willing to submit to. They want to get something done, the world is full of urgent problems which appeal to us as matters of life and death, for the world if not for ourselves: hunger, over-population, disease, war, tyranny.

Indeed practical Humanism, like politics, is an art of the possible. But Humanism is also a theory of existence, a philosophy. And I believe that a good practice cannot follow from a weak and mistaken theory. We have by now a great deal of social machinery built on intentions and studies which look, and often are, excellently humane. But of all men and women, humanists ignore at their peril that any machinery or organization, technical or social, can become the rider instead of the mount. We want, don't we, to free the human animal, to stop him being just a collection of habits or conditioned reflexes?

So that the humanist, of all people, must maintain, in his most social and moral activities, a certain detachment, a certain criticism of himself, his motives and his own conditioning. The alternative is a futuristic panglossism, a hope in the sweet by-and-by which we know in our hearts will be deflected if not wholly disappointed. Do we want to finish up with Teilhard de Chardin in the dream of a world-brain? Some leading humanists who ought to know better have relaxed criticism of this dream-state so far that they appear to be not far off it themselves already.

Hence art-language may be the only really lively language for a humanist because it is more instructive, not because poets or imaginative writers are more encouraging about the human animal at his present stage of development. The blackest (or even the bluest) contemporary novel, if it is honest, can teach you more than the most painstaking piece of sociological research, because it tells you about some human being's struggle to see for himself in some no doubt limited direction, and not be fobbed off by any kind of abstract generalizing language. *If it is honest.* Much contemporary fiction and poetry is extremely unconsoling and not at all inspiring (and often boring). But the moral advantage of remaining in touch with it is that one may acquire a sounder taste in authenticity and learn to tell when black is just the fashionable colour or when, on the other hand, the writer is duly providing the natural and necessary antithesis to our own hypocrisy or our inevitable unresistant panglossism.

This may sound a dreadfully clinical, at best a therapeutic, idea of the function of literature in our time. But I have found that a certain purge is needed in the humanistic-social attitude towards the arts. Humanists, especially if they are scientists, are much more inclined than artists to talk about 'beauty' or to believe that an artist sets out to establish harmony; more seriously, that he is somehow in collusion with the Future of Man ('better, happier and wiser' as Snow prophesied, than we know now). A significant work of art, an authentic poem or novel, is discouraging to this kind of hubris, and therefore may act on us with an ultimately sobering realism.

# Faith Lost— Imagination Enriched

BRIGID BROPHY

## Brigid Brophy

Novelist and critic.

Publications include: *Black Ship to Hell*; *The Finishing Touch*; *Flesh*; *The King of a Rainy Country*; *The Snow Ball*; *Hackenfeller's Ape*; *Don't Never Forget*; *Mozart the Dramatist*; *Religious Education in State Schools*; various articles and reviews in literary journals and newspapers.

# Faith Lost—Imagination Enriched

## BRIGID BROPHY

'But what would you put in its place?'

Every experienced secularist-humanist will recognize this standard response to any proposal to demote religion from its privileges in school, state or individual heart. Evidently human nature deplores a vacuum. Sometimes the standard response is crossly brandished at you, in expectation of nailing you on it; sometimes it is brought forth as a moan, from which you guess the questioner really has apprehended your words to be inexorably pumping out from his bell-jar some atmosphere of mind without which he feels his mental life would stifle.

It is tempting to answer the question, if only for sheer weariness of it, with 'Nothing'—a reply that withdraws behind the impregnable inner defences of cold reason. For in cold reason we are absolutely entitled to show that the religious hypothesis is improbable, and we do not thereby incur the faintest obligation to offer an alternative account of anything at all. But when there is pain in the tone of the question, one would much prefer to answer it with Pamina's ringing soprano syllables, 'die Wahrheit'—running up a flag over that cold fortress of reason as a signal that, no matter how bleak it may look from down there at skirmish-level, there is a transcendent altitude at which the truth (whatever it may turn out to be—one has to dash off the gesture of writing a blank cheque) is so purely *attractive* that one is forced to acknowledge it as a species of beauty, and Keats as right after all.

Perhaps we secularist-humanists ought to put out more flags and be more mindful of Keats.

I do not, of course, mean that the secularist–humanist organizations as such ought to go in for gestures. Gestures are the best language for works of art, because they are so highly condensed; but for the same reason they are far too liable to misinterpretation to be very frequently used for signalling messages. The secularist–humanist movement, which has definite practical and prosaic social aims to fulfil, cannot *be* a work of art, and would rapidly make a fool of itself if it tried. But there is no reason why the secularist–humanist mind (by which I mean any mind, whatever its native tenor, when it is thinking in an official secularist–humanist capacity) must be, as it often seems to show as being, tone-deaf to all the arts.

This is not to accuse the movement of aggressive philistinism. Its philistinism is of the passive, by-default variety, and consists in the movement's conducting its own business, drawing up its programmes and propounding its arguments all in terms that would not need to be changed a jot were the human aesthetic faculty declared abolished tomorrow. And equally the movement neglects to bring home to the Christians how strongly they rely, though without admitting to any such thing, on an appeal to aesthetics.

I suspect that in its oblivion of the very existence of aesthetics the movement cannot distinguish very sharply between what is aesthetics' business and what is reason's. It cannot, therefore, insist on its opponents' observing the distinction. And in many of its own affairs it seems to have been frightened into a diluted, de-theologized Christian goodwill on the very issues where it ought to take its stand most coldly and austerely on reason, while, on the occasions where it ought to be mentally rioting in a baroque, a positively Rubensesque bacchanal, it offers instead a sensuously repellent world of high thinking in scratchy tweed trousers and uncomfortable moquette armchairs, a world resembling the interior decoration of the mind of the young H. G. Wells.

The very adoption of the name 'humanist' (a *fait accompli*, now, which one can only make the best of) was perhaps an occasion when we let ourselves be scared. The name is inept because ambiguous: even now, I daresay, there is in every humanist audience one poor person who has come expecting a lecture on Erasmus. And I imagine we were scared into ineptitude by a bogey bidding us not call ourselves by negative names but be seen to be proposing something positive.

That bogey, however, is neither reason nor psychology; it's a mere trick of the advertising trade, an adage against writing negative copy, a concern with images in the sense of 'image' received on Madison Avenue, not in Freudian Vienna. In reason we shouldn't be afraid to negate a proposition we think untrue. Psychologically, we of all people should see deeper than the simple-minded dichotomy which is having a vogue in the lukewarm afterglow of, in combination, Christianity, Buddhism and the Boy Scout movement, and which divides acts according to their literal content, into good-loving-outgoing-constructive or bad-destructive-aggressive-negative.

By that feeble-minded type of thinking, surgeons are brutes because they don't feel squeamish about blood. In reality, of course, a positive act may be registered by a vote of No: it all depends on the terms in which the motion was couched. In Britain, where Parliament starts its sessions with prayers and sees fit to legislate that the only other organizations in the country compelled by force of law to do likewise are the state schools, the motion is clearly proposed by the religionists. Irreligionists can't be justly accused of negativism if they register their No by calling themselves unbelievers or atheists. By dodging those names we perhaps lost a chance to push the issue into greater clarity. And it is possible we actually lost on the swings as well as the roundabouts, damaging even our Madison-Avenue-sense image by letting ourselves be labelled with a genteel euphemism. Atheists, I suspect, go to the lavatory; humanists use the toilet.

And then there is our graphic label, that little British Humanist Association symbol whose official nickname is 'the Happy Man'. No one, of course, would wish him unhappy. Yet here, too, conceivably, we have been scared or lured into competing with the Christians on their own ground, and have thereby forfeited an opportunity to point out that their ground is incorrect. For I think our basic reproach against them must be that they propose as truths doctrines they have ultimately no better authority for believing than that believing makes them happy.

A Christian will often tell you 'I couldn't live without my faith' with the implication he is making a statement about the Christian faith; he is, of course, making a statement strictly about himself. It was Christianity which in the first place confused this issue (with later help from popular misconceptions of popular democracy), with its insistence that what those literal 'witnesses', the martyrs, bore witness to was the Christian faith. In reality a Christian martyr bears witness to his own faith, in the sense of an emotion inside his own personality, and certainly to his own courage. His brave behaviour does not comment either way on the truth of the propositions he has faith in—any more than the equal bravery of the witches who were martyred by the Christians does anything to establish the validity of witchcraft.

Sooner or later in most Christian–atheist conversations the Christian will say 'But you can't *prove* God doesn't exist'. The atheist must in honesty confess that indeed he can't; but he is also entitled—indeed, obliged—to go on and say to the Christian, 'Neither can you prove that Astarte or the king of the fairies doesn't exist, but you're quite willing to take it for granted that they don't.' In other words, the Christian is tacitly relying on an extension of the notion that martyrs bear witness to the faith. This time it is not the believers' deaths but the continuing lives of a succession of believers which are being pressed into service as a sounding-board for the validity of the propositions they believe. We are being surreptitiously asked to swallow Christianity because the historical chain of believers in it is still extant. Had the Christian lived when the worship of Astarte was extant, he would have had as much call to ask us to swallow that. Even now he has, but doesn't exercise (and that he doesn't marks his behaviour as a caprice, an application of aesthetic judgement where rational judgement is required), the same justification for bidding us believe what the stars foretell, a probably even older supernatural system than Christianity and one whose survival into a scientific age and in the teeth of the evidence might be claimed to argue spiritual validity and even supernatural support rather more plausibly than those can be argued on behalf of Christianity, which since the death of Julian the Apostate has always possessed official backing and the power to put down anyone who disagreed.

One of the prime responsibilities of a rationalist movement is to insist that the appeal to martyrdoms or extantness or (the democratic extension) public opinion polls is irrelevant. It is the Christians who subtly, chiefly through their insidious and intellectually horrifying notion that faith is a virtue, seek to create a magical world in which wishing—especially communal wishing—will make a thing so. Prayers are simply wishes; it is when 'two or three are gathered together' that those who pray expect their requests to be granted. Religionists often apprehend your lack of faith as some threat to their own, which is why they are more equivocal about toleration than atheists are. And in a sense anyone who abstains from faith *is* a threat to them: he is like the abstainer or the scoffer in a theatrical audience, the one who won't laugh or won't join in the community singing, who won't merge his own in the group's identity and thereby makes it hard for the others to do so and hard for them to succumb to the illusion that the dramatic performance is true. But of course suspension of disbelief in a drama is a voluntary and temporary act. Religionists are always trying to turn it into literal belief, a necessary and lasting act; but the questions by which they allure you into belief are proper not to judgements of truth but to aesthetics—'Don't you find this an appealing story? Is he not a sympathetic and good character? Would it not all be neater and *nicer* if there were a god?'

We, in contrast to this, are surely the ones who ought to proclaim that the test of whether there are fairies at the bottom of your garden has nothing to do with whether it would be nicer if there were; nothing to do with whether you can or can't live by the belief there are; nothing to do with whether a belief in fairies is still extant. Our case against compulsory religious worship in schools ought to be simply that it is immoral to impose on children what both sides agree to be a matter of faith, and not of demonstrable or rationally arguable—and rationally rescindable, if better evidence turns up—fact. Our case may mention in passing, but ought not to rest much of its weight on, how small a fraction of the citizenry bothers to attend voluntary religious worship. If that were the correct criterion, we might be put in a very awkward position any day now, were a public opinion poll to establish, as it very well might, that 90 per cent of the population voluntarily consults its horoscope in the newspapers; we would be in honour bound to start campaigning for compulsory horoscope lessons.

Likewise with the size of our own fraction of the population. We atheists bear a special responsibility not to be intimidated by consensus politics. It is good public relations to present a happy, flourishing, branching secularist–humanist movement, but it is poor rationalism to do it by withdrawing emphasis from the fact that our propositions might still be correct even if they were confined—as truths sometimes have been in the course of history—to a single ugly, unhappy, snarling, intensely neurotic head. While so many forces, commercial and social as well as religious, propagate magical thinking, it particularly falls to us to insist that the fact of God's existence or non-existence will not be altered either by the numbers of Christians or atheists or by the happiness with which they live by their creed or non-creed. That humanist Happy Man is all very well, so long as he doesn't obscure that atheism might still be correct and that we would still have, if we saw them in that way, to accept the facts, even if doing so made us all utterly miserable.

Only, it seems to me, when we have firmly planted this rigorous and austere plinth for our rationalism do we become morally free to riot into the creation of a baroque statue to stand on it. And here, precisely where it should liberate its fantasy, our movement is inclined to be at its timidest nineteenth-century academic bronze. Perhaps, in holding back from the grimness of proclaiming it *would be* atheist even if that did make it miserable, it has got cramp and can't move freely enough to actually *be* happy.

Surely we are no longer to be constrained by that lugubrious Victorian idiom, 'loss of faith'? Surely we need not shun the names 'atheist' and 'agnostic': the knowledge that grammar labels the *a-* prefixed to them 'privative' surely need not put it into our heads that we are deprived? Surely we should once and for all issue by our very behaviour a denial of the notion that being an atheist means picking your way carefully among the austere furniture, taking care not to stumble into the fleshpots of religious ritual or imagery? For it isn't we who are the primitive, magical taboo-thinkers. It isn't we who have to utter the spell 'lead us not into temptation', nor we who have to take care our consciousness never entertains certain images except 'in', as Gracie Fields used to say when she switched from ribaldry to singing the Lord's Prayer, 'all reverence'.

Precisely, in fact, the opposite. We are (of all the synonyms the one I most prefer to 'humanist') freethinkers. We are deprived of nothing. We have lost nothing. Exactly *because* we are not primitive thinkers, we do not need to have a thing genuinely present to our eyes or to be hallucinated before we can hold it in mind as an object of thought. We are liberated into and given the freedom of the whole kingdom of the imagination, which includes the imagery of religion.

The religionist is pinned down by his literal belief in the images of one religion and forced to shun those of all the other contradictory religions as false idols. We, by dissolving literal belief, become free to offer aesthetic belief to them all. Where there is no literal belief, there are no contradictions. Specifically religious emotions or experiences do not exist for us to be excluded from. Religious emotions are simply aesthetic ones which their owners have misinterpreted. As soon as we have understood Coleridge correctly we become free to offer the voluntary suspension of our disbelief for the moment, at no violence to truth, wherever beauty compels us.

We can, as a matter of fact, instruct our own imagination if we take the lesson implicit in the works of imaginative masters. Veronese, it is clear, in one sense 'believed', with equal vividness, in Venus and in Christ. Probably he always managed to hold the two distinct in his consciousness and to offer literal belief to one but not the other. Leonardo imaginatively believed in both Leda and the Virgin, and literally believed in neither. We, who cannot help being, in the imaginative sense, instantly convinced by Veronese's Venus, do no violence to our atheism if we are convinced also by his risen Christ. They are all—pagan myth-figures and Christian myth-figures, depicted by the Christian painter and by the atheist painter—images that impose poetic faith on us.

Equally we are free to make whatever use we can, private or communal, of religious forms. And of course we do use them psychologically—or, strictly, we use the psychological mechanisms which are the common ancestors of all religions, and, thanks to the history of our culture, it often comes most readily to us to use the as it were Christian branch of the family. Everyone prays when he is in love—though perhaps in that case it is (our culture is as much Greek as Christian) Aphrodite whom he invokes. Love even makes one revert to pre-religious superstition—'if I don't see a black cat before I reach the corner, the letter will come'. And from our communal point of view, what is Tom Paine to the freethinking movement if not patron saint or, in the Greek sense, hero? Ought we not to secularly-canonize George Eliot? And beatify Henry James? ('Blessed Henry James', murmured a young man I knew, as the waiter lit the candles on the dinner table over which we were having a literary discussion, 'pray for us'.) We need fear neither supernatural vengeance (or a trap) on the part of the things themselves, for we don't believe them to *be* supernatural, nor the sniping of Christians telling us we remain obsessed and can't get religion out of our heads. Why should we? Our heads are human, and we've always maintained religion is a human psychological phenomenon. To admit we're all, in some degree, ritualists and mystics is simply to say we're all, in some degree, obsessional neurotics and hysterics. *Humanisti sumus; humani nihil a nobis alienum putamus.*

Communal rites (a freethinker's litany? a freethinker's commination?—there's no need to confine such efforts as we do make to the occasion of death) are always in the danger that they will turn out to be funny. But then why not? Our great advantage is that we are under no obligation to be reverent. Self-satire is a cogent art-form, low comedy perhaps even more.

But while the freethinking movement awaits its satirist or low comedian, why shouldn't it turn impresario? We are right to support humane and compassionate enterprises like the excellent Humanist Letter Network which was the simple, sensible idea of Kit Mouat; why shouldn't we *also* mount a music festival? A quintessentially freethinking week-end's music would consist of *The Passion According to Saint John*, some of George Harrison's Indian-mysticism-in-music, some Benjamin Frankel, a Haydn mass, and *Die Zauberflöte.* Freethinkers are the people who voluntarily become protestants, Jews, flower people, Roman Catholics and Freemasons as the spirit of beauty moves them, just as they are the people the nape of whose neck tingles with a numinous frisson alike in the Parthenon and in Canterbury Cathedral, in front of Bernini's *Saint Teresa* and in front of an Egyptian sacred cat.

I suspect the correct answer to 'What would you put in the place of religion?' is 'What have we put in the place of belief in fairies?'—not by way of a rhetorical debating point but because, if you anatomize the answer, it indicates what we *ought* to put in the place of belief in God. One branch of the answer implies that we have used our scientific imaginations. We have replaced belief in fairies by historical–anthropological–linguistic–psychological hypotheses about the origin of fairy images and names, and also by a number of more plausible, less extravagant practical hypotheses than folklore could provide about why the milk disappears overnight from the saucer you put out for the fairies on the window-ledge. The other branch of the answer refers to the other branch of our imagination, with its faculty for lending aesthetic belief. The lovers' story of what happened in the wood near Athens 'More witnesseth,' remarks Hippolyta, 'than fancy's images, And grows to something of great constancy.' And indeed Shakespeare's poetry bears witness to more and to something of greater constancy than literal-minded belief. It performs the psychological, non-supernatural miracle of creating in us poetic faith. We have replaced belief in fairies by *A Midsummer Night's Dream.*

# In Our Image?

CHRISTOPHER LONGUET-HIGGINS

## H. C. Longuet-Higgins

DPhil, FRS. Royal Society Research Professor at the University of Edinburgh. Professor of Theoretical Physics at Kings College, London, 1952–1954. Professor of Theoretical Chemistry at Cambridge 1954–1967. Harrison Memorial Prizeman (Chemical Society), 1950. Editor of *Molecular Physics*, 1958–1961.

Publications: papers on theoretical physics, chemistry and biology in scientific journals.

word. If he were to intervene and type the next letter or next few letters correctly, this would save you a little time—though if his predictions were wrong you would find his help distinctly irritating. My CAT is like that person looking over my shoulder. I sit at the typewriter and type (in lower case) the words 'tomorrow and'. Nothing happens until I begin the next word, which starts with t. The CAT has learnt just one word starting with t, so he fills in the rest of it (in block capitals, so that we can see who typed what). Result: 'tOMORROW'. I am satisfied, and proceed to the next word. The moment I type 'a', the CAT supplies 'ND', because 'and' is the only word that it knows beginning with a. Again I am satisfied, and start the next word with a t. The CAT fills in 'OMORROW'. When I come to 'creeps' I have to type the whole word myself, because the CAT doesn't know any words beginning with c. Likewise with 'in'. When I try and type 'this' I am interrupted after the t with the letters 'OMORROW'. I smack the CAT with a stroke (/) and he gives me back a 'T' so that I can type the rest of the word the way I want it; result: 'This.' And so on. The rules are simple; if I have typed one or more letters, and the CAT only knows one word starting with those letters, he fills in the rest of the word; if he does it wrong I smack him thus / and he realizes he has to learn a new word beginning with those letters, which he types out again to save me the trouble. At the end, on the signal ** from me, he asks if I would like a fair copy of our joint effort, and if I say 'yes', or rather '1', he provides it while I sit and watch.

You may have noticed—I only just have—that in telling you about the CAT I have sometimes spoken of 'it', but more often of 'he'. Just a literary device? Yes and no. I could have used it on purpose, but actually I didn't; the word 'he' simply slipped out. How ridiculous! Who in his right mind could imagine that my CAT is anything but neuter—a simple gimmick, an automaton, a mere mechanical artifice. Of course that's all it is, and a pretty elementary one at that. We humanists know better than to be deluded into imagining that computers 'think'; they merely process information—to use the jargon of the experts. Human beings are different, utterly different. To begin with, computers have no souls. WHAT did I say? SOULS? Every good humanist knows that the soul is an outworn relic of religious superstition. I'd better try again. Computers have no minds. That sounds less controversial, but perhaps we'd better make quite sure.

It would be an elementary philosophical blunder to suppose that the word 'mind' has the same meaning as the word 'brain'. You might, if you were a cannibal, serve up my brain on a plate with Worcester sauce, but the best chef in the Congo could not cook my mind. The fact that we sometimes say 'There goes a first-class brain', meaning 'That person has a first-class mind', does not alter my contention; people are incorrigibly sloppy about words—or poetic, if you prefer to put it that way. Of course if you removed my brain you would destroy my mind, but this is no reason to identify the two. Indeed it is only a few hundred years since it was firmly believed that the brain's function was merely to cool the blood. Nowadays we realize that mental activity depends upon the possession of a brain, but having a brain does not guarantee that one will be able to think clearly, or indeed to think at all, if one happens to be the victim of accident or disease.

One has to say these rather obvious things in order to avoid it being supposed that 'Computers have no minds' means 'Computers have no brains'. It would be merely boring to point out that however hard you search inside a computer you will find nothing that would afford nourishment to a carnivore. Naturally you will find no such thing. But you will find something that might properly be called a brain, if we take that word to imply a physical system which can be—and is—used for processing information. So if I had said 'Computers have no brains' you could have shot me down straight away by asking me to define the word 'brain' in a non-trivial way, and then pointing out that the works of a computer ought to count as a perfectly good brain. Of course I could have tried to escape by saying that 'brain' means not merely a system for processing information, but one which was enabling somebody or something to think. But that would have been cheating, and anyway it would have brought us back to the proposition which we have actually decided to discuss, namely that computers have no minds. (I shall treat this proposition as equivalent to the statement that they cannot think, without apology to any philosophically expert reader.)

The argument as to whether computers can 'really think' or not has raged without interruption for twenty years and more. The only sensible way that I can find to approach this question is to consider how you and I would decide whether a person was 'really thinking' or not. We would, I suggest, suspect him of *not* really thinking if he were to give apparently random or apparently automatic responses to questions or stimuli. When I was a schoolboy I often used to panic when asked a question in class, and give a silly answer. I can still hear my maths master's lisping reproof: 'Think, Higginth! Think!' What upset him was not that my answer was wrong, but that it was apparently random, having no close connection with the question. But I had a friend who got into similar trouble in a subtly different way. The occasion was a Divinity lesson in which he was attempting to translate one of Pilate's utterances from the Greek, in front of the rest of us. The Greek words to be translated were '*ὅ γεγραφα, γεγραφα*' ('What I have written, I have written') and quick as a flash my friend translated them as 'O Jerusalem, Jerusalem!'. Not completely thoughtless, but symptomatic of a somewhat parrot-like frame of mind; the appearance of the Greek sentence, particularly the 'o' at the beginning, triggered off the one item in his memory that would fit this particular pattern. The reason why clichés are so tiresome is that when hearing them we have the horrid suspicion that the speaker's mind is out of action between the beginning and the end of the cliché; and if we are not careful our own minds go out of action too. This phenomenon is of immense value to politicians, salesmen and ecclesiastics, but its exploitation is an insult to the human mind.

The only way of telling whether someone else is really thinking or not is to observe his responses, verbal or otherwise, to situations in which we can imagine ourselves being placed. If random or automatic responses are both signs of mental inactivity, then we must regard their opposites as signs of thought, even in non-biological systems, unless we are to be accused of a quite irrational anthropocentrism. We may, of course, discover that overt behaviour which seems thoughtful is in fact automatic; Grey Walter's artificial 'tortoises', which explore their cage and make for the electric point when they run out of power, look as if they were thinking about what to do next, though of course they are 'mere' automata. Conversely, we may discover that behavioural responses which are apparently random are actually systematic, that there is method in their madness, and we will then have to revise our opinion of the mental incapacity of the system under study. But we must be very careful about concluding that a system which *seems* thoughtful is in fact mindless just because we have reason to believe that its behaviour is automatic; this conclusion might ricochet on ourselves in a most embarrassing way. I know very well, and so do you, that my CAT is no more than a set of instructions which I have coded on to a piece of paper tape and fed into a computer; and we know that the computer itself is a mere automaton obeying the laws of mechanics and electricity. It does not scratch, or bite, or mew, or produce KITTENs, so I need not be frightened of it, or feel that I have any obligation to look after it kindly. But ought I to say dogmatically that it doesn't think about what I give it to read? Its responses to what I type are certainly not random, and after it has read a few thousand words it responds in a way which I could certainly not predict in detail. If I didn't know that it is a mere automaton I might very well suspect that someone else was interrupting my laborious typing efforts.

The trouble is, you see, that I am more than likely to come under the same accusation as my CAT. It is fashionable nowadays to say that the Uncertainty Principle, or the complexity of the human brain, or the current state of ignorance about neurophysiology, lets me off the hook—lets me think of myself not as an automaton conforming slavishly to deterministic laws but as a free agent, and in a sense this is true; but only in a sense. A necessary condition for me to behave intelligently and responsibly is that my brain should work 'properly'— or so there is every reason to suppose— which means that its functioning is not subject to capricious interruption by 'quantum jumps' in the atoms and molecules which compose it. I should feel most unhappy if I had reason to suppose that my brain were not working as smoothly and inevitably as I expect my digestion—or my CAT—to work. If my brain were diseased, or somehow excused from the laws of physics, I could not regard myself as a free and responsible agent; I should have to plead that my behaviour was not controllable, and expect to be treated accordingly.

So perhaps we are not going to find it so easy, after all, to make a hard and fast distinction between human beings and computers based on the assertion that we can think and computers cannot do so, even when they are programmed to carry out some non-trivial task. (My CAT is admittedly a rather trivial program. The triviality of a task is not an easy quality to assess, but simple arithmetic is certainly trivial compared with playing chess—an activity for which moderately successful programs are now being written, though a good player can still beat them without much difficulty.) Should we therefore explore some other tack, so as to establish to our satisfaction that we really are superior in some way to our artefacts, and to any artefacts that our descendants might ever construct?

Most people who reach this point in their thinking stop and say to themselves: 'I really can't see the point of trying to prove by philosophical argument something that is so patently true; why should I bother?' A reasonable enough attitude, if one is sure of the outcome. Some other people, who feel less sure where the argument might lead, think: 'At the moment I feel reasonably secure in my position and that of my fellow human beings; please don't disturb me with worrying doubts.' The good humanist ought to grasp the nettle, and see if it really is a nettle or not. Does he really wish to emulate the dogmatic theologian, who starts with his conclusion and does everything he can to support it with *ad hoc* arguments of various kinds? So let us try to be good humanists for a moment, and see whether we have found a real bogey or a sham one.

Computers can do many jobs very fast and very efficiently, and they are going to get faster and more efficient. But this is not quite true. They don't work on their own; they have to be programmed, and intelligently programmed. In this respect a computer is like a car; it won't drive itself from London to Edinburgh; you have to drive it. But you would have a great deal of trouble in getting from London to Edinburgh without a car if there were a transport strike. The computer, in fact, puts a new kind of tool at the service of man, an extension of his intellect. If that were all to be said, the mountain would have given birth to an intellectual mouse, and you would be well justified in slamming this book with irritation. But we cannot avoid the lurking thought that machines which imitate our brains are for some reason to be taken rather more seriously than machines which imitate our arms or even our kidneys. Why do we have this feeling? Is it just a sense of competition? I suggest that there is more to it than that. It is because for the first time we have been made to think really hard about our own nature—what it is that entitles *us* to serious consideration. Let me, in the pages that remain, attempt to explain what I mean.

In the pre-scientific age—though its end is difficult to place exactly—the proper study of mankind was man. It was mildly eccentric, but quite harmless, to weigh bodies in water, to roll spheres down inclined planes and to speculate on the motion of arrows; nobody minded very much unless, as sometimes happened, a natural philosopher went too far and encroached on the orthodox view of man's relation to the universe and its Maker. We like to think that that Golden Age is now over, and has been replaced by an even better Platinum Age, in which our entire world view has been shaped (at least in outline) by the clean bright chisel of modern science. Nothing could be further from the truth. If man is the most significant phenomenon in the universe, and his own proper study—as most of us would like to think, then all the knowledge and insights of science have brought us only to the outer fortifications of our castle. We know, and the knowledge has been hard won, how oxygen is carried in the blood, how electrical impulses travel along nerves, and how it is that we can distinguish colours while most other animals cannot. But we have virtually no idea how we recognize a face, or a tune, or attach meanings to words, or do the hundred-and-one other easy tasks that a worm, say, could never do however hard it tried. We can poke electrodes into people's heads and record their brain waves, but nobody has the slightest idea why some kinds of wave appear only when a person's eyes are shut, and disappear when he opens them or when he is asked to do some mental arithmetic. We do not know what sleep is for—though there are plenty of hazy theories—and we haven't the faintest idea how we learn to ride a bicycle. And as to the writing of poems, or symphonies, or sermons . . .

When one is faced with a really difficult problem in science a good thing to do is to sit back and ask oneself whether one has stated it correctly; stating a problem properly is half the job of solving it. Let us imagine ourselves as eighteenth-century naturalists trying to understand the flight of birds. What should we say to one another? What observations would we make? How should we attempt to piece together some plausible hypotheses? Argument by analogy, often a helpful dodge, would be useless, because apart from bats, which are equally remarkable, birds are the only things that fly. We might obtain some intuitive insight by comparing a bird in flight to a man swimming under water, but how would we set about testing our ideas? Without the resources of modern technology we would be fatally handicapped, and could do no more than present our crude notions to the Royal Society in elegantly modulated prose.

What is the present state of affairs? Do we yet understand bird flight? Yes, fairly well. How has this come about? Through the development of modern aerodynamics. But aerodynamics did not come into existence by the unaided efforts of mathematicians; it evolved by a process of collaboration between mathematicians, engineers and inventors. Nothing at all would have happened unless people had set themselves the formidable task of constructing heavier-than-air flying machines. As it is, we now have at hand some highly sophisticated aerodynamical concepts, and without these—in particular the concept of aerodynamical instability—we could never hope to have understood the remarkable manoeuvrability of a swallow on the wing. (I refer to the work of John Maynard Smith.)

The moral of this is that in order to understand our mental and perceptual processes in detail we may find it most profitable to try and make working models of them. By working models I do not mean just electronic devices, but carefully designed programs which express what we think may happen when we look, listen, speak or act. Testing such programs demands, inevitably, some computing machinery, but it is not very useful to regard the machinery itself as the counterpart of the human brain. The fruitful analogy, it seems to me, is between the programs we write and the mental processes that they are meant to simulate. Acceptance of this analogy allows us to reinstate the mind above its servant, the brain, because a program, unlike a computer, is a set of logical instructions, and the main interest of a computation lies in its logic rather than in the machine which carries out these instructions.

Now that our argument has come full circle, let us see where it has taken us. Computers and the programs which we feed into them are our own brain children. Some of these children are impressively precocious. Professor A. C. Aitken, probably the greatest human mental calculator in history, regarded their competition as thoroughly unfair. So we must not underestimate our artefacts, or adopt a holier-than-thou attitude towards them. Equally, there is no need to be frightened of them, any more than we need fear cranes or typewriters; they add power to our thoughts just as a mechanical digger adds power to our elbow. What we should do is to try and learn from them—to learn more about ourselves. Each of the great scientific revolutions of the last 500 years has given man a new view of himself. The Copernican revolution placed him in a much bigger universe, though not at its centre. The Newtonian revolution established the faithfulness and universality of natural law, so that he could feel secure against the arbitrary whims of supernatural forces. The Darwinian revolution placed him at the peak of a vast evolutionary development. Relativity and quantum mechanics re-established him as the observer who cannot be omitted from any complete account of matter and motion; and the computer revolution enables him to think of his own mind in a logical and systematic way, rather than in terms of dark nebulous concepts such as the Ego and the Id.

My CAT is mewing; I must go and see what is the matter.

# Rock of Ages?

KINGSLEY MARTIN

## Kingsley Martin

Journalist and author. Editor of the *New Statesman and Nation*, 1930–1960. Lectured at London School of Economics. Was on the staff of the *Manchester Guardian*, 1927–1931.

Publications include: *The Triumph of Lord Palmerston*; *French Liberal Thought in the Eighteenth Century*; *The Magic of Monarchy*; *The Press the Public Wants*; *Harold Laski—A Memoir*; *The Crown and the Establishment*; and two volumes of autobiography: *Father Figures* and *Editor*.

# Rock of Ages?

## KINGSLEY MARTIN

One September morning I was awakened by the BBC Choir. This is what they sang:

> Rock of Ages, cleft for me,
> Let me hide myself in Thee;
> Let the water and the blood,
> From Thy riven side which flowed,
> Be of sin the double cure,
> Cleanse me from its guilt and power.

The writer of this hymn, the Reverend Augustus Toplady, was an eminent eighteenth-century Divine who is said to have been inspired by the experience of taking refuge from a violent thunder-storm under a rock in Blagdon Gorge in Devon. Visitors are still shown the rock. I am sure that he knew why he wanted to be cured more than once, and what was the significance of the combined water and blood which is reported by St John to have flowed from the wound in Christ's side. I am equally sure that very few of those who listened to his verses, sung by the BBC Choir, had even the vaguest notion of what the hymn was all about. But it took me back to my childhood.

Hymns, whether Christian or those of other religions, have an emotional impact, not because they are sensible but because their associations are emotional. I can still feel tears prickling behind my eyes when certain words of a completely unintelligible character are sung to familiar tunes of no considerable musical value. My father, who was a good, rationalist-type, Nonconformist Minister, used to omit the more meaningless and bloodthirsty hymns, though he had to accept others which the congregation liked. He himself preferred a revolutionary hymn like Blake's *Jerusalem* or

*When wilt Thou save the people?* At times, when the congregation was particularly sparse, he liked to announce from the Adult School Hymnal that we should all sing *God send us men.*

The function of hymns is to put one in a generally-religious state of mind. William James remarked that such a state of mind should at least find expression in a kind word to your aunt. Unhappily, I do not think that this is always the effect of feeling religious. A practical result should follow. If there were ever a more mean, backbiting lot of unChristian scandalmongers than many among the congregation in Nonconformist chapels in Hereford when I was a boy, I hope never to meet them. Of course, there were some exceptions; people to whom God meant a comforting reassurance that they were not alone in the world, that they should see their relatives after death and that the sorrows of this troubled world would be compensated for in a blissful eternity. They gained, too, by an act of communal worship; it made them feel that they belonged to an élite of the uncommonly good. What should also be said for Christianity is that it is one of the chief conductors of the revolutionary idea of good neighbourliness, even towards members of other tribes. This has certainly had useful results among some primitive peoples who otherwise assume that they gain merit chiefly by killing members of rival tribes. But the basic code of civilization is common to civilized people and it has been the height of absurdity to teach Christianity to Buddhists, and has had no noticeable effect on the constant wars of Western nations.

I was amused once by an incident which illustrated the limitations of Christian teaching when applied to primitive people. I found myself sitting one day in a car with a member of the Kikuyu tribe in Kenya. He told me that he was not only a Christian, but a Scottish Presbyterian. While I was pondering over the extraordinary fact that our obscure sectarian quarrels of the seventeenth century should have been perpetuated in twentieth-century Kenya, he added that he no longer attended the Scottish Presbyterian Church because its pastor had wished to interfere with the old

African and horribly cruel custom of female circumcision. He really couldn't allow his Christianity to be applied to tribal customs, any more than people would put up with my father insisting, as he did in season and out of season, on Christian principles having a relationship with the wages which his church members paid to their workers, or with the Christian wars that were being fought in South Africa or Europe.

One of the oddest paradoxes of history is that the progressive West has adopted a mystical faith of love and non-violence; it is Christians who have conquered and tyrannized over less-energetic peoples and Christians who have so far fought the bloodiest wars. One here enters upon one of the most controversial historical problems; have religions anywhere had any considerable effect on the conduct of organized groups of people? Faith has clearly affected the lives of many individuals, but whether its overall influence has been good or bad can be endlessly debated. When you survey the bloody story of Christendom, the cruelty of the Churches and their obstruction of truth, you are inclined to agree with Gibbon and regard the acceptance of Christianity by Constantine as a disaster. But it is not difficult to put up a counter-case and argue that the world might have been even worse if paganism had triumphed.

I got interested in this problem at a comparatively early age and in adolescence decided that God was merely a word we used to explain anything we didn't understand. People often used to be puzzled by what is known as 'The Problem of Pain'. Why, if God is all-powerful and all good, did He make such a horrible world? The common answer still is that He has a hidden purpose which mortals cannot understand and which, in the full glory of time, will be revealed to them. We, as individuals, must accept this as an article of faith and co-operate with Him in some day bringing about the unspeakable glory which is promised us. Even as a child I found this unsatisfactory. I could not see why the toothache I had today would be compensated by pie in the sky tomorrow. If God had really created this cruel universe, he was not a god at all, but a devil, and anyway, why were our problems solved by assuming a Creator who must presumably Himself have been created? Who was God's mother?

I might have been less ribald on this subject if I had been granted the mystical experiences or profound sensations of awe and reverence which have made some people intensely concerned with religious problems. Some people are not readily satisfied with the usual psychological explanations, even though they well know that their personal experience provides no objective evidence of anything transcendental. I remember suddenly getting angry as a boy, reading Keats, who wrote:

> There was an awful rainbow once in heaven:
> We know her woof, her texture; she is given
> In the dull catalogue of common things.
> Philosophy will clip an Angel's wings.

This seemed to me—and still seems to me today—sheer nonsense. A rainbow is a glorious and splendid sight; why the fact that science can now explain its physical characteristics should detract from its beauty or make it a common thing defeats my comprehension.

I never felt that the mystics were important, but I could not escape the fact that many people had 'a God-shaped hole' inside them. They cannot face a blank world of science, and have had increasing difficulty in finding adequate inspiration in any materialistic answer. There was a time when the religion of Progress seemed adequate. In the 'eighties, Mrs Sidney Webb saw Socialism as a new religion which was taking the place of the old idea of personal salvation. Improvement of environment would lead, if not, as the eighteenth century put it, to the perfection of man, to an improvement in world society so great that we need not worry about the pains and frailties that would still remain. Though Mrs Webb herself ceased, I think, to find satisfaction in this gospel, it remained the basic faith of most intelligent people at least until the First World War and they did their best to cling to it in the next decades. No one expressed it with anything like the fervour and brilliance of H. G. Wells; he did, in fact, make a religion of science and believed that only greed and prejudice and tradition prevented us from achieving a life on earth of undreamed-of felicity. We lay becalmed, like a ship outside the harbour, lacking only a little education and honest thinking to enter into port. This faith, like others, has now died because we understand (more than Wells did) the aggressive tendencies of human nature, and the depth and strength of emotional drives which hinder our progress.

We no longer believe in a life after death and no longer have faith in the future of mankind on earth. To what must we gear our lust for righteousness? We have always held, and I think rightly, that our difference from the beasts has depended primarily on the development of reason. We have also come to doubt now whether reason has not taken charge too dictatorially in our decisions. Let me take an example from contemporary life. I was once taken to task for suggesting, in the *New Statesman*, that on an ordinary calculation of consequences, Mao Tse-tung might be justified in the wholesale liquidation (I use this word because the Chinese word appears to mean 'disposing of', whether by execution or by some less-drastic method) of armed men who were ready to fight for Chiang Kai-shek if he began an invasion from Formosa or Japan. There is no doubt that Chiang constantly threatened invasion and prophesied a successful counter-revolution, relying on a potential fifth column inside Communist China. These supporters of Chiang were said to have refused to give up their arms and I believe that after their 'liquidation', the threats ceased. Obviously, I said in the *New Statesman*, they should have been peacefully disarmed, if possible; obviously Mao should try all other methods before cold-blooded murder and no doubt his motives were mixed and he may not have been sure enough about the invasion threat. But supposing these precautions had been taken and invasion was impending, how was one to argue that he was not justified in preventing a renewed civil war by this appalling preventive stroke? I still find this a difficult problem of ethics, as well as politics.

Let me take another, more immediate example. There is no doubt that some Americans today believe that they are at least attempting to make a third world war less likely by establishing themselves in Vietnam and elsewhere in South-east Asia, so that China will not be tempted to expand at the expense of her weaker neighbours. I disagree totally with this analysis, but I am not concerned with its accuracy. I am impressed today with the appalling situation in which President Johnson created for himself. I am told that he receives on his desk a regular 'appreciation' of the situation, based on computers which are, in fact, a vast extension of human reason. Never have so many facts been known and carefully marshalled as a basis for action. The computer will have taken into account the possibilities of a compromise involving the virtual defeat of Hanoi; it will tell him exactly what are the military results of his latest escalation and make a calculation about the length of time it will take him to achieve victory and what will be the effects of victory or defeat on the United States reputation in the outside world and in America itself, where no doubt the next election chances will certainly be affected. Johnson will also have to consider, on data built in to the computer, whether he can afford to scrap his home welfare promises and to expend so many men and so much treasure on the next step in Vietnam. The net result amounts, in his case, to an order from On High—something which he does not dream of disputing.

It is clear enough that war and not peace has been fed into the computer, that none of the imponderables can be measured statistically and that neither love nor compassion could be included in this fantastic calculation. It is no wonder that President Johnson's face, as we saw it on television, seemed every week to become more bewildered, more conscience-stricken and more bedevilled.

One result of the attempt to make world decisions without taking into account the motives and emotions which, combined with reason, must be our guide if humanity is not to destroy itself, is the flight of many of the younger generation from reason altogether. Adolescents of every generation are moved by the horrors of the world and when they see no outlet for their revolt, they may decide to differentiate themselves from their elders by some extravagance of behaviour such as the Flower Children today like to demonstrate. Those who suffer less from the excess of affluence in our society organize demonstrations and seek to create a climate of opinion in which the riches of the state are not spent on tanks and bombs. So powerful and so well-justified is their protest that at any earlier time since the birth of democracy we should have prophesied that they must be successful. It has always been a commonplace of sociology that in any free society no large-scale war could be organized without the virtual unanimity of a population; atrocity propaganda, for instance, had to be used on a large scale in the First World War in order to persuade the public that it was their duty to kill and die in a national war. It is not today certain that this axiom can be maintained; it sometimes seems as if the computer was taking charge and that humanity could be forgotten.

There is, of course, a limit to this process; social welfare and human revolt cannot yet be disregarded. We are at present still some way removed from 1984. But if the President is one day convinced that it is his computerized duty to drop nuclear bombs on China's industrial and now nuclear installations, there would be nothing to stop him, and he would have even less to deter him from making use of the biological weapons now being evolved in the United States and which might have the advantage that their use would not affect the Americans, as well as the Chinese people. The recent conference at Pugwash was, I understand, more concerned with biological and bacteriological poisons than with the danger of universal radioactivity.

We shall not find the solution to this world-problem by singing songs about Luv-luv-luv, or by religious escapism or even by Indian meditation in expensive hotels in the Himalayas. What I take Humanism to be is an effort to feed humanity, with all its emotions and built-in search for righteousness, as well as reason, into our personal computer. Somehow we have to get away, as a good and sincere pacifist, Max Plowman, once said, from the 'nag of consequences'. That is to say, there must be a point when we do things because they are good in themselves, not because they are the lesser of two evils. All the historical events which we most admire have been done by those who acted just because they thought they were acting rightly, not because, having worked out the results, they thought they were doing rather less harm by one action than by another. Plowman once rightly remarked that 'such an item as the Crucifixion' would not have occurred if Jesus had bothered about the results of his violent death. So much mythology has been built up round the story of the Cross that I do not myself find it particularly moving or inspiring. I much prefer the story of Socrates, who quietly decided that he preferred to die rather than to yield on a question of principle. Socrates, it is true, spoke of a private God who instructed him in such matters. This clearly was not any of the deities in which people of his age believed; it was merely a personification of his own conscience, perhaps of his pride and consciousness of his own dignity as a human being. What has happened, I wonder, to our own scientists, who at one time resolutely opposed the idea of making nuclear weapons? Did they forget this deity of conscience which they knew should be supreme in their lives, when they became members of the Establishment and had discarded the idea that they were servants of the world? They seemed to think that they must accept the notion that it was their duty to regard as an enemy another state, which, as history wonderfully shows, might change in a decade to be an ally? Humanism must bring society back to the idea of a world society which, whatever the consequences to a particular state or individual, must always be given the first place.

In a remarkable, and nowadays usually-forgotten, essay which Bertrand Russell wrote as long ago as 1903, he advanced an argument, strangely illogical from a great logician. We were, he said, helpless puppets of the Natural Order, and yet somehow we would achieve freedom 'on the firm foundation of unyielding despair'. In *A Free Man's Worship* he does not tell us whence comes man's freedom, but he defines it:

> If power is bad, as it seems to be, let us reject it from our hearts. In this lies Man's true freedom; in determination to worship only the God created by our own love of the good, to respect only the heaven which inspires the insight of our best moments. In action, in desire, we must submit perpetually to the tyranny of outside forces; but in thought, in aspiration, we are free, free from our fellow-men, free from the petty planets

on which our bodies impotently crawl, free even while we live from the tyranny of death. Let us learn, then, that energy of faith which enables us to live constantly in the vision of the good; and let us descend, in action, into the world of fact, with that vision always before us.

Personally, I find this outlook on the world the most satisfying. There is no God who created the world, there is a Natural Order whose origin, maybe, scientists may someday understand and which is totally indifferent to us, but there is a strange, unexplained desire in men for a righteousness whose victory in the world seems highly problematic. If there is a God, we invented him, and he is a personification of our insistence not to accept as final the infinitely more powerful forces around us. If we have a problem, it is to explain, not the origin of evil, but the origin of good. If we find any comfort in projecting that maybe unreasonable but most admirable aspect of our own nature and calling it a struggling and defeated deity, I see no harm in that.

# The Cambridge Heretics (1909-1932)

P. SARGANT FLORENCE

# P. Sargant Florence

PhD, Hon LittD, Hon DSocSc. Professor of Commerce, 1929–1955, and Dean of the Faculty of Commerce and Social Sciences, 1947–1950, at the University of Birmingham. Visiting professor at the universities of Cairo, Johns Hopkins, Malta and Rhode Island. President of the economics section of the British Association for the Advancement of Science, 1937. Member of the Council of the Royal Economic Society, 1930–1961. Consultant to the Jordan Development Board and to the US National Resources Planning Board.

Publications include: *Economics of Fatigue and Unrest*; *The Statistical Method in Economics and Political Science*; *The Logic of Industrial Organisation*; *Industry and the State*; *Ownership Control, and Success of Large Companies*; *Post-war Investment of Industry*; *Economics and Sociology of Industry*.

These twelve became the first members of the Heretics. The inaugural public meeting, held in December 1909, was addressed by Miss Jane Harrison and Dr J. E. McTaggart. Subsequent meetings were of two kinds: public, held four or five times a term in various lecture-halls during the mid-week; and private, in which every member had an opportunity of singing, held regularly on Sunday evenings in C. K. Ogden's rooms, first over the Pepysian Library in Magdalene, then in 'Top Hole' over the fish shop in Petty Cury. By 1913 the membership was considerable, over 200, a large figure considering the smaller total of undergraduates then than now, and the much higher proportion of 'muddied oafs' and pass men. Newnham girls joined from the outset, but chaperonage rules at first checked the attendance of Girtonites. Later, however, my aunt Ethel Sargant, an Honorary Fellow of Girton, took charge; and the society's hundredth meeting was a party at her house, the old Girton Rectory.

Going through the green-printed programmes of triptych form I am struck by the galaxy of honorary members appearing on the right-hand flap and by the quality of the speakers in the triptych middle panel. Both lists were mainly the achievement of Ogden, who here and later as an editor proved himself a master in spotting intellectual winners. Many of the outstanding Cambridge speakers to be mentioned later were honorary members, but besides these the honorary membership included, even as early as January 1911, the Master of Emmanuel, J. B. Bury (the Regius Professor of History), Sir Francis Darwin, Patrick Geddes, E. W. Hobson, A. C. Seward (subsequently Master of Downing), W. McDougall, G. H. Hardy, J. T. Sheppard (subsequently Provost of King's), G. Lowes Dickinson and J. M. Keynes. The fact that the development of the Heretics was largely the creation of Ogden must be firmly stated as the 'Portrait of Ogden' broadcast by the BBC in December 1962 and March 1963 completely omitted any reference to him as a heretic and organizer of heresy. This omission was soon pointed out in a letter to *The Listener* by Dora Russell. She was secretary of the society in 1918–1919, and with Bertrand Russell started such a lively discussion (in March 1922) on

'Industrialism and Religion' that the meeting had to adjourn to college rooms.

Ogden was the first secretary of the society and when its original president, Pittiotto, turned mystic after two years, Ogden, then in his third undergraduate year, became president and continued so from 1911 to 1924, when I took over. During this period, including the lean war years (when Brian Downes, later Master of Christ's was secretary), he not only recruited honorary members and speakers but reported programmes and meetings in the *Cambridge Magazine* of which he was proprietor and editor, and had many of the papers printed including—in the 'Today and Tomorrow' series—J. B. S. Haldane's 'Callinicus' and 'Daedalus', read before the society in February 1923 and November 1924. When I was secretary between 1912 and 1914 and, on returning to Cambridge, again from 1921 to 1924, it was a delight, a great relief—*and* an education—to have such a resourceful president. In the BBC 'portrait', Professor Ayer was right to call him an intellectual entrepreneur.

A further source of delight was C. K. O's gaiety. Bertrand Russell mentioned in the BBC 'Portrait' that the *Cambridge Magazine* was 'great fun'. The magazine reflected a certain impishness, as did Ogden's own writing and also the various newspaper cuttings and incongruous pictures and notices he pinned on his walls. His *nom-de-plume* for many of the more heretical magazine articles, and for the joint authorship in 1915 of a pamphlet on *Fecundity versus Civilization*, was Adelyne More. When readers began to suspect the existence of anyone with such an appropriate name, Ogden displayed his secretary's photograph duly signed Adelyne, and when suspicions continued, an affecting news item appeared in the Magazine of Adelyne's white wedding in Great St. Mary's and probable retirement from public life.

Unfortunately these pranks have led to Ogden being thought a mere eccentric who happened to have tossed off the *Meaning of Meaning* and Basic English. His importance as a heretic and a creator of heretics, among at least six generations of Cambridge men and women, impels me to protest here and now, while I still can, against this superficial tag.

His gay sense of fun certainly helped infectiously to spread heresy and Humanism; but Ogden's brand of both was firmly built on reasoning, wide reading and well-informed critical judgement.

After, initially, considerable wrangling, members were persuaded by Ogden to adopt the simple stated Law 4, that 'membership of the society shall imply the rejection of all appeal to Authority in the discussion of religious questions'. This condition prevented many dons from accepting honorary membership, but proved a useful practical test separating heretical goats from essentially orthodox sheep; and for the first twelve years, till birth control and psycho-analysis appeared on the agenda, no honorary member, I believe, resigned in protest at any activities.

Law 2 read 'that the object of the society be to promote discussion on problems of religion, philosophy and art', and the activities of the Heretics may conveniently first be considered in II, III and IV under these three heads.

## II

Today, the revolutionary impact may not be appreciated of the discussion of religion upon the majority of the society's membership. Most of the audience at the meetings were 'public school men', previously subjected for seven to ten years according to their stretch at a preparatory school, to compulsory chapels and more or less Arnoldian 'moral earnestness'. Arnold is one of Lytton Strachey's four Eminent Victorians and as Strachey says 'the final, the fundamental lesson could only be taught in the school chapel, in the school chapel the centre of Dr Arnold's system of education was inevitably fixed'. At Rugby itself we were given nine chapels a week together with seven twenty-minute evening prayers in our houses. One of the weekly full-length sermons was, I still remember, a diatribe against Ernst Haeckel, author of the *Riddle of the Universe*, which triumphantly identified him with Antichrist. Poor Haeckel had no chance to defend himself and the prosecutor, one of the dozen or so Rugby assistant masters in Holy Orders, made out a case that overwhelmed us. This preacher subsequently became headmaster of an equally 'top' public school.

Every year during Lent the Prayer Book's commination service was duly recited affirming the curse of God to be due on ten sorts of vices including that, apparently of Humanism.

> Minister: Cursed is he that putteth his trust in man and taketh man for his defence, and in his heart goeth from the Lord.

After we had, as prescribed, 'answered and said Amen' to each of the curses, the headmaster was in top form reading out the fate of the accursed. 'Snares', 'fire and brimstone', 'unquenchable fire', 'utter darkness', 'weeping and gnashing of teeth' are some of the details. They can still be found in the *Book of Common Prayer*. But the ultimate in brain-washing was reached for every boy (except the few orthodox Jews and non-conformists) in his preparation for Confirmation. My tutor for the purpose, I recollect, told us we *must* believe in a personal God. Belief in a personal Devil was optional, though he himself did so believe. No doubt this helped him bridge the credibility gap.

What a relief it was, after all this, to join the Heretics and hear Edward Clodd question God's design in creating gadflies as expounded in a religious tract: 'In order to move cattle from spot to spot and preventing them growing too indolent;' or to hear Bertrand Russell's crack that the Ten Commandments were like the customary rubric for a ten-question examination paper: 'only six need be attempted'.

Compulsory chapel-going continued a sore subject and Chawner's lead was soon followed up. A paper by F. M. Cornford on *Religion in the University* read to the society on October 25th, 1911, pointed out that Anglicanism was

> just a local form of Christianity . . . and if colleges had an Anglican chapel they ought also to have a mosque, Hindu temple, a Baptist chapel and so on with an official attached to each. Either that or none at all.
>
> In practice the existing system was a mild and gentlemanly attempt to repress complete freedom of thought and inquiry, by slight hindrances, trivial fines, and social pressure. Ritual

is a powerful means of suggestion, working by the emotional appeal of early associations, and the extraordinary beauty of some parts of the Liturgy. This emotional stimulant is valued as having the effect of tiding young men over a critical period in their lives when they ought to be overhauling all their beliefs till they leave the University to earn their living, and have no time to think about beliefs at all.

Discussion of religion, however, broadened out from the compulsory chapel issue, though in several colleges that issue remained. In a paper *De Heretico Comburendo* read in October 1913 G. M. Trevelyan, subsequently Master of Trinity, castigated attendance at Church merely to set a good example to the lower orders—particularly at the village church 'where the presence of gentlefolk is noted and their absence might be remarked'. It was particularly 'bad form' for women to be absent.

Religion was discussed tolerantly *pro* as well as *con*. The Rev. R. J. Campbell appeared in February 1911 to speak on the 'Possibility of a Liberal Interpretation of Christianity', and Father Waggett (in his own Presbytery) on the 'Scientific Method in Religion' in November 1912. In May 1926 the society heard Dr Joseph Needham, now Master of Caius, maintain under the text the 'Limitations of Optick Glasses' that scientific and religious glasses might, each used alone, be equally fallacious.

In February 1914 a debate with the X Club of Oxford decided, if I remember rightly only by a small majority, to support the motion proposed by Hubert Henderson that 'the Churches today are doing more harm than good'. But before 1914 the set piece among all the religious discussions was the debate between H. G. Wood and J. M. Robertson, MP, on the 'Historicity of Jesus'. Robertson had written three books in which he presented Professor Drew's views of the Christ-myth and these had been criticized by Wood at an early meeting. The two were brought to a confrontation on November 25th, 1911. The match I then thought (and still think after rereading the published accounts) ended in a draw. If the evidence of the Dead Sea Scrolls were pursued more honestly to god, the match might reach a decision yet!

## III

Next to religion the Heretics proposed to discuss philosophy. Thanks to Ogden's know-how and know-who, the society had by March 1912 tapped contemporary resources at Cambridge, in McTaggart and Bertrand Russell, and, elsewhere, in F. C. S. Schiller (speaking on 'Pragmatism, Humanism and the Religious Problem) and J. A. Hobson. Discussion of papers by G. E. Moore occurred later.

Unlike some almost contemporary groups at Cambridge the Heretics really did leave matters open to discussion and had no particular philosophy dominating them like a religion. We learn from Maynard Keynes' memoir, *My Early Beliefs*, how G. E. Moore's particular 'religion' was accepted by his friends that 'nothing matters except states of mind'[2] and that 'there was not a very intimate connection between being good and doing good.' Since the publication of this memoir, Bertrand Russell has complained in his *Autobiography*[3] that 'those who considered themselves his disciples ignored aspects of Moore's doctrine. Moore gave due weight to morals and his doctrine was not one of a life of retirement among fine shades and nice feelings.' Moore spoke to the Heretics in February 1914 on the 'Philosophy of Commonsense,' again in January 1916 on 'Intrinsic Value' and again in January 1921 on 'Some Problems of Ethics'. But other schools of thought were represented by C. D. Broad (on Francis Bacon) in October 1926 and Wittgenstein (on Ethics in October 1929); and in November 1931 Prince Mirsky introduced Dialectical Materialism to Cambridge.

Though hearing and discussing many philosophies and keeping open minds, many, if not most of us had a slightly utilitarian Benthamite bias for 'doing' rather than 'being' good. For practical purposes, we used as a criterion the greatest happiness of the greatest number or, at any rate, the least unhappiness of the least number. Later on, in his centenary lecture at University College, London, in 1932 Ogden certainly expressed his admiration of Jeremy Bentham 'for the humanity of his manner as well as matter'.[4]

It was, however Bentham's Theory of Fictions and not his Felicific Calculus that excited Ogden's greatest enthusiasm and set the tone of Heretics discussion. Fictional words like rights, spiritual, morals, sin, were criticized for 'their magical potency' particularly in putting over religious authority. This line of philosophical discussion was thus consistent with the society's religious line, as it was with Bentham's rejection of 'Mother Church' and other ecclesiastical fictions in his fight against 'Jug'. To quote Ogden, 'Jug' 'was Bentham's abbreviation of Juggernaut for the ruthless march of organized religion'; and certainly has current applications. Among other ways of 'suppressing contrary opinion' is 'insinuating theological departments even into the most dexterously devised academic constitutions.'[5]

The Heretics' philosophic discussions were as I remember them interlarded with the appeal 'what precisely do you mean by N or M, or V or W (whatever the questionable names or works)'. C. E. M. Joad spoke to the society in January 1930 and his use of this refrain in the Brains Trust during the Second World War rang, to me, a familiar bell. This careful use of words, largely a legacy of Moore's teaching, comes vividly to mind when I recall a heated exchange in 1911 across the wide spaces of the Cambridge Guildhall after G. K. Chesterton's address. A good heretic in the audience insisted that Chesterton was wrong in supposing that he, the heretic, knew he existed; he had no knowledge of this but only an intuition. The long argument closed with Chesterton's final 'cherish it, my dear Sir, cherish it.'

The line of Semantics, under the title of Significs conferred upon it by Lady Welby, was taken up early in the society's life in a paper by Ogden on the 'Progress of Significs.' I remember going over to Oxford to hear him read a similar paper and possibly, on that basis, start a Heretics Society there. For his pains he was told to take it all back to Tabland, though an Oxford Heretics seems to have eventuated. In April 1920 Ogden returned to the charge with I. A. Richards in a paper to the Cambridge Heretics on 'The Symbolic Movement.' Their joint interest blossomed shortly after in the *Meaning of Meaning*. Though this book, published in 1923, was not, as many seem to believe, the ancestor of Basic English, Ogden's thinking on Significs was; and in his centenary lecture he claimed Bentham as 'the true father of Basic English'.[6] Certainly the philosophy of many of us Heretics began with the analysis of words. I find in my own paper 'Sociology and Sin' (discussed by the Heretics in 1928 and published, too timorously, as *Uplift in Economics*) a plea for the social sciences to avoid words involving praise or blame. I counted up from Roget's Thesaurus thirty-five synonyms of virtuous and a hundred and nine of vicious.

## IV

Art was the third problem the Heretics set out to discuss. Apart from thus following in the footsteps of the Renaissance humanists, this was a natural reaction since the public schools from which most of us were drawn had fed us on the forms of dead languages, grammar—and games, and starved us of culture and especially contemporary literature. Neither Shaw, now Wells' social novels were allowed in my house library at school; A. C. Benson was our strongest meat. Nor was much art taught officially at the University. With organists attached to the various colleges, music and discussions of music were available. But no chair of English existed in Cambridge when the Heretics began and the existing Slade Professorship of Fine Art was very much part-time.

For those not particularly excited by demolition of religions, or abstruse philosophizing, the positive interests of pictures, plays, literature and music were perhaps the chief attraction of the Heretics. Within the first two years undergraduates or recent B.As had read papers on, and discussed, Oscar Wilde (then almost a tabu subject), Poe and Thomas Hardy (as the Poet of Heresy); not to mention aesthetics and Aristotles' Poetics. A then revolutionary point of view appeared in T. E. Hulme's *Anti-Romanticism and Original Sin* and 'a long and lively discussion followed in which Mr Hulme expended much energy in convincing the uninitiated that their questions were irrelevant'.[7] The 'Top-Hole' meeting I remember best, however, was Rupert Brooke's on the 'Drama Present and Future', in March 1913. Ibsen, he said, was famous for his economy of characters, props and incidents, but there usually had to be a child, a stove and a suicide. Why did he not write the supremely economical play and let the child commit suicide in the stove?

The efforts of junior members of the University were interlaced with papers read usually at the more public meeting by critics and the creative writers or artists they criticized. In attracting people famous or soon to be famous I am again amazed by Ogden's wide contacts. During the four years 1920–1923 while he was yet president, the society had heard, among others, in chronological order:

1920 Walter de la Mare, Bonamy Dobrée, Lytton Strachey.
1921 Arthur Waley, Edith Sitwell, Clive Bell.
1922 E. J. Dent, Eugene Goossens, Nugent Monk, W. J. Turner.
1923 Virginia Woolf, Roger Fry.

At Fry's meeting Maynard Keynes tried to elicit the name of any good living artist under forty—but as far as my informant's memory goes—in vain. Virginia Woolf's paper was 'Mr. Bennett and Mrs. Brown', published shortly afterwards, putting Arnold Bennett to the test by his own criterion that novels were about character. He did not score very highly. Another interesting (academic) year for literary discussion, with Ogden now an honorary member and adviser, was that of 1926—7 which included papers by Wyndham Lewis, Richard Hughes, Herbert Read and Leonard Woolf. However, I do not think we were too impressed by big names; and, anyway, some of them only became big names subsequently. During discussions, in fact, the chair had occasionally to intervene in defence of the speaker.

## V

I must now recount how the Heretics exceeded their threefold plan of discussing religion, philosophy and art, and pioneered into new fields.

In his paper on 'Religion in the University', F. M. Cornford said that 'theology is already taking its place as a branch of anthropology'. Cornford and his fellow classics, Jane Harrison and Gilbert Murray certainly led off well but the Heretics were pioneers in calling upon professed anthropologists to discuss the dogmas of religious authority. In October 1910 Dr A. C. Haddon spoke on the 'Moral Ideas of Savages', in May 1911 Dr W. H. R. Rivers on the 'Primitive Conception of Death' and in October 1922 Elliott Smith on the 'Story of the Flood'. But anthropologists also came to discuss the validity of their own authorities, if one may judge from Malinowski's paper read in November 1926 on 'Heterodox Professions of a Schismatic Anthropologist'. This introduction of anthropology is significant first as foreshadowing the modern swing towards the social sciences generally, though 'social stinks', as we used to call them, did not appear in the original Rule 2 as subjects for discussion, any more than the natural sciences. With papers by R. A. Fisher, William Bateson, Julian Huxley, A. S. Eddington and J. B. S. Haldane to start discussions, the Heretics certainly did not neglect natural science; but it was in the social sciences that they broke new ground.

The discussion of anthropology was significant, also, in taking as a model a true social science, based on observation not speculative ratiocination. Humanistic rationalism is often laughed at as old fashioned in assuming man to be rational. This sort of rationalism, though certainly Benthamite, was not that of the Heretics. With anthropologists, social historians and, later on, psychologists and psycho-analysts we were quite prepared to find men irrational. What we did believe was that irrationality could be studied rationally as the irrationality was studied of primitive, or for that matter medieval, man, beginning with detailed and, if possible, measured, observation.

Social history forms the next stage logically (if not chronologically) after anthropology in the observation of human activities, rational or irrational, and Ogden 'talent spotted' Eileen Power at Girton. She read papers on the 'Cult of the Virgin' in October 1915, 'Women in the Middle Ages' in

November 1919, 'The Nun in Literature' in March 1920, 'In Defence of Medievalism' followed in May 1920.

Psychology, seldom discussed at meetings before 1912, was represented in February 1912 by Dr C. S. Myers, founder of the National Institute of Industrial Psychology speaking on 'The New Realism'; and psycho-analysis soon came into the picture. Papers were read by Dr Ernest Jones (November 1922 on 'Narcissism'), by Dr James Glover (May 1925 on 'Biological Lying'), by Adrian Stephen (February 1930; 'A Description of Freudian Analysis'). I also remember a meeting with Dr Alfred Adler when the Cambridge Malting House experiment in uninhibited schooling was in full swing. Its staff was present and disputed his contention that in early childhood *mens sana*, free from any inferiority complex, depended largely on *corpore sano*.

Sociology has not till quite recently been recognized officially by the University of Cambridge and the word, being a Latin–Greek hybrid, was not used in polite academic society. However, I find from a Heretics programme that I offered to discover the 'Key to Sociology' in November 1914. My memory has (probably mercifully) censored what it was I presumptiously disclosed. But the papers by Julius West ('the Russian Intelligentsia', June 1916) Leonard Woolf ('Hunting the Highbrow', in October 1926) and S. K. Ratcliffe ('The Lower Middle Classes', March 1917) would certainly count today as sociology.

Graham Wallas, professor of political science in London, was for me the dominating empirical realist. In his *Human Nature in Politics* he had broken the rationality-assumption barrier and, addressing the Heretics in May 1918 on 'Rational Purpose', he expressed his horror at the vast forces at the disposal of single individuals of like passions with ourselves. The technical revolution in transport and communications had given effect to momentary whims over thousands of miles and tens of millions of persons. The Heretics were thus early, in the midst of the First World War, led as the *Cambridge Magazine* put it 'to the conception of a World State—a state in which relations of the past were not left to God (as in the days of Canning or Cobden) nor to the blind play of economic forces (as in the philosophy of Lenin and Trotzky).'

In 1921 an Economic Section was founded, which met in my own house till it was merged in 1927 with the new Marshall Society, of which I was the first president. The section was heretical in criticizing theory based entirely on the assumption of a rational economic man. Barbara Wootton, for instance, read a paper on 'The Proper Place of Economic Theory' foreshadowing her book *Lament for Economics*. Our attitude was not purely negative, and we realized the importance of social institutions and of integrating economics with the social sciences. Frank Ramsey spoke on 'G. D. H. Cole's Social Theory', mainly his belief in Guild Socialism, Maurice Dobb on the *Decline of Capitalism*. The subjects under discussion (they have now become orthodox as 'micro-economics') were often the practical problems of the industrial firm. Miss Audrey Wedgwood, for instance, introduced us to the technical problems of designing, making and selling pottery. I remember her telling us that cheap, bad, china could always be detected by holding it up to the light when it would shine green. We had offered coffee all round and casually, to illustrate, she held her cup to the light. A ghastly green shone out over our guests.

It was at this section that M. Albert Thomas spoke (in French and a large examination hall) about the International Labour Office of which he was the first director; and that Joan Robinson and Dorothea Braithwaite told the tale of Beauty and the Beast irreverently in the jargon of orthodox economic theory, and on the assumption of perfectly rational man.[8] When her father told the Beauty that 'the degree of hairiness of the Beast was not above the normal for that class of person', she was 'just willing to accept the bargain'. Both of them realized that 'she was on the margin'. More hairiness 'an additional (small) increment of disutility, would have outweighed the satisfaction to be obtained from obedience to filial duty'.

## VI

With the new social sciences at their back, their critical attitude to religion, and their somewhat utilitarian philosophy, the Heretics were 'natural' humanists in discussing morality without religion. In 1956[9] Julian Huxley hailed the change of title of the *Literary Guide* to the *Humanist* 'as attaching importance to all essential human attributes and values, morality as well as science, art as well as reason'. Forty years earlier the Heretics were in fact discussing the values and morality of certain English attributes, traditions and institutions. To discuss current politics was redundant, for most members belonged to political societies including the War and Peace Society and the Men's League for Women's Suffrage. Indeed, I can remember the difficulty of getting a committee that was not predominantly Fabian. But outside the morals of government policies, there was scope enough for practical humanist heresy—for instance on education. In February 1914 J. H. Badley, the founder of Bedales School, answered a previous Heretics paper by C. Reddie whose assistant master he had originally been at Abbotsholme School. This led to an interchange of letters in the *Cambridge Magazine*. Mr. Reddie said at the Heretics that there was a kind of 'electric leak' in co-educated boys. In the *Cambridge Magazine* for November 29th, 1913, three Bedales alumnae (one of them my sister Alix Strachey, and all of them Heretics) wrote from 'first-hand knowledge'.

> The boys do not lose vitality or forfeit their manliness. The fact that co-education exerts a mildly civilising influence upon them may be misleading to some, but it is a matter for congratulation rather than anxiety.

Dr Reddie answered in a letter concluding:

> if the British Empire is not to perish, we must fill it up with Britishers. This is women's work. If they cannot marry in England, let them go to the colonies. This was the pith of my lecture.

Education continued to exercise the Heretics during and after the war. Rebecca West spoke early in 1918 on 'Emotion in Education.' We heard from Dr Faithful that education was 'psychological rape' and discussed a paper by Henry Morris, the founder of the Cambridgeshire Village Colleges, on 'The Tragedy of Education.' The Heretics were also concerned, as humanists are today, with the press, crime and population. Kingsley Martin led a discussion on the 'Psychology of the Press in January 1922, Margorie Fry on 'Prisons and Punishment' in January 1923, Dr Norman Haire on 'Rejuvenation', and Dr Marie Stopes on 'Birth Control'. It was these last two papers that led to the resignation of one or two honorary members.

With four 'don' presidents following Ogden the Heretics lasted altogether twenty-two years. For a society so essentially a humanist deviant from the then establishment, and catering for a body of undergraduates rejuvenated or, rather, rejuveniled every three years, this was an uncommonly long life. The moral of the story is that senior members of universities should take some responsibility for the stability of humanist societies from one fleeting generation of undergraduates to another. But it must be admitted that few senior members are likely to be found with quite the genius of C. K. Ogden.

## REFERENCES AND NOTES

1. Printed at the Cambridge University Press.
2. 'Roughly described,' quoting Moore himself, 'as the pleasure of human intercourse and enjoyment of beautiful objects'. *Op. cit.*, pp. 83, 84, 89.
3. Vol. 1, pp. 70, 71.
4. 'It was Archbishop Whately, a divine full of Christian charity, who said "the more I see of men, the more I like dogs"; for my part the more I read of the older Benthamites . . . the more I feel it essential that one should have read the very humorous and very human Bentham'. C. K. Ogden, *Jeremy Bentham*, Kegan Paul, p. 17.
5. *Op. cit.*, p. 24.
6. *Op. cit.*, p. 44.
7. *Cambridge Magazine*, March 9th, 1912, p. 201.
8. The paper was published many years later in Professor Robinson's *Collected Economic Papers*, Vol. I, pp. 225 ff.
9. *Humanist*, October 1956, p. 6.

# On the Impossibility of Proving Survival

THEODORE BESTERMAN

## Theodore Besterman

HonDLitt, HonLLD., D.ès L.h.c. Director of the Institut et Musée Voltaire at Geneva. Head of the Dept. for Exchange of Information, UNESCO, 1946–1949. President of the International Congress on the Enlightenment 1963–1967. Corresponding member of the Institut de France and the Académies of Dijon, Lyons and Marseille. Hon. member of the Society for French Studies. Chevalier de la Lègion d'Honneur.

Publications include: *Mrs Annie Besant, a Modern Prophet*; *Some Modern Mediums*; *Pilgrim Fathers*; *A World Bibliography of Bibliographies* (5 vols); *Index Bibliographicus* (2 vols); *Voltaire's Notebooks* (2 vols); *Voltaire's Correspondence* (107 vols); *Studies on Voltaire and the 18th Century* (founded and edited).

# On the Impossibility of Proving Survival

THEODORE BESTERMAN

Though Humanism has great difficulty in getting a hearing on radio and television, spiritualism has recently been given a good show. Clergymen (including a bishop), mediums and other impartial persons have assured us that human survival after death is no longer a mere article of religious faith, but a proved fact. Bereaved persons have been encouraged to consult spiritualistic mediums. Even some so-called evidence has been produced, but the experiences cited served only to show once again that some minds are impenetrable to any notion of scientific method. Apart from the value of such evidence, a much wider question must be asked: Is it in fact possible to obtain evidence for human survival beyond the grave? It would be unscientific to assert as a fact that this is impossible, but I do say that it appears to be impossible in the light of existing knowledge. And I will now show why.

The surviving personality of a dead man is by definition discarnate. Living people are, or have, or function through bodies—we need not trouble ourselves for this purpose about the exact nature (if we knew it) of the mind-body relationship. Communication between incarnate and discarnate personalities can therefore take place only by some method which is not peculiar to only one of the two sets of personalities. Hence, if we obtain information only through our senses, then, since discarnate entities have no senses, communication between the two categories of beings cannot take place.

It follows that the transference of information from the dead to the living can take place only by extra-sensory methods. In other words, if the spiritualists' claim that the dead do communicate evidence to us is true, we *must* have means of acquiring information by methods other than those of the senses. But in that case, of what is the information so obtained evidence? Obviously, if a dead man wants to convince his living wife that he is really the man he claims to be, it is useless to tell her things that only he knew subjectively. For if these things never existed outside his own mind, how is she to determine whether he is telling the truth? Clearly, the dead man must tell her about objective things theoretically known only to him, but which, being objective, can be verified on earth. And here we come to the crucial difficulty. The dead husband imparts this knowledge direct to his wife, or through the intermediary of a medium, but in either case by means transcending the senses. But if such means exist, how can one be sure that the knowledge has not been obtained by the wife or medium direct from the object, without the participation of the discarnate husband?

Let us consider a specific case, which will also serve to illustrate the nature of evidence in this field. One of the mediums who recently appeared on television recounted the following incident, which she claimed to be irrefutable evidence of survival: a woman unknown to her telephoned this medium, who there and then obtained clairaudiently (that is, by non-sensory 'hearing') from the woman's dead husband the information that he had put a certain paper into his wallet. The widow inspected it and found such a paper. As evidence of survival, far from being convincing, this incident is quite worthless.

In the first place, we are not entitled to assume that this telephone conversation took place as described. The medium was no doubt doing her best to tell the exact truth, but the fallibility of human testimony is notorious, and has been established experimentally. In an experiment I myself conducted some years ago, in connection, it is true, with more complex events, an average of 33·9 per cent of accuracy was obtained, ranging from 5·9 per cent for the worst witness to 61 per cent for the best.[1]

If the medium's account of what happened was strictly

[1] Described in my *Collected Papers on the Paranormal* (1968).

accurate, what then? The paper in question was the receipt for a deposit paid on a motor-car. We were not told when this payment was made, nor how much time elapsed between the payment and the man's death, nor how long ago this had taken place. These facts must necessarily affect our evaluation of the total situation, but apart from this, is it so unusual to put a receipt of this kind into one's wallet and even to keep it there until needed? Moreover, it does not appear that the nature of the paper was specified by the medium. The whole thing thus boils down to this: what are the odds *against* the statement that a widow on looking into her late husband's wallet, would find there an 'important' paper? Would anyone be prepared to offer any odds against the truth of such an assertion?

In any case, how can we be sure that the wife did not know that the paper was in the wallet? It may well have been the husband's practice to put such papers into it. Indeed, when given a receipt in a showroom, where else is a man to put it? The wife may even have seen him put it there. Was she present when he ordered the car? We need to know many such details before arriving at any conclusion. It may also be that the man kept his wallet in his desk, and put the receipt into it on getting home. In either event the wife may have seen it and forgotten, or she may have seen it as it were unconsciously. But supposing she was not there, and knew nothing about it, is it not hard to believe that she had not thought of looking in the wallet when searching for the paper?

These are *normal* difficulties, of the kind that always have to be weighed before proceeding from a fact to a hypothesis, and in this case these difficulties are such that the case is quite worthless as evidence of survival. Let us now suppose that it would have been impossible for either the widow or the medium to have had any knowledge of the whereabouts of the paper. What then? Then we are thrown back on the same insuperable difficulty. If the medium were able by extra-sensory means to obtain the information from the dead man, it would be quite unjustifiable to assume that she did not obtain it direct from the object. On the latter hypothesis we need to assume 'only' the existence of extra-sensory methods of communication; on the former hypothesis we have to assume this *plus* the survival of a personality able and willing to communicate, and able to pick the exact time and place for making the communication effective. The former assumption is enormous, but it is vastly economical in comparison with the latter.

Here two points must be made. First, even if telepathy, clairvoyance (in this case, clairaudience), etc., are facts of nature (of which I am not at all convinced), we know absolutely nothing of their rationale or even their *modus operandi*. No limits can therefore be placed on the working of these supposed faculties. Second, the survival of personality after bodily death is, scientifically and philosophically, so immeasurably unlikely, that any other explanation of a given situation must be preferred. I am prepared to argue that survival of personality is even more improbable than the existence of a god—though admittedly in these regions the language of probability ceases to have much meaning.

Let us nevertheless consider whether it is possible to conceive of any evidence which would triumph over such a degree of improbability. The existing evidence has convinced some very good minds, including one or two for whom I have the greatest respect. I will name only Eleanor Mildred Sidgwick, though she became convinced of survival only in old age. Yet I must point out respectfully that no mind is good all through. A man who always reasoned at 100 per cent efficiency would go mad, and that is perhaps why Newton and Faraday, to mention only two of the world's greatest men of science, each had a water-tight compartment in his make-up in which he was in fact mad: Newton believed fervently in and wrote extensively on Biblical prophesy, and Faraday was a professed Sandemanian, that is, a member of one of the most eccentric of the antinomian sects.

I say unhesitatingly that no such evidence exists; that no kind of evidence yet devised can possibly produce such a result; and that I cannot, after many years of reflection about this problem, suggest any line of research likely to lead to the discovery of such evidence. The only possibility I can discern may appear paradoxical. I have argued that extra-sensory communication tells against survival. However, this is true only in so far as this 'faculty' remains unproved. If these alleged phenomena could be incorporated into the body of scientific knowledge, if they could be delimited, and if their scope could be determined, it might then ensue that certain other phenomena would be seen to fall outside their orbit. But all this is in the region of rarified speculation. I can hold out no real hope that such a situation will ever exist.

# The Meaning of Death

F. A. E. CREW

# F. A. E. Crew

FRS, TD, MD, DSc, PhD, DIH, FRCPE, FRSE, Hon D.Se, Hon LLD. Professor of Animal Genetics, 1928–1944, and Director of the Institute of Animal Genetics, 1921–1944, at the Edinburgh University; Professor of Public Health and Social Medicine at Edinburgh University 1944–1955. Visiting professor at Cairo University and WHO visiting professor at Rangoon and Bombay. Chairman, Board of Management of the Edinburgh Central Group of Hospitals, 1946–1956. Member of scientific societies of Poland, Czechoslovakia, India. President 8th International Genetical Congress, 1939. Freeman of the City of London in the Co. of Apothecaries.

Publications include: Official (Army) *Medical History of the War*; *Health, Its Nature and Conservation*; *The Foundations of Genetics*; textbooks on Animal Genetics, Genetics of Sexuality, Organic Inheritance in Man, Sex Determination, Genetics in Relation to Clinical Medicine and essays in Social Medicine and Hygiene.

# The Meaning of Death

F. A. E. CREW

Now that I have reached the age of 80, not too badly scathed, I have begun, after many postponements, to think seriously of preparing myself for my inevitable encounter with death. I have not given much thought to this matter since I was a child when, I remember, I found it irresistibly attractive and very frightening. Such information concerning it as I could extract from the adults around me was so vague and puzzling that I found it quite unconvincing. I only ceased worrying about it when, as I grew, I became increasingly engrossed in the adventure of living. But in recent years and especially since retirement from an active academic life thrust me into the shadows, the almost continuous stream of obituary notices of my contemporaries has evoked in me a sense of deepening loneliness and has seemed to be writing on the wall warning me that my days are likewise numbered.

I have been obliged to recognize the progressive decay of vitality in me, the stigmata of senility such as the waning of creative intellectual power, the decrease of physical agility, the increasingly leisurely nature of sexual performance, breathlessness on exertion, the loss of acuity of vision and hearing. All these signs of biological ageing tell me that I am old and since the true measure of age among the over 50s is the likelihood of dying in the immediate future, this increasing as age advances, I am forced to acknowledge that my life-expectancy is, in all probability, very small.

I find it interesting to examine my reactions to this prospect of an early demise. They are, of course, determined by my opinion concerning the meaning of death and this, in turn, is necessarily in accord with my opinions concerning the meaning of life, the nature of man and man's place in nature.

All these opinions have been fashioned by the operations of two forces, the particular culture to which I have been exposed and the particular career—that of an academic biologist—which I was privileged to follow.

Death is defined as that state of the animal or plant in which there is a total and permanent cessation of all vital functions. But now that it is possible to maintain the circulation and respiration artificially, to transplant whole organs, such as the kidney, to implant artificial valves in the heart and to delay irreversible brain damage, due to oxygen lack, by hypothermia, it has become difficult to determine when a given individual actually died, a matter of some importance legally. However, no matter what kind of intervention occurs, every individual sooner or later dies. It has been suggested that only when there has occurred a total and permanent disappearance of all spontaneous functioning of the brain, as revealed by an electro-encephalic tracing, can an individual be said to be indubitably dead.

Of death there are two forms, natural and premature or untimely. Natural death is the culmination of the process of biological ageing, it marks the end-point of the life-cycle of the individual which begins with conception and which is characterized by this progressive deterioration as the individual passes successively through the phases of immaturity, maturity and senescence. Since this process is progressive it follows that there must necessarily be a predetermined life-span. The maximum life-span of mankind is a little over a hundred years and seems not to have changed much over the ages. But natural death is exceedingly rare and the vast majority of individuals die prematurely from causes other than progressive deterioration. What has changed is man's survival rate at various ages for the reason that liability to disease and injury, which are the major causes of premature death, are age-specific. In an 'advanced' country the chances of dying between the ages of 1 and 50 do not increase significantly with advancing age because the diseases that especially affect individuals within this age-range have been brought under control through rising standards of living, and the conquest of squalor, poverty, famine and infection. After the age of 50 the killing diseases are of quite a different kind, the most important being degenerative in nature-diseases of the circulatory system, such as coronary embolism, hypertension, rupture of blood-vessels in the brain (stroke), which account for more than half the total deaths in this age-range, and cancer, about 16 per cent. These, together with pneumonia, about 3·6 per cent, and accidents, about 2·5 per cent, must be brought under control before the figure for life-expectancy can be expected to rise much further.

The causes of this process of biological ageing are not yet known. The wear and tear theory attributes the process to the repeated stresses to which all organisms are subjected, each illness or injury leaving permanent defects which accumulate until some vital organ fails. The individual can be regarded as an association of a number and variety of mutually inter-dependent parts, tissues, organs and organ-systems, each of which makes its own special and essential contribution to the functioning of the whole and not one of which is self-sufficient. Should a component part develop a fault in its own functioning the whole organism can be affected and if the fault is sufficiently serious and is not repaired it can lead to the death of the individual.

Other suspected causes are the progressive deterioration of cells that are not replaced by mitotic division and that seems to have a built-in life-span of their own—the cells of the central nervous system are of this kind—certain specific chemical and physical changes at the molecular level; and imperfections of mitosis in renewable cells—mutation and mal-distribution of chromosomal material.

It seems probable, therefore, that even at my advanced age, I shall die prematurely from heart disease, often swift and painless, from cancer, long drawn out and often gruesome, from a terminal pneumonia following a chill due to some indiscretion or following a fracture of a hip due to a fall or as the consequence of an accident of one kind or another. Should I escape these hazards then mine will be a natural death following a period during which I am housebound and a misery to myself and a burden to those taking care of me. The act of dying is not as a rule attended by physical pain, it is suffused with serenity as the carbon-dioxide in the blood-stream acts upon the central nervous system; it is very much like falling asleep. But the approach to death can be heavily loaded with anxiety and anguish and great pain. What manner of death will be mine I do not know. When it comes I hope to meet it with a steady eye and forfeit life with grace.

Should chronic infirmity threaten to rob my life of all serenity and delight and to render me altogether too dependent upon the care and attention of other people I shall certainly request that all effort to prolong my life shall cease forthwith and my thoughts will turn to suicide since, in my view, only by self-destruction could I display that consideration for others that is the hallmark of the civilized person. I am fortunate in that because of my professional qualifications there will be no need for me to involve others and to think of euthanasia, assisted suicide. I possess the means and the knowledge of the way in which these should be used. One of the greatest gifts of pharmacological science to mankind has been the provision of the means of self-destruction, freed from ugliness and distress. I am firmly of the opinion that suicide for rational motives is altogether different from 'pathological' suicide, for it springs from altruism and not from the depression and the failure that unbalance the mind. It can rightly be regarded as an honourable and praiseworthy act.

In this country today there are thousands of very old, lonely, chronically infirm and miserable people to whom life has no more to offer. Were it not for the disgrace which is felt by the relatives of a person who takes his own life, many of these old, unwanted people would destroy themselves, if the means of doing so were readily available. As things are they are condemned to live. In my view the right of such people to choose the time and the manner of death is unassailable. Being greatly interested in the problems created by the unplanned increase in population size I think that the self-removal for rational motives of a completed life is as great a contribution to the control of this size as is the prevention of the origin of a new one.

It is my wish that my carcase shall be incinerated, without any kind of ceremony or sign of mourning, and that my ashes shall be strewn in the garden from which I have derived so much pleasure.

I grew up in a society in which death was so unwanted and so feared that much effort was expended in attempts to defer it, its being accepted that death could not be prevented. The influence of the Church, though waning, was still strong. Its theistic religion, based upon the belief that there exist supernatural beings capable of influencing natural events and also upon the belief in the reality of supernatural events such as incarnation and resurrection from the dead, provided a picture of man and of his origin, nature and destiny that, to very many people, seemed to make sense. Man was created by God and was endowed with an immortal soul. The purpose of life was to glorify God. Death was not to be feared by the virtuous since it was the gateway to an unending and much preferable life beyond the grave.

Since religious instruction was encountered in the school curriculum long before any introduction to biological science and since church-going was then the habit of the social class to which my parents belonged, this was the doctrine that I absorbed. I came to understand that one of the more important functions of traditional religious belief was to allay the fear of death. But in the later years of my schooldays and during my undergraduate years I encountered much that I could not reconcile with this doctrine. I was offered alternative explanations of the meaning of life and death, of the nature of man and of human destiny and these seemed to me to be far more credible and rational and far preferable for they were supported by evidence that I could examine and weigh.

I found Darwinism completely satisfying. Evolution I accepted as an inescapable fact. I found the evolutionary process comprehensible and, as a concept, all embracing. Man, like all the plants and other animals that have inhabited this earth, is the product of this evolutionary process. He is the highest dominant type of living thing on this earth to be produced by millions of years of the slow biological improvement that has been the outcome of the blind workings of natural selection. Religions, theistic and non-theistic, are inventions of man, face to face with problems too vast for his understanding, to provide a comprehensive picture of human significance and human destiny. They have played an exceedingly important role in the development of civilization, providing a cohesive force which has held a society together and being the source of codes of morality which have greatly facilitated the development of the aggregate life.

It seemed reasonable to accept the teaching that the initial stages of life on this earth were protein compounds born of fantastic thunderstorms playing upon the soup-like seas several thousand millions of years ago and that countless numbers of these prototypes must have failed to become established before a structure appeared, by chance, that proved itself able to survive and evolve further; that life had its origin in chemical synthesis and that all living things, including man, are organized pieces of worldstuff. Biochemists have demonstrated conclusively that all the basic chemicals required for the making of a living thing of the simplest kind can be formed quite easily in conditions that simulate those that, it is reasonable to think, existed in the earth's atmosphere at the time when life first made its appearance. Among astronomers, physicists, chemists and biologists there is rapidly developing the opinion that it is by no means improbable that that which has happened on this earth has also taken place on some of the billions of planets that crowd the skies; that it is quite possible that the evolutionary process has produced intelligent forms of life and civilizations elsewhere in the universe though these dominant forms of life may well be very different from ourselves. If this should turn out to be so and if it becomes possible to establish communication between them and ourselves by means of radio signals, our views concerning the position of *Homo sapiens* in the universe may need profound modification.

It was the Darwinian teaching concerning the common ancestry, the relatedness, of all living things, including man, that caused me to give less thought to the uniqueness of *Homo sapiens* and more to the attributes he shares with other living things. Since they have a life-span which ends in death, it follows that the study of death cannot be restricted to man. The life-span differs greatly from species to species, ranging from a few hours to well over a hundred years. But whatever it is, it is related to the time of attainment of the ability to reproduce and to make an adequate contribution to the next generation. Animals in the wild do not live long enough to become old; they die prematurely of violence, starvation, exposure or infection. When domesticated, kept as pets or in zoos and protected against these hazards, they live much longer and display all the signs of biological ageing. Death among them, be it premature or natural, is exactly identical with mortality in man.

An inquiry concerning death and involving many species inevitably leads to certain firm conclusions. If a species is to flourish it is essential that the individuals of a generation shall reproduce their kind. The individual animal or plant is so constituted that efficiency in reproduction is ensured. But this efficiency wanes with increasing age after maturity is reached and is ultimately extinguished. The essential feature of reproduction is the transmission by parent to offspring of a genetic endowment. When the individual has contributed adequately to the stream of life the purpose of being an individual has been served. In my opinion there is no valid reason for excluding *Homo sapiens* from this generalization. To demand that (biological) man shall be the sole exception to the rule seems, to me, to be an instance of indulgence in unjustifiable and arrogant egocentricity. Natural death, therefore, can be interpreted as the means whereby such as have ceased to be reproductively efficient are removed from the population. By so doing it confers an advantage on the species.

The habitats in which animals and plants have their being are, and always have been, subject to sudden or gradual change of considerable magnitude. If a species is to flourish its characterization must be in harmony with the conditions of the environment, it must therefore be capable of change and be able to adjust and adapt to change. Many are the species that have perished for the reason that they were unable to harmonize themselves with changed environmental conditions. The capacity to adjust and to adapt is at its peak in the young and becomes progressively diminished with advancing age. It is well known that among nomadic peoples the hastening of the premature death of the old has been a world-wide custom. Natural death can therefore be regarded as the removal from the population of such as are incapable of adjusting to changing conditions. Had the conditions on this earth been completely and permanently stable there would have been no need for the development of the ability to adjust, to learn new tricks in order to be able to cope, but in the external physical world (and also in the social world invented by man) change is everywhere and all the time, and so in order to ensure that a species shall be biologically efficient there came into being a system of replacement. The old, inefficient in respect of the abilities to reproduce and to adapt, are removed by natural death and replaced by the young, efficient in reproduction and adaptability.

In a country such as this where the life-expectancy has become so greatly lengthened and in which the rate of change of all kinds has been so exceedingly rapid, a great gulf has developed to separate the young adult and the senescent. Communication between the two age-categories has become exceedingly difficult for their systems of ideas and even their vocabularies are very different. Even if the 75s and over had some special contribution of social or cultural value to offer it is doubtful that it would be welcomed or accepted. But this age-range has no monopoly of the wisdom extracted from experience; between wisdom and age there is no linear correlation. Whatever quality is possessed by the 75s and over is displayed to an equal or even greater degree by the 50–60 age-range. These two age-categories are distinguished, in the main, by differences in general vigour and healthiness. It seems improbable that the population would be seriously disadvantaged if from it the great majority of the 75s and over were removed. What seems to be urgently necessary is the discovery of the means whereby the progressive enfeeblement, accelerating as age advances, can be halted or slowed down so that the vigour and healthiness of the 55s shall become the possession of the 75s.

This biological invention of replacement, which involves birth, sex, sexual reproduction and natural death, occurred long after life first appeared on the earth. The multicellular organism evolved out of the unicellular. Among the unicellulars natural death is unknown for when the individual has reached maturity it divides into two daughter cells each of which is a new individual of the next generation. The parental individual has ceased to exist but since there is no corpse there is no death. In the multicellular organism, reproduction provides ample opportunity for the occurrence of gene mutation and aberrent chromosome distribution during the formation of the gametes, and sexual reproduction makes it possible for such mutations and aberrations to become widely dispersed in the population. For the evolutionary process to occur there must be variants in the population, individuals differing from the standard characterization in respect of some heritable detail of structure or function. The forces of natural selection in the environment act upon these differences so that some are favoured and others are oppressed. Such variants are produced by this mutation and mal-distribution of the chromosomes. This replacement system is a thoroughly efficient mechanism for ensuring that evolutionary progress shall occur.

I am persuaded that when once life is launched it must reach its final destination which is death and that death implies the extinction of the individual and the dissolution of the worldstuff of which he is composed into its primordial elements which return to the universe, dust to dust and ashes to ashes. In the young the fear of death is normal and useful. It threatens to cheat them of the best things in life and in its absence life would be risked unnecessarily, and premature death from accident and the like would tend to become too frequent for species survival. This fear derives from a fear of the unknown, a fear of anguish, an unwillingness to relinquish life and a sadness at leaving all the things that bind the individual to this world.

But such fears are not for the likes of me. Because I am old

I can accept the idea that death is the end of me as an individual without any undue disquiet. I have lived a long and a very full life. I have loved and have been loved. I have passed on a genetic endowment to posterity—there are now two great grandchildren—and so have ensured continuance. A few of the results of my activities as a scientist have become embodied in the very texture of the science I tried to serve—this is the immortality that every scientist hopes for. I have enjoyed the privilege, as a university teacher, of being in a position to influence the thought of many hundreds of young people and in them and their lives I shall continue to live on vicariously for a while. All the things I care for will continue for they will be served by those who come after me. I find great pleasure in the thought that those who stand on my shoulders will see much further than I did in my time. What more could any man want?

The god-hypothesis, invented by man to provide an explanation of the meaning of existence, has served its purpose and is destined to disappear. The old-established religious faiths, in general, are failing to control human thought and action. The decline of Christian theology in the Western World has left a void and since most people need something above and beyond themselves, some ideal, some cause, to which to attach their loyalty and since there can be no return to the simple faith of their forefathers, some new and alternative philosophy must be found.

For my part, I find complete satisfaction in the thought that man has taken charge of his own further evolution and also the further evolution of this planet. Than this there could not possibly be a greater adventure, one that must tax to the utmost all the resources that man can muster, knowledge, reason, imagination, aspiration, hope, faith and a love of mankind. In this adventure all the geographical varieties of *Homo sapiens* must become united. Mankind must tackle the problems that arise and must plan its future unaided by any supernatural power and in so doing must greatly increase its own stature. Engaged in such an adventure the life of the individual must become meaningful and purposeful and in making his own contribution to the creation of a world that would be optimal for the development of those human qualities that are to be admired, every one would surely secure great emotional and intellectual satisfaction. In a world so organized that everyone equipped to do so would be able to enjoy life at least as much as I have done, there would be very few who would hanker after an existence beyond the grave for the life lived on this earth would be complete in itself.

# Humanism and the Future

H. J. EYSENCK

## H. J. Eysenck

PhD, DSc, Professor of Psychology at the London University's Institute of Psychiatry since 1955. Director of the Maudsley Hospital psychology department since 1946. Visiting Professor at the Universities of California and Pennsylvania. Chief editor of *Behaviour Research and Therapy*, and editor of *International Monographs of Experimental Psychology*.

Publications include: *The Structure of Human Personality*; *Uses and Abuses of Psychology*; *Sense and Nonsense in Psychology*; *Dynamics of Anxiety and Hysteria*; *Perceptual Processes and Mental Illness*; *Behaviour Therapy and the Neuroses* (editor); *Crime and Personality*; *Causes and Cures of Neurosis*; *Fact and Fiction in Psychology*; *Smoking, Health and Personality*; *The Biological Basis of Personality*; *Description and Measurement of Personality*.

grounded in historical factors which have certainly ceased to operate to any significant extent. Consider Fig. 1. It reports the results of an experiment carried out by R. H. Thoulless, in which subjects were asked to indicate their agreement or disagreement with each of a number of propositions on a seven-point scale ranging from 'I strongly approve of the proposition' (+3 points) through 'I am on the whole in favour of this proposition' (+2 points) and 'I am uncertain, but if forced would probably vote for the proposition' (+1 point) to 'I am uncertain, but if forced would probably vote against the proposition' (−1 point), 'I am on the whole against the proposition' (−2 points), and 'I strongly disapprove of the proposition' (−3 points). The propositions themselves related to a variety of social issues on none of which could it be said that scientific evidence clearly indicated a true answer; on rational grounds therefore most responses should have clustered around the +1, 0 (No vote), or −1 region. In actual fact, the distribution of 22,208 votes was as shown in Fig. 1, i.e. the majority of votes cast indicated extreme certainty of agreement or disagreement! This was in conformity with Thoulless's 'Principle of Certainty': 'When, in a group of persons, there are influences acting both in the direction of acceptance and of rejection of a belief, the result is not to make the majority adopt a lower degree of conviction, but to make some hold the belief with a high degree of conviction, while others reject it also with a high degree of conviction.' This principle of certainty applies to religious matters, but not only to them; it is the principle of superstition and of anti-scientific attitudes in general.

Nor are rationalists and humanists free from the shackles which this law imposes on our thinking. Consider the following proposition which (among others) I once put to a group of knowledgeable university members of the British Humanist Association: 'Negroes in the United States are born with the same intellectual potentialities as whites, and their failure to do as well on intelligence tests is due to poor educational facilities and other environmental factors.' On the same 7-point scale as that used by Thoulless, hardly a Jack or a Jill failed to endorse the +3 (or, more rarely, the +2) position—just as among working class subjects most endorsed the −3 or the −2 position. Yet such evidence as there is (and a very great deal of quite sophisticated research has been done in this field) indicates that −1, or even possibly −2, would be the correct answer! (Scandalized readers may like to read

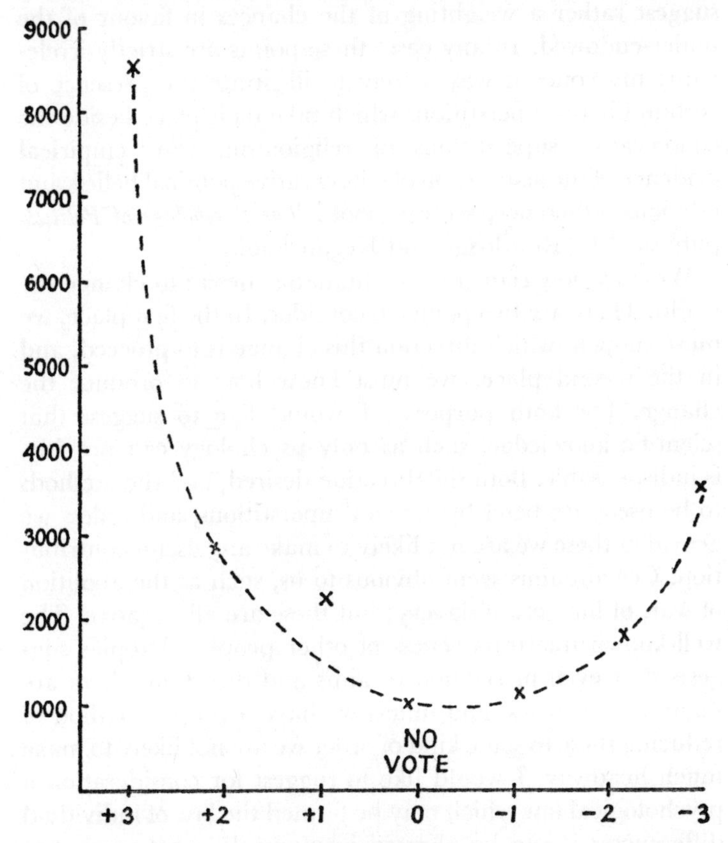


Distribution of 22,208 votes on a 7-point attitude scale

the recently published second edition of Audrey M. Shuey's *The Testing of Negro Intelligence*, published in New York by the Social Science Press, for a scholarly account of the evidence.) It should hardly be necessary to add that this statement relates entirely and exclusively to the results of research, and does not carry any of the implications which many people (as in South Africa, for instance) may read into it; group differences in intelligence, even if congenital, do not by themselves justify apartheid or any other political perpetuation of inferior status. The fact of unequal endowment (between individuals as well as between races) does not justify a doctrine of unequal opportunity; to many people it may suggest rather a weighting of the chances in favour of the under-endowed. In any case, these points are strictly irrelevant; my concern was merely to illustrate the presence of certain liberal superstitions which take their place beside the conservative superstitions of religionism. (For empirical evidence of the association of conservative political beliefs and religious adherence, see my book: *The Psychology of Politics*, published by Routledge and Kegan Paul.)

We may now return to the humanist desire to change the world. There are two points to consider. In the first place, we must know in which direction this change is to proceed, and in the second place, we must know how to produce the change. For both purposes, I would like to suggest that scientific knowledge, such as only psychology can provide, is indispensable. Both the direction desired, and the methods to be used, are beset by ancient superstitions, and unless we get rid of these we are not likely to make any useful contribution. Certain aims seem obvious to us, such as the abolition of war, of hunger, of slavery; but these are all negative. The well-known unattractiveness of other people's Utopias suggests that even in relation to aims and directions there are many divergencies, and unless we have a proper method of reducing these to some kind of order we are not likely to make much headway. I would like to suggest for consideration a psychological law which may be termed the law of individual differences; it can be phrased in many different ways, but for the present purpose the following wording may perhaps be the most useful: 'The vast majority of psychological laws, rules, prescriptions, principles and generalizations are only valid for some of the people some of the time, and require to be qualified in terms of individual differences between people.'[1] A few examples may make this law clearer, and show how it can be applied to actual social problems of the day.

[1] An alternative wording; 'One man's meat is another man's poison!'

I have recently argued that the well-known differences between extroverted and introverted people are due to congenital threshold differences in the excitation of the brain-stem reticular formation, whose function it is to keep the cortex in a suitable state of arousal; the consequence of these differences is that the introvert has a cortex which under identical conditions is in a state of higher arousal than the average, while the extrovert has a cortex which under identical conditions is in a state of lower arousal than the average; there is much physiological and psychological experimental evidence for this theory (presented in detail in my book on *The Biological Basis of Personality.*) One consequence of this low arousal on the part of the extrovert is that he quickly accumulates reactive inhibition when sensory input consists of identical or similar stimuli; in other words, he is quickly bored by monotonous stimulation, and craves change. This can be shown quite easily in the experimental laboratory—show your subject two pictures in such a way that he can change from viewing one to viewing the other by pressing a button, and you will find that the extrovert presses the button much more frequently. This of course is not particularly interesting, or of much social importance. But he also changes his domicile more frequently, and his work; he is much more likely to change his girl friend, and to get a divorce. He is much less happy with a monotonous job, needs excitement, bright lights, loud music. His Utopia is entirely different from that of the introvert, and the fact that most Utopian books have been written by introverts (extroverts would probably not have the patience!) may account for their utter unacceptability by extroverts as a description of an ideal society.

Humanists (like most other people) make the frequent mistake of assuming that fundamentally other people are like themselves (the purest form of anthropomorphism), and that if only other people would listen to them, or had had the benefit of their upbringing, then everything would be well. This simply is not so. People are fundamentally, constitutionally, congenitally different in the most profound way from each other; no general rule or law can cover all these different needs, desires, motivations. In another experiment subjects could press a lever at a rate chosen by themselves; if this rate did not exceed a certain number of presses a minute, they were left in silence and darkness, but if it did exceed that number, then bright lights would come on for a short time, and loud juke box music. Extroverts pressed the lever like mad, while introverts hardly touched it. How now for pirate radio stations! Extroversion–introversion is only one dimension of personality along which one person may differ from another; emotionality–stability is another. And these are undoubtedly not the only ones; there may be many more. Without an understanding of these profound differences our notion of the proper direction of change is not likely to appeal to many people, and may make the situation worse rather than better. Even war possibly gives rise to behaviours which appeal to many people, and thus has a certain attraction to some; William James' 'moral equivalent of war' may be needed if we really want to eliminate all types of war-like behaviour. Administrators who build new towns for old slums often cannot understand why so many people prefer the old slums; they assume the universality of their own likes and dislikes, forgetting entirely the law of individual differences. The list of mistakes made along these lines is endless; most readers will be able to add to it from their own experience.

It may be possible to formulate a general rule from these considerations, a rule to cover the direction in which humanists should desire to go. This rule takes into account the law of individual differences, and states, simply, that the maximum diversity of behaviour compatible with survival is an important desideratum in any future Utopia. This would contain as a rider, the desirability of not conditioning any superstitious beliefs into young members of the community, because these superstitions curtail, even more efficiently than laws, the maximum diversity of behaviour which we have declared to be desirable. In other words, education should emphasize scientific ideals, not religious ones (taking that word in its widest meaning); one man's ideal is another man's pet aversion. Let us educate our children to give answers ranging from +1 to −1 on a seven-point scale; that will ensure that tolerance of variability which alone can incorporate our innate diversity.

This is of course not the only, nor is it likely to be the most important, law of humanistic ethics. The point to be stressed is that however desirable the elaboration of such an ethics may be, the accomplishment of such an aim depends entirely on the development of our scientific knowledge of psychology. To wish to work out in any detail a humanistic ethics at this stage of development is equivalent to asking for television, flying machines and laser beams at a time when men still thought that the earth was shaped like a saucer and carried on the back of a gigantic elephant; the future of humanistic thought on this subject is completely bound up with the growth of psychological knowledge—without this it must remain nothing more than an alternative superstition.

The same applies to the second of our points, i.e. the manner to be adopted for changing the world, assuming that we knew in what direction to change it. Here too it probably needs a psychologist to realize how utterly governed by superstitions our approach is, and how pitifully small our stock of scientific knowledge. Consider such an eminently commonsense notion as the widespread belief that punishment deters. Does it? Consider the following experiment. A rat is put at the bottom (starting point) of a T-maze; when he reaches the top he can turn right or left. We place some food on the right, and want to teach him to learn always to turn right. One group of rats is simply replaced time and time again at the bottom of the T; they are allowed to eat the food when they turn right, but receive nothing when they turn left. A second group is punished by an electric shock when they turn left, in addition to being allowed to eat when they turn right. A third group is punished when they turn right, as well as being allowed to eat the food. If punishment deters, then this third group should learn less quickly than the first group, and the second group, which is punished for doing the wrong thing, should learn fastest of all. Nothing of the kind; in actual fact the group which is punished for doing the right thing learns just as quickly as does the group which is punished for doing the wrong thing, and both learn more quickly than the group which is not punished at all!

Does punishment then always facilitate learning, regardless of what is being punished? Nothing of the kind. Consider the following experiment. Dogs are put in compartment A, which is divided from compartment B by a low wall which they can easily jump. They are given a signal, and a few seconds later the floor of compartment A is electrified; this makes them jump over the wall into the safety of compartment B. Dogs quickly learn this habit, and soon jump immediately the signal is heard. Now we wish to teach them *not* to jump to the signal. For one group we simply turn off the electric shock permanently, so that dogs which linger a little before jumping after receiving the signal do not get shocked any longer; the dogs soon catch on and learn not to jump. For a second group we also turn off the electric shock in compartment A, but we also actually punish them for jumping to B by giving them a shock when they land in B! If punishment for jumping into B is effective in making them learn not to jump, then they should give up this habit even more quickly than the dogs which did not receive the punishment. But this is not what happens at all. The dogs punished for jumping to B continued jumping and never learn that it is safe to remain in A! In other words, they behave like recidivists who return to criminal activity each time they are punished for their criminal behaviour.

I have discussed some of these facts in *Crime and Personality* (Routledge and Kegan Paul), and hinted at the possibility of using such knowledge as we possess for the more efficacious stamping out of crime; the sad truth, after all, is that after three thousand years or more of using common sense in trying to eradicate crime, violations of the laws are probably more widespread than ever, and constantly on the increase. Our efforts to deal with this situation are characterized by superstition, not by scientific knowledge. 'Punishment' is vaguely advocated as a universal remedy, but punishment may have exactly the opposite effect from that intended. Punishment, under certain circumstances, can 'stamp in' the behaviour we are punishing, rather than stamp it out, just as it did in the case of the dogs. In other studies, the infliction of pain has been shown to result in a tremendous increase in *aggression* as a direct, reflex effect of the punishment; put two rats in a box and shock them through their feet, and they will turn on each other and fight furiously in a rage of destructiveness. Is that the effect we wish to produce when we call for a resurrection of 'the birch' or even the cat o' nine tails?

Crime is one example of our unwillingness to apply even the little knowledge that we have of scientific principles in the field of changing human behaviour; education is another. What we do today is still very much what we did three thousand years ago; changes in policy are dictated by political shibboleths rather than by factual knowledge. Are humanists different? Do humanists base their views entirely on the scientific evidence, and thus endorse the $+1$ and $-1$ positions on a seven-point scale when discussing educational practices, or advocating changes? If not, then superstitions govern their conduct just as much as they do that of the despised religionists; humanists, just as much as religionists, often fail to obey the tenets of the only religion they owe allegiance to—the religion of the open mind. Only psychological research can tell us the answers to these questions; do humanists in fact try to acquaint themselves with the results of such research, in order to base their opinions on the best facts available—or to be able to assert that in fact no worth while facts are known in this particular field?

Of course the position is very difficult. Not only are we woefully short on accepted principles, but even worse, the law of individual differences holds sway here too. Are children more motivated by praise or blame? Well, it appears that introverted children are more motivated by praise, extraverted ones by blame. Is teaching machine instruction more efficient than the traditional kind? Well, it appears that introverts benefit more by machine instruction, extraverts more by the traditional kind. The list of established differences is already very long; the methods to be adopted in order to change the behaviour of people must be adapted to the kind of person we are dealing with—universal penaceas should be treated with the greatest reserve! Stick and carrot may both work for the donkey, but some donkeys respond better to the one, others to the other. If we pay no attention to these factors we may in fact have exactly the opposite effect to the one intended.

What, then, is the upshot of the arguments advanced so far? It is, essentially, that the kind of society rationalists and humanists should work for is one based on science rather than on superstition—where superstition includes not merely religion but also most of our treasured everyday beliefs about social, national and political matters. This in turn means that we would have to work for a society based on experiment rather than on vague empiricism. This distinction is not always clear to people not trained in the social sciences, and an example may make it clear. Educationalists who favour comprehensive schools often refer to the setting up of the large number of such schools in recent years as an 'experiment in education'. Now if the word 'experiment' meant nothing more than 'trying out something new and different' this would be a reasonable and accurate description. But 'experiment' also carries the implication of control—we want to be able to come to some more or less certain conclusion as the result of our experiment. That means that we want to compare the results we obtain from our comprehensive schools with the results from some other types of school; clearly it is only if the results are in some clearly defined sense 'better' that we would want to indulge in wholesale reorganization. But in order to obtain such comparisons we would have to proceed very carefully indeed, making sure that allocation of pupils to type of school was randomized, that different ability levels were equally represented in different types of school, that parental status and many other variables were properly controlled, and so on. Vaguely turning large numbers of schools into comprehensives does not answer any serious questions; that is not an experiment at all, but an exercise of social judgement. No doubt a shift in the political wind will lead to a reversal of this social judgement, and a new, and equally inconclusive 'experiment', consisting in the disestablishment of comprehensives. The final result will be that both sides will remain convinced of the virtues of their preconceived opinions, and no knowledge at all will have been gained on an important point of educational policy.

In a similar way, it is often assumed that judges know more than laymen, or even social scientists, about the consequences of their decisions, and can with advantage be appealed to when changes in the law are contemplated. But clearly they know as little as anybody about the actual consequences of their decisions, possibly even less than most people because they are protected with elaborate care from consorting with actual wrongdoers; only careful follow-up studies of matched groups of criminals sentenced according to different principles can tell us if these differences are relevant to our particular concerns. Any change in the law not accompanied by such careful scientific investigation of its precise effects is not 'experimental'; it does not lead to any improvement in our knowledge, and is therefore beyond the pale of scientific thought.

It is sometimes objected that it is not in line with democratic values to make human beings into 'guinea pigs', and the notion of making the schooling or sentencing of people into an experimental exercise is regarded as being inhuman and unethical. It needs little thought to discover that these objections are valueless. There is nothing sacred about our present institutions, to which we subject children and criminals; neither is there anything sacred about such changes as we do in fact make from time to time—such as the move towards comprehensive schools, for instance, or the change in the laws affecting homosexuality between consenting adults. All that is suggested is that when changes are contemplated, they should not be implemented in too wholesale a fashion, but should be introduced along carefully considered experimental lines, so that definitive knowledge could be obtained on the actual effects of the changes. The steel industry has been nationalized, de-nationalized, re-nationalized, and will probably again be re-de-nationalized, without any scientific knowledge being gained as to the advantages of nationalization in this sector. Schools are being turned into comprehensives, and may again be de-comprehensified, without all these changes being used to give us some worthwhile knowledge of the results of doing all these things. In other words, the state is using us as guinea-pigs in any case (and inevitably), but in experiments which are useless, because they are not properly organized and designed. It is difficult to see any objection against organizing and designing the experiment in such a way that the effort is not wasted, but can be used for securing an improvement in future planning.

Politicians, of course, are temperamentally opposed to the very notion that conduct can and should be based on scientific evidence; this after all would deprive them of their prime function, which is to trade upon the superstitious prejudices of the population to secure their election. Politicians *par excellence* are the people who give +3 and −3 answers to questions the answers to which are not known, and try to persuade the voters to follow them in this foolish endeavour. Politics, as Bismarck said, is no exact science; this should not prevent us from making it as exact as is humanly possible. Nor should it make us take pride, as many politicians do, in the unscientific and intuitive nature of their craft or art; the sad consequences of political superstitions are only too obvious to the unprejudiced observer of the modern scene.

This, then, is my notion of the future of Humanism. If Humanism is not to become identified in the popular consciousness as a relic of Victorianism no less antiquated than the established religion it opposed, then it must go forward and attack other superstitions which are less weak and long in the tooth than religion. In order to fulfil a positive function as pace-setter in 'changing the world' Humanism must adopt whole-heartedly the scientific method; that means (because nearly all the problems Humanism is concerned with are psychological problems) that it must identify with scientific psychology. It is a good sign that more and more students are seeking to enrol in courses leading to a degree in the social sciences; the message which I have been trying to spell out in this brief chapter is clearly not falling on deaf ears as far as modern youth is concerned. So far, alas, Humanism is not showing many signs of following this path; perhaps an internal debate might be in order to discuss this and alternative proposals for harnessing the emotional vigour of humanists in a more positive endeavour than the mere opposition to organized religion.

# Emancipation through Knowledge

SIR KARL POPPER

## Sir Karl Popper

Kt 1965, PhD, DLit, Hon LLD, FBA. Professor of Logic and Scientific Method in the University of London (The London School of Economics and Political Science). President, British Society for the Philosophy of Science, 1959–1961; and of the Aristotelian Society, 1958–1959. Visiting professor at various times to the universities of Yale, Princeton, Chicago, California, Minnesota, Indiana, and Denver. Annual Philosophy Lecturer to British Academy, 1960; Herbert Spencer Lecturer at Oxford, 1961. William James Lecturer in Philosophy at Harvard, 1950. Hon. Member of American Academy of Arts and Sciences, 1966, and Fellow of the International Academy of Philosophy of Science. Member Harvard Chapter of Phi Beta Kappa, 1964. Co-editor: *Ratio*; *Studies in the Foundations Methodology and Philosophy of Science*.

Publications include: *The Open Society and Its Enemies*; *The Poverty of Historicism*; *The Logic of Scientific Discovery*; *On the Sources of Knowledge and of Ignorance*; *Conjectures and Refutations*; *Of Clouds and Clocks*.

# Emancipation through Knowledge

KARL R. POPPER

The philosophy of Immanuel Kant, and with it, his philosophy of history, is often looked upon in Germany as antiquated, and as superseded by Hegel and his followers. This may well be due to the surpassing intellectual and moral statue of Kant, German's greatest philosopher; for the very greatness of his achievement was a thorn in the flesh of his lesser successors, so that Fichte, and later Hegel, tried to solve this irritating problem by persuading the world that Kant had been merely one of their forerunners. But Kant was nothing of the sort. On the contrary he was a determined opponent of the whole Romantic Movement and especially of Fichte: Kant was in fact the last great exponent of that much reviled movement, the Enlightenment. In an important essay entitled 'What is Enlightenment?' (1785) Kant wrote:

> Enlightenment is the emancipation of man from a state of self-imposed tutelage. This state is due to his incapacity to use his own intelligence without external guidance. Such a state of tutelage I call 'self-imposed' (or 'culpable') if it is due not to lack of intelligence but to lack of courage or determination to use his own intelligence without the help of a leader. *Sapere aude*! Dare to use your own intelligence! This is the battle-cry of the Enlightenment.

This passage from Kant's essay shows what was for him the

A broadcast delivered in German on the Bavarian Broadcasting Network in February 1961, in a series of broadcasts *On the Meaning of History*, and published in German in *Der Sinn der Geschichte*, edited by L. Reinisch. (Not previously published in English).

central idea of the Enlightenment. It was the idea of *self-liberation through knowledge.*

This idea of self-liberation or self-emancipation through knowledge remained for Kant a task as well as a guide throughout his life; and although he was convinced that this idea might serve as an inspiration for every man possessed of the necessary intelligence, Kant did not make the mistake of proposing that we make self-emancipation through knowledge, or any other mainly intellectual exercise, the whole meaning or purpose of human life. Indeed, Kant did not need the assistance of the Romantics for criticizing pure reason, nor did he need their reminders to realize that man is not purely rational; and he knew that mere intellectual knowledge is neither the best thing in human life, nor the most sublime. He was a pluralist who believed in the variety of human experience and in the diversity of human aims; and being a pluralist, he believed in an open society—a pluralist society that would live up to his own maxim: 'Dare to be free, and respect the freedom and the autonomy of others; for the dignity of man lies in his freedom, and in his respect for other people's autonomous and responsible beliefs, especially if these differ widely from his own.' Yet in spite of his pluralism he saw in intellectual self-education, or self-emancipation through knowledge, a task which is indispensable from a philosophical point of view; a task demanding of every man immediate action here and now and always. For only through the growth of our knowledge can we liberate our minds from their spiritual enslavement: enslavement by prejudices, idols, and avoidable errors. Thus the task of self-education, though certainly not exhausting the meaning of life, could, he thought, make a decisive contribution towards it.

The analogy between the expressions '*the meaning of life*' and '*the meaning of history*' is worthy of examination; but I shall first examine the ambiguity of the word 'meaning' in the expression 'the meaning of life'. This expression is sometimes used in the sense of a deeper, a hidden meaning—something like the hidden meaning of an epigram, or of a poem, or of the *Chorus Mysticus* in Goethe's *Faust.* But the wisdom of some poets and perhaps also of some philosophers has taught us that the phrase 'the meaning of life' can be understood in a different way; that the meaning of life may not be something hidden and perhaps discoverable but, rather, something with which we ourselves can endow our lives. We can bestow a meaning upon our lives through our work, through our active conduct, through our whole way of life, and through the attitude we adopt towards our friends and our fellow men and towards the world.

In this way the quest for the meaning of life turns into an ethical question—the question, 'What tasks can I set myself in order to make my life meaningful?'. Or as Kant puts it: 'What should I do?' A partial answer to this question is given in Kant's ideas of freedom and autonomy, and of a pluralism which is limited only by the idea of equality before the law and of mutual respect for the freedom of others; ideas which, like the idea of self-emancipation through knowledge, can contribute meaning to our lives.

We can understand the expression 'the meaning of history' in a similar way. This, too, has been often interpreted in the sense of a secret or hidden meaning, underlying the course of world history; or perhaps of a hidden direction or evolutionary tendency which is inherent in history; or of a goal towards which the world is striving. Yet I believe that the quest for the hidden 'meaning of history' is misconceived, as is the quest for the hidden meaning of life: instead of searching for a hidden meaning of history, we can make it our task to *give* it a meaning. We can try to give an aim to political history—and thereby to ourselves. Instead of looking for a deeper, a hidden meaning in political history, we can ask ourselves what could be worthy and humane aims of political history: aims both feasible and beneficial to mankind.

My *first thesis* is, therefore, that we should refuse to speak of the meaning of history in the sense of something concealed in it, or of a moral hidden in the divine tragedy of history, or in the sense of some evolutionary tendencies or laws of history, or of some other meaning which might perhaps be discovered by some great historian or philosopher or religious leader.

Thus my first thesis is negative. I contend that there is no hidden meaning in history, and that those historians and philosophers who believe they have discovered one are deceiving themselves, and others.

My *second thesis*, however, is very positive. I believe that we ourselves can try to give a meaning to political history—or rather a plurality of meanings; meanings that are feasible for, and worthy of, human beings.

But I go even further than that. For my *third thesis* is that we can learn from history that the attempt to give history an ethical meaning, or to set ourselves an ethical aim, need not be vain. On the contrary, we shall never understand history if we underrate the historical power of ethical aims. No doubt they often have led to terrible results, unforeseen by those who first conceived them. Yet in some respects we have approached more closely than any previous generation to the aims and ideals of the Enlightenment represented by the American Revolution, or by Kant. More especially the idea of self-emancipation or self-liberation through knowledge, the idea of a pluralist or open society, and the idea of ending the frightful history of wars by the establishment of eternal peace, though perhaps still far distant ideals, have become the aim and the hope of almost all of us.

By saying that we have got nearer to these aims I am not, of course, venturing to prophesy that we shall soon, or ever, attain them. Certainly we may fail. But I think that at least the idea of peace which Erasmus of Rotterdam, Immanuel Kant, Friedrich Schiller, Bentham, the Mills and Spencer, and in Germany Berta von Suttner and Friedrich Wilhelm Foerster, have fought for, is nowadays openly acknowledged by the diplomats and politicians of all civilized states as the aim of international politics. This is more than those great fighters for the idea of peace expected, and it is more than we could have expected even twenty-five years ago.

Admittedly, this great success is only a very partial one, and it has been brought about not so much by the ideas of Erasmus or of Kant as by realizing that a nuclear war might put an end to mankind. But that does not alter the fact that this aim is now generally and openly recognized, and that our difficulties are mainly due to the failure, so far, of diplomats and politicians to find a means to its realization. I cannot discuss those difficulties here; yet a more detailed explanation and discussion of my three theses might make it possible to understand them and to see them in perspective.

My *first thesis*, the negative assertion that there is no hidden meaning in political history—no meaning which we might look for and discover—nor a hidden tendency, contradicts the various *theories of progress* of the nineteenth century—for example the theories of Comte, Hegel and Marx. But it also contradicts Oswald Spengler's twentieth century theory of the *Decline of the West* as well as the classical theories of *cycles* propounded for example by Plato, by Giovanni Battista Vico, and by many others.

I regard all these theories as completely wrong-headed and even, in a way, pointless. For they answer a question that is wrongly put. Ideas such as 'progress', 'retrogression', 'decline', etc., imply judgement of value; and thus all these theories, whether they predict historical progress or retrogression, or a cycle consisting of progress and retrogression, must necessarily refer to some scale of values. Such a scale of values can be moral, or economic, or perhaps aesthetic or artistic; and within the realm of the latter values it can refer to music or painting or architecture or literature. It may also refer to the realms of science, or of technology. Another scale of values may be based upon the statistics of our health or our mortality. Obviously, we can progress, in one or several of these fields and, *at the same time*, retrogress and reach rockbottom in others. (Thus we find in Germany at the time of the greatest works of Bach, 1720–1750, no very outstanding works in literature or in painting.) But much more important is the fact that progress in some fields—say in the fields of economics or of education—has often to be paid for with retrogression in others; just as we purchase progress in the speed, spread and frequency of motor traffic at the expense of safety.

Now what is true of the realization of technological or economic values also holds, of course, for the realization of certain moral values and especially for the fundamental postulates of freedom and human dignity. Thus many citizens of the United States felt that the continuance of slavery in the Southern States was intolerable, and incompatible with the demands of their conscience; but they had to pay for the abolition of slavery with a most terrible civil war, and with the destruction of a flourishing and unique civilization.

Similarly, the progress of science—itself partly a consequence of the ideal of self-emancipation through knowledge—is contributing to the lengthening and to the enrichment of our lives; yet it has led us to spend those lives under the threat of an atomic war, and it is doubtful whether it has on balance contributed to the happiness and contentment of man.

The fact that we can progress and simultaneously retrogress shows that the historical theories of progress, the theories of retrogression, the theories of cycles, and even the prophecies of doom, are all equally untenable, since they are clearly wrong in the way they pose their questions. They are all pseudo-scientific theories (as I have tried to show elsewhere).[1] These pseudo-scientific theories of history, which I have called '*historicist*' theories, have a rather interesting history in their turn.

Homer's theory of history—like that in *Genesis*—interprets historical events as the immediate expression of the erratic will of some highly capricious man-like deities. This type of theory was incompatible with the conception of God of later Judaism and Christianity. And indeed, to view political history—the history of robbery, war, plunder, pillage and of ever-increasing means of destruction—as the direct work of God is nothing short of blasphemy. If history is the work of a merciful God, it can be so only if His will is for us inscrutable, incomprehensible and unfathomable. This would make it impossible for us to understand the meaning of history, should we try to see in history the direct action of God. Thus a religion which tries to make the meaning of history really comprehensible to us (rather than leave it inscrutable) must try to understand it not as a direct revelation of the divine will of an omnipotent God but as a struggle between some good and some evil powers—powers that act in us and

[1] See *The Open Society and Its Enemies*; also *The Poverty of Historicism.*

through us. This is what St Augustine tried to do in his book *De Civitate Dei*. He was influenced not only by the Old Testament but also by Plato, who interpreted political history as the history of the fall from grace of an originally divine, perfect, harmonious and communist city state, whose moral decline was caused by the worldly ambition and selfishness of the leading citizens. Another important influence on the work of St Augustine derives from his own Manichean period: from the Persian–Manichean heresy which interpreted this world as an arena for the struggle between the good and the evil principles, personified by Ormuzd and Ahriman.

These influences led St Augustine to describe the political history of mankind as the struggle between the good principle of the *civitas dei*, and the evil principle of the *civitas diaboli*. And almost all later theories of the evolution of history—perhaps with the exception of some of the more naïve theories of progress—can be traced back to this almost Manichean theory of St Augustine. Most of the modern historicist theories simply translate his metaphysical and religious categories into the language of natural or social science. Thus they may merely replace God and the devil by morally or biologically good races, or races fit to rule, and morally or biologically bad, or unfit, races; or by good classes and bad classes—proletarians and capitalists. But this hardly alters the character of the theory.

The little that may be allowed to be correct in these theories is their inherent assumption that our own ideas are powers that influence our history. But it is important to realize that good and noble ideas may sometimes have a disastrous influence on history; and that, conversely, we can sometimes find an idea, a historical power, which wills the Bad and works the Good (as Bernard de Mandeville was perhaps the first to see); just as we can often find that an error leads to the discovery of truth.

So we must guard carefully against viewing our highly pluralist history as a drawing in black and white, or as a picture painted in a few contrasting colours. And we must be even more careful not to read into it historical laws that can be used for the prediction of progress, cycles, or doom, or for any similar historical prediction.

Yet unfortunately the general public expects and demands, especially since Hegel, and still more since Spengler, that a real scholar—a sage or a philosopher or a historian—should be able to play the role of an augur or soothsayer: that he should be able to predict the future. And what is even worse, this demand creates its own supply. In fact the insistent demand has almost led to a glut of prophets. Without much exaggeration one could say that nowadays every intellectual of repute feels an irresistible obligation to become an expert in the art of historical prophecy. And the abysmal depth of his pessimism (for not to be a pessimist would be practically a breach of professional etiquette) is always matched by the abysmal profundity and the general impressiveness of his oracular revelations.

I think it is high time to make an attempt to keep soothsaying where it belongs—in the fairground. I do not of course mean to say that soothsayers never predict the truth: if their predictions are sufficiently vague, the number of their true predictions will even exceed that of their false ones. All I assert is that there does not exist a scientific or historical or philosophical method which might help us to produce anything like the ambitious historical predictions in Spengler's vein.

Whether a historical prediction will come true or not is neither a matter of method nor of wisdom or intuition: it is purely a matter of chance. These predictions are arbitrary, accidental and unscientific. But any of them may well achieve a powerful propagandistic effect. Provided a sufficient number of people believe in the decline of the West, the West will decline; even if, without that propaganda for its decline, it would have continued to flourish. Prophets, even false prophets, can move mountains; and so can ideas, even wrong ones. Fortunately there are some occasions when it is possible to fight wrong ideas with right ones.

In what follows I shall express some rather optimistic ideas; but they are, most emphatically, not to be taken as predictions of the future, for I do not know what the future holds, and I do not believe in those who believe they do. I am optimistic only about our ability to learn from the past and the present; we can learn that many things, both good and bad, have been and are possible, and that we have no reason to give up hoping, striving and working for a better world.

My *second thesis* was that we can give a meaning and set an aim to political history; a meaning and an aim or several meanings and aims, which are beneficent and humanitarian.

Giving a meaning to history can be understood in two different ways: the more important and fundamental one is the *imposition of an aim* through our ethical ideas. In another and less fundamental sense of the expression 'giving a meaning', a Kantian philosopher, Theodor Lessing, has described the writing of history as '*The Giving of Meaning to the Meaningless*' (*Geschichte als Sinngebung des Sinnlosen*). Theodor Lessing's thesis (with which I am inclined to agree even though it differs from mine) is this: we may read a meaning into the written, traditional books of history, even though history is meaningless in itself; for example, by asking how our ideas—say, the idea of freedom and the idea of self-emancipation through knowledge—have fared throughout history's tortuous course. If we are careful not to use the word 'progress' in the sense of a 'law of progress', we may even give a meaning to traditional history by asking what 'progress' we have made, or what set-backs we have suffered, and especially what price we had to pay for making progress in certain directions. Part of the price we have paid is revealed by the history of our many tragic errors—errors in our aims and errors in our choice of means.

A similar idea has been beautifully expressed by H. A. L. Fisher, the great English historian who rejected historicism and with it all the alleged laws of historical evolution, yet who did not shrink from judging events in history from a critical point of view, applying to them the yardstick of ethical, economic and political progress. Fisher wrote:

> Men wiser and more learned than I have discerned in history a plot, a rhythm, a predetermined pattern . . . I can see only one emergency following upon another as wave follows wave, only one great fact with respect to which, since it is unique, there can be no generalizations, only one safe rule for the historian: that he should recognize . . . the play of the contingent and the unforeseen.

Here Fisher states that there are no intrinsic developmental tendencies. Yet he continues as follows:

> This is not a doctrine of cynicism and despair. The fact of progress is written plain and large on the page of history; but progress is not a law of nature. The ground gained by one generation may be lost by the next.[1]

Thus some progress—by progress Fisher means here social betterment in the field of freedom and justice, and also economic progress—may occur within the senseless and cruel emergencies of war or power-political strife. But since there are no historical laws which ensure that this progress will continue, the future fate of progress—and with it our own fate—will largely depend on ourselves.

I have quoted Fisher not only because I believe that he is right, but also because I want to show how his idea that history depends, in part, on ourselves, is much more 'meaningful' and 'noble' than the idea that history has its inherent, and inexorable laws—whether mechanical, dialectical or organic; or that we are puppets in a historical puppet-show; or victims of superhuman historical powers, such as the powers of Good and Evil, or the collective forces of proletarians and capitalists.

Thus in writing and reading history, or books of history, we can give a meaning to it. But now I come to the other and more important sense of 'giving a meaning to history': I mean the idea that we can set ourselves tasks not only as individuals living personal lives, but also as citizens and, particularly, as citizens of the world, who regard the senseless tragedy of history as intolerable and see in it a challenge to do our best to make future history meaningful. The task is difficult, mainly because good intentions and good faith can

[1] H. A. L. Fisher, *History of Europe*, Vol. 1, p. vii.

lead us tragically astray. And because I support the ideas of the Enlightenment, of self-emancipation through knowledge, and of a critical rationalism, I feel it all the more necessary to emphasize the point that even the ideas of the Enlightenment and of rationalism have led to the most terrible consequences.

It was Robespierre's rule of terror that taught Kant, who had welcomed the French Revolution, that the most heinous crimes can be committed in the name of liberty, equality and fraternity: crimes just as heinous as those committed in the name of Christianity during the Crusades, the various eras of witch hunting, and the Thirty Years' War. And with Kant we may learn a lesson from the terror of the French Revolution, a lesson which cannot be repeated too often: that fanaticism is always evil and incompatible with the aim of a pluralist society, and that it is our duty to oppose it in any form—even when its aims, though fanatically pursued, are in themselves ethically unobjectionable, and still more so when its aims coincide with our personal aims. The danger of fanaticism, and our duty always to oppose it are two of the most important lessons we can learn from history.

But is it possible to avoid fanaticism and its excesses? Does not history teach us that all attempts to be guided by ethical aims must be futile, just because those aims can play a historical role only when they are believed in and upheld fanatically? And does not the history of all religions and all revolutions show that the fanatical belief in an ethical idea will lead not only to the perversion of this idea, but again and again to its transformation into its very opposite? That it will make us open the prison doors in the name of liberty, only to close them again behind the new enemies of our new liberty? That it makes us proclaim the equality of all men, and also, that some men 'are more equal than others'; and further, that this equality is a jealous god who commands us to visit the inequity of some of the less equal fathers upon the children unto the third and fourth generation? That it will make us proclaim the brotherhood of all men; and also, that we are the keepers of our brother—as if to remind us that our desire to rule over him is fratricidal? Does not history teach us that all ethical ideas are in reality pernicious, and the best of them often the most pernicious? Can we not learn from the French and Russian and more recently from some African revolutions that the ideas of the Enlightenment and the dreams of a better world are not merely nonsense, but criminal nonsense?

My answer to these questions is contained in my *third thesis*: we can learn from the history of Western Europe and the United States that the attempt to give to our history an ethical meaning or aim need not always be futile. That is not to say that we ever have realized, or ever will fully realize, our ethical aims. My assertion is very modest. All I say is that an ethically inspired social criticism has been successful in some places, and that it has been able to eliminate, at least for the time being, some of the worst shortcomings of social and public life.

This then is my third thesis. It is optimistic in that it is a denial of all pessimistic views of history. For obviously all theories of cyclical evolution, and of decline, are refuted if it is not quite impossible for us to impose successfully an ethical aim, an ethical meaning, upon history.

But there are certain very definite prerequisites for the imposition of ethical aims, for the successful betterment of social relations. Social ideals and social criticism were crowned by success only where people had learned to respect opinions that differ from their own, and to be sober and realistic in their political aims: where they had learned that the attempt to create the Kingdom of Heaven on earth may easily succeed in turning our earth into a hell for our fellow men.

The first countries to learn this lesson were Switzerland and England, where some Utopian attempts to create a Kingdom of Heaven on earth soon led to disenchantment.

The English Revolution, the first of the great modern revolutions, did not bring about the Kingdom of Heaven but the execution of Charles I and the dictatorship of Cromwell. Thoroughly disenchanted, England learned its lesson:

it was converted to believe in the need for a rule of law. The attempt of James II to re-introduce Roman Catholicism in England by force foundered on the rock of that attitude. Tired of religious and civil strife, England was ready to listen to the arguments for religious tolerance of John Locke and other pioneers of the Enlightenment, and to accept the principle that an enforced religion can have no value; that one may *guide* people into church, but must not try to *force* them into it against their convictions (as Pope Innocent XI expressed it).

The American revolution managed to avoid the trap of fanaticism and intolerance.

It can hardly be accidental that Switzerland, England and America, which all had to go through some disenchanting political experiences, are the countries which have succeeded in achieving, by democratic reforms, ethical-political aims which would have been unattainable by means of revolution, fanaticism, dictatorship and the use of force.

At any rate we can learn not only from the history of the English-speaking democracies but also from the history of Switzerland and Scandinavia that we can set ourselves aims, and that we can sometimes achieve them—provided that these aims are neither too wide, nor too narrow, but conceived in a pluralist spirit—that is, that they embody respect for the freedom and convictions of all sorts of people with widely differing ideas and beliefs. This shows that it is not impossible to give meaning to our political history; which is, precisely, my *third thesis*.

In my view it is the Romantic School and its criticism of the Enlightenment which was superficial, and not the Enlightenment, even though its name has become a synonym for superficiality. Kant and the Enlightenment were ridiculed as superficial and naive for taking seriously the ideals of liberty: for believing that the idea of democracy was more than a transient historical phenomenon. And nowadays we can hear again a lot about the necessary transience of these ideas. But instead of explaining their necessary transience and prophesying their impending decline, it would be better to fight for their survival. For these ideas have not only shown their vitality, and their power to survive terrible attacks: they also have turned out to provide, as Kant thought they would, the necessary framework for a pluralist society; and *vice versa*: the pluralist society is the necessary framework for the working out of political meanings and aims; for any policy which transcends the immediate present; for any policy which reads a meaning into our past history, and which tries to give our present and future history a meaning.

Enlightenment and Romanticism have one important point in common: both see the history of mankind mainly as a history of contending ideas and beliefs; as a history of ideological struggles. In this respect they agree. But it is in their attitude towards these ideas that Enlightenment and Romanticism diverge so widely. Romanticism values the power of faith as such: it values its vigour and depth, independently of the question of its *truth*. This it seems is the real reason why the Romantic School is so contemptuous of the Enlightenment. For the Enlightenment views faith and the power of faith with some diffidence. Although it teaches tolerance and even respect for other peoples' faith, its greatest value is not faith, but truth. And it teaches that there is something like absolute truth, even though it may be unknown to us; and that we can get nearer to it through correcting our errors. This, in fact, is the fundamental thesis of the philosophy of Enlightenment; and in this lies its greatest contrast with the historical relativism of the Romantics.

But the approach to truth is not easy. There is only one way towards it, the way through error. Only through our errors can we learn; and only he will learn who is ready to appreciate and even to cherish the errors of others as stepping stones towards truth, and who searches for his own errors: who tries to find them, since only when he has become aware of them can he free himself from them.

The ideal of our self-emancipation through knowledge is therefore not the same as the ideal of our mastery over nature. The former is, rather, the idea of a spiritual self-liberation from error, from superstition, and from false idols.

It is the idea of one's own spiritual self-emancipation and growth, through one's own criticism of one's own ideas—though the help of others will always be needed.

Thus we see that Enlightenment does not reject fanaticism and fanatical forms of belief for purely utilitarian reasons, nor merely because it has found that better things can be achieved in politics and in practical affairs by a more sober attitude. Its rejection of fanatical belief is, rather, the natural corollary of the idea that we should search for truth by criticizing our errors. This self-criticism and this self-emancipation are possible only in a pluralist society, that is, in an open society which tolerates our errors as well as the errors of others.

The idea of self-emancipation through knowledge, which was the basic idea of the Enlightenment, is in itself a powerful enemy of fanaticism; for it makes us try hard to detach ourselves or even to dissociate ourselves from our own ideas (in order to look at them critically) instead of identifying ourselves with them. And the recognition of the sometimes overwhelming historical power of ideas should teach us how important it is to free ourselves from the overpowering influence of false or wrong ideas. In the interests of the quest for truth and of our liberation from errors we have to train ourselves to view our own favourite ideas just as critically as those we oppose.

This is not a concession to relativism. In fact, the very idea of error presupposes the idea of truth. Admitting that the other man may be right and that I may be wrong obviously does not and cannot mean that each man's personal point of view is equally true or equally tenable and that, as the relativists say, everybody is right within his own frame of reference, though he may be wrong within that of somebody else. In the western democracies many of us have learned that at times we are wrong and our opponents right; but too many who have digested this important truth have slipped into relativism. In our great historical task of creating a free pluralist society, and with it a social framework for the growth of knowledge and for self-emancipation through knowledge, nothing is more vital for us than to be able to view our own ideas critically; without however becoming relativists or sceptics, and without losing the courage and the determination to fight for our convictions, even though we realize that these convictions should always be open to correction, and that only through correcting them may we free ourselves from error, thus making it possible for us to grow in knowledge.